Bureaucracy
and Professionalism

Bureaucracy and Professionalism

The Evolution of Public School Supervision

Jeffrey Glanz

Rutherford • Madison • Teaneck
Fairleigh Dickinson University Press
London and Toronto: Associated University Presses

© 1991 by Jeffrey Glanz

All rights reserved. Authorization to photocopy items for internal or personal use, or the internal or personal use of specific clients, is granted by the copyright owner, provided that a base fee of $10.00, plus eight cents per page, per copy is paid directly to the Copyright Clearance Center, 27 Congress Street, Salem, Massachusetts 01970. [0-8386-3419-2/91 $10.00+8¢ pp, pc.]

Associated University Presses
440 Forsgate Drive
Cranbury, NJ 08512

Associated University Presses
25 Sicilian Avenue
London WC1A 2QH, England

Associated University Presses
P.O. Box 39, Clarkson Pstl. Stn.
Mississauga, Ontario,
L5J 3X9 Canada

The paper used in this publication meets the requirements of the American National Standard for Permanence of Paper for Printed Library Materials Z39.48-1984.

Library of Congress Cataloging-in-Publication Data

Glanz, Jeffrey.
   Bureaucracy and professionalism : the evolution of public school supervision / Jeffrey Glanz.
      p. cm.
   Includes bibliographical references (p.   ) and index.
   ISBN 0-8386-3419-2 (alk. paper)
   1. School supervision—United States—History. 2. School management and organization—United States—History. 3. Public schools—United States—Administration—History. 4. Bureaucracy—United States—History. I. Title.
LB2806.4.G53   1991
379.1′5′0973—dc20   90-55989
                                                                                             CIP

PRINTED IN THE UNITED STATES OF AMERICA

For my wife: Lisa.
For my children: Daniel, Joshua, Noah, Rena.
For my parents.
For my in-laws.
For my teachers.
For my students.

Contents

List of Illustrations 9
Acknowledgments 11
Introduction 13

Part 1: The Bureaucratization of Supervision
1. Bureaucracy and School Supervision: Antecedents for Current Practice 37
   Superintendent as Supervisor 38
   Managing the Urban Schools: Influence of the Bureaucrats 53
   Authority versus Freedom: An Intractable Problem for School Supervision 66
   The Bureaucratization of Supervision 73

Part 2: The Drive Toward Professionalism
2. From Cautious Optimism to Confirmed Despair: The Supervisor's Newly Found Status within the School Organization 79
   Progressivism, Educational Growth, and the School Supervisor 80
   Bobbitt and School Supervision 89
   Teacher Rating as a Function of Supervision 94
   The Attack on School Supervision 99
   The Dubious Attempt to Improve Instruction 103

3. The Fall of Autocracy and the Emergence of Efficient, Cooperative, Democratic Methods and Scientific Supervision: The Supervisor's Dream 107
   The Professional Orientation 110
   Science and School Supervision 115
   The Distinction between Supervision and Administration 118
   The Democratic Impulse 120
   The Problems of Efficiency, Democracy, and Science 124
   The Status of School Supervision 126

4. The Alliance between Supervisors and Curriculum Workers: The Quest for Professionalism Revisited 129

CONTENTS

The Supervisory Dream Shattered: Three Possible
    Explanations 129
Curriculum as the New Supervision 135
The Society for Curriculum Study and the Joint Committee 140
The End of an Era 144

Epilogue: Bureaucracy and Professionalism Revisited   **147**

Notes   **161**
Bibliographical Essay   **184**
Bibliography   **201**
Index   **209**

Illustrations

1. A Superintendent's Rating Sheet　　　　　　　　61
2. A Superintendent's Rating Form　　　　　　　　63
3. Allen's Typology of School Supervision　　　　113
4. Spears's Cartoon　　　　　　　　　　　　　　121

Acknowledgments

I wish to acknowledge the support, advice, assistance, and criticism of certain people who have made substantive contributions to this book. The sole responsibility for any errors or misrepresentations in this study rests with this writer.

First among the individuals I wish to thank is my mentor Professor Emeritus Arno A. Bellack, of Teachers College, Columbia University, who questioned, developed, and incisively critiqued my early work on the present topic. Professor Bellack's high standard of excellence, discerning criticism, and patient guidance will always be held in deep esteem.

Two other scholars must also be recognized: Prof. Dwayne Huebner for his provocative ideas that led me to investigate supervision in an historical context, and Prof. Gary A. Griffin for his support and encouragement and, specifically, for his stimulating insights into the organizational framework of schooling. Special thanks are also due to my friend and colleague at Columbia, Leigh Altadonna, for the many interesting discussions that helped several vague notions develop into workable hypotheses.

I am grateful to the many librarians at various institutions who provided me with invaluable assistance in tracking down specific journals and obscure references to supervision. Special thanks to Sanford Goin, who issued me a rare stack pass to the Teachers College library. I would like to thank Drs. Alice Miel and Florence Stratemeyer for graciously sharing their ideas and experiences concerning public school supervision. I also appreciate the lengthy response I received from Dr. Hollis L. Caswell to my letter, regarding his involvement with the Department of Supervisors and the Directors of Instruction, and the Society for Curriculum Study. Also, thanks are extended to Profs. Michael B. Katz, David B. Tyack, Edward A. Krug, and Herbert M. Kliebard for their reactions, by correspondence, to my general thesis, as well as for several valuable leads. Appreciation is also extended to Bob Gill who typed portions of the manuscript and who made numerous editorial suggestions. Without his expertise in computers this book would have just been another good idea. Thanks to colleagues and friends for their instructive criticism: Robert O'Donnell, Dawn Cucciniello, Jeffrey Shurack, and Lois Goldstein.

I would also be remiss if I didn't acknowledge Ronald Evans, Principal of P.S. 92 in Brooklyn, for providing me with my first opportunity to deal with the very challenging responsibilities of supervising an urban public school. His leadership and guidance have been a source of inspiration. To my colleagues Shirley Goldstein and Norma Adams Clemons, Assistant Principals at P.S. 92, I extend my admiration and respect for displaying the very best qualities that supervisors, in my estimation, can possess. Thanks to Gilbert Haber, Assistant Principal of P.S. 55 in the Bronx, who inspired me to pursue a career in administration.

Thanks to Dr. Shan Nelson-Rowe, Assistant Professor in the Department of Social Sciences at Fairleigh Dickinson University, for his extensive and incisive criticisms which, in the end, brought greater substance and focus to this work. Thanks to Dr. Harry Keyishian of Fairleigh Dickinson University Press, and Mr. Michael Koy, of Associated University Presses, for directing this work to its successful conclusion.

Finally, I wish to acknowledge all future scholars who may, in some small way, be so influenced by the publication of this book, that they will join in the provocative venture of exploring the history of school supervision.

Introduction

I
Setting the Tone

People in various fields of study, such as physics, sociology, or education, have varying opinions regarding their historical traditions. The degree to which educators, in general, have attempted to examine their inherited modes of behavior and action has certainly been minuscule. Different attitudes have been manifested concerning the lack of historical awareness into educational problems and issues. On the one hand, some historians tend to lament the ahistorical nature of educational thought and practice. On the other hand, some educators express ambivalence concerning the useful and pragmatic consequences of historical inquiry. Nevertheless, the number of historical studies in education has markedly increased. Interest in American educational history has focused attention, albeit to a limited extent, on subspecialties within the field of education. The field of curriculum is a prime example.[1] To a greater degree than ever before, history, as a mode of inquiry, has been recognized as a valuable resource for the contemporary educator.

Despite this interest in history, the important and pervasive school function of supervision has escaped historical investigation. Indeed, those currently concerned with school supervision as a professional enterprise and field of study are in a state of "historical unconsciousness."[2] Although not convinced that historical exploration will necessarily alter existing conditions in our schools, I do believe that analyzing the past is crucial for understanding present conditions and future possibilities and, perhaps, might even help avoid some of the pitfalls of the past.

Although many books discuss the history of supervision, much of this history is plagued by generalizations, inaccuracies, and a lack of critical analysis. Such scholarship lacks a basic understanding of the significant factors that have shaped public school supervision in this country. Supervision has been influenced by the centralized control of urban schooling, scientific and measurement movements, industrialization, flurries of reform, wartime activities, postwar depressions, and other noneducational forces. The history of supervision is clearly a history of the interaction of the broad social and intellectual movements within American society. My purpose in this book is to offer an interpretive analysis of the factors that have shaped and influenced public school supervision from the late nineteenth century to the present. The sixty years, from about 1875 to 1935 are of particular importance to the development of supervision. During this time two related, but sometimes opposing, forces, bureaucracy and professionalism, helped shape the nature of public school supervision in the United States. From a functionalist point of view, school supervision in this country has served to maintain, support, and perpetuate the educational bureaucracy. By contrast, professional supervision has been less important as a source of educational improvement. The tensions created for supervisors by membership in a bureaucratic organization are central to this study. This book examines a persistent problem in public school supervision; namely, the unresolved dilemma between the demands of the organization (bureaucracy) and the drive for professionalism.

Throughout most of the nineteenth century, city school systems were controlled by loosely structured, decentralized ward boards. Superintendents were relatively unimportant in public school policy or decision making. Supervision, for the most part, was controlled by local politicians and ward (school) boards. In the late nineteenth century educational reformers sought to transform schools into a tightly organized and efficiently managed centralized system. Educational historians have described this period as a time when the movement toward centralization in large urban cities gained considerable momentum. David Tyack, for example, described the centralization movement as one that enabled the superintendent to expertly administer urban schools.[3] As centralization increased in urban city schools, more power and authority to run the schools was placed in the hands of city superintendents. In general, reformers during this period sought to remove the schools from what they considered to be harmful and corrupt influences of pervasive lay control. Centralizers, such as Nicholas M. Butler and Andrew S. Draper, sought to "remove the school from politics" by allowing the superintendent to have the power to control, legislate, and assume responsibility. Indeed, these reformers eventually succeeded in shifting the direction and responsibility of schooling to the superintendent.[4]

Americans view bureaucracy with a great deal of ambivalence. On the one hand, the bureaucratic form of organization has been viewed by many as the "most efficient form of administrative organization" because of its hierarchical structure that clearly defines the role of each individual.[5] Bureaucratic organizations are programmed to result in the calculability of behavior, regimented operations, and a stable and predictable environment. Reformers in the late nineteenth century promoted these characteristics of bureaucracy as the panacea for the problems of urban education. Bureaucracy, as Tyack notes, became the "one best system" to solve the ills of a school system beset by corruption and inefficiency.[6] The pervasiveness of bureaucracy, then, was the chief characteristic of schooling in the late nineteenth century. Bureaucracy has also been criticized for its rigidity, red tape, waste, inefficiency, and stifling of individual initiative.

The book begins with an analysis of this period in which bureaucracy emerged as the chief form of school organization. Although the centralization of urban schools in the late nineteenth century has been explored by historians, the importance of supervision in the movement toward centralization and bureaucracy has been overlooked. Supervision was an indispensable means by which superintendents gained control over schools and infused bureaucratic values and ideas therein.[7] Supervision did not create the injustices generally associated with bureaucracy, although it certainly had a systematic part in perpetuating them. Supervision, then, was an essential part of a larger tendency to bureaucratize schooling.

Chapter 2 describes a shift in the role of supervision in public schools. Not until the turn of the century did supervision become the responsibility of a functionary other than the superintendent. Supervisors, general and special, and principals who bore responsibility for supervising teachers, increased both in number and importance as the school system grew in size and complexity. However, the problems and tensions confronting the supervisor also grew. Teachers and other educators sharply criticized administrators during the first two decades of the twentieth century for the increasing bureaucratization of urban schools and for rating procedures used by supervisors. Supervisors found themselves in an awkward position. Torn between administrative duties and instructional responsibilities, they occupied a precarious status in the bureaucratic hierarchy. In a direct response to mounting criticism, they sought to professionalize and gain control over their work as a means to counteract bureaucracy.[8]

In the 1930s, supervisors came to fully understand the meaning of professional membership in a bureaucratic organization. The tension between wanting to improve the instructional process, while at the same time maintaining bureaucratic role relationships reached its peak in 1937, when the members of the Department of Supervisors and the Society for Curriculum Study met to work on a yearbook on curriculum. The eventual merger of these two groups, composed of middle-management personnel, indicates their desire to combine forces in order to bolster professional interests and objectives. Subsequently, supervisors had difficulty securing what the Association for Supervision and Curriculum Development (ASCD), during the 1950s and 1960s, called "the professionalization of supervisors and curriculum workers." Chapter 4 explains the ways in which bureaucracy inhibited the efforts of supervisors to professionalize.

The book ends on a dubious note. Supervision needs direction. Indeed, schooling needs direction. The shape, manner, and form of this direction will be determined by several important factors that currently affect educational practice. I will discuss the future of public school supervision by analyzing these forces and issues.

An historical examination of public education since the nineteenth century indicates that bureaucracy has been the dominant form of school organization. This study will reveal, in particular, a characteristic tension experienced by supervisors, in their attempts to find legitimacy within the school bureaucracy. In most cases, supervisors wished to improve instruction and help teachers, but they were confronted by an unyielding organizational structure which, by its very nature, impeded individual autonomy. It is not my intention to portray the supervisor as the victim of circumstance. On the contrary, the history of supervision reveals that supervisors were in fact participants in the maintenance of bureaucratic role relationships. The important point to be made is that, intended or not, bureaucracy was perceived as a phenomenon *sui generis;* that is, it confronted educators with a reality that seemingly could not be altered or reduced to other terms. The tensions of bureaucracy and the desire to professionalize, became crucial concerns for public school supervisors.

The conflict between professionalism and bureaucracy is reflective of a much broader issue that has troubled educators from Horace Mann and William T. Harris in the nineteenth century, to John Dewey and George Counts in the twentieth century: how to find a balance between order and freedom. Dewey referred to this dilemma when he said that "the problem of education is the harmonizing of individual traits with social ends and values."[9] In other words: How can we accentuate individuality and at the same time maintain an effective organizational framework? Different generations of educators sought different solutions to the problem. Still, the end result remained the same; that is, the dominance of order, authority, and organization over freedom, autonomy, and the individual. This dominance has provoked questions about the inevitability of the bureaucratic framework of schooling and the search for alternative forms of management. Indeed, this issue remains a vital and critical problem facing educators today. It is not my purpose to provide the solution. Rather, my goal is to rephrase and interpret the issue in terms of a specific group of school functionaries, namely supervisors, and point out salient facts that must be evaluated by current educators.

Historiographical controversies concerning order and freedom have flourished and will continue to do so. Profound differences in points of view are never gratuitous. For one person, bureaucracy may be the road to freedom; for another, the road to oppression. In terms of the school bureaucracy, there appear to be four basic alternatives. First, one may completely and wholeheartedly accept the bureaucratic form of organization as a necessity and, generally, a "good thing." Undeniably, many people assumed this position throughout the history of public school supervision. Conformity and compliance to established rules of conduct were essential to these educators. From this perspective, "everything is running smoothly!" The system, in other words, is operational and efficient.

Second, by adopting a noncommittal stance, one can detach oneself from bureaucracy. As a result, bureaucratic rules and regulations become meaningless to the individual. Fortunately, most educators have not succumbed to such a position. This second alternative or hermitlike existence, for some, postpones any decisions that have to be made. It is believed, at least in this context, that this alternative was not adhered to by most supervisors.

Third, the most radical alternative has been the perceived need to transform societal structures. The possibilities range from Ivan Illich's deschooling society in favor of "educational networks," to Samuel Bowles's and Herbert Gintis's proposal for the "dismantling of the capitalist system and its replacement by a more progressive order."[10] Related to the history of supervision in this country, this alternative has never received adequate attention. Supervisors, rarely if ever, sought to transform the school bureaucracy.

Fourth, educators have sought to manipulate the system in order to make it work. The number of possibilities within this fourth alternative are voluminous. Today, as in the past, educators readily perceive this to be a viable alternative. Choices range from examining one's existential possibilities to specific strategies used by change agents in order to make the bureaucracy work. This fourth alternative considers the bureaucracy as a given, or at least an unalterable state, and desires to change internal components rather than structural dimensions.

These, then, are the possibilities available to educators. The history of supervision reveals that most supervisors either accepted or attempted to manipulate, in some manner, the school bureaucracy. Few, if any, proposals were advanced to challenge the bureaucratic structure. It may seem, however, unreasonable to assume that supervisors would discard a system of organization that provided stability during a time in which schools were beset by confusion and unpredictability. Bureaucracy, as an elitist philosophy focusing on centralized expert control over the schools, overrode older concerns of democratic individualism. Bureaucracy inculcated values of discipline, control, and civic harmony. Individual interests became subservient to the new bureaucratic machine. The implementation of bureaucracy as the chief form of school organization meant a diminution of personal liberties that would have serious ramifications for future generations of educators. As American education continues to grow in response to heavy demands that are continually being placed on it, educators of the future will have to decide whether or not bureaucracy will occupy a position of central importance. One can only hope that there is a clear understanding of both the past and present so that future choices can be made intelligently, honestly, and with vigor.

II
What Is Supervision and Who Is the Supervisor?

The difficulties in obtaining an accurate picture of who the supervisor is and defining the function of supervision are compounded by the fact that supervision has meant many things to different people and has been performed by individuals with a great variety of titles. Daniel Tanner and Laurel Tanner in their recent book entitled *Supervision in Education: Problems and*

Practices, attest to the lack of clarity in both the role and function of supervision. They state that while "a very small district may have only one person working in the area of supervision and curriculum improvement, and that person may be called the supervisor," it is conceivable, if not a certainty, that at another location "the supervisor may be called the deputy superintendent of curriculum and instruction, with essentially the same functions as the supervisor in the first district. . . ."[11] According to Evelyn F. Carlson, writing an introduction to the 1965 yearbook published by the ASCD, there is no uniformity in either title or function regarding public school supervision. For example, it is not uncommon to find individuals with identical titles performing different functions within the same school district. "There are supervisors who are generalists and supervisors of specific subjects; there are supervisors of services and supervisors of instructional media. However, all are usually known simply as supervisors or consultants."[12] Despite these difficulties, however, it is possible to delimit and define supervision for purposes of this study.

Supervision is an inevitable function in human organizations. To quote William H. Payne, the author of the first published text on supervision: "Organization implies subordination. If there is to be a plan, someone must devise it, while others must execute it . . . the many must follow the directions of the few."[13] To the nineteenth-century urban school reformer, supervision was axiomatic. Josiah L. Pickard, a teacher, principal, superintendent, first president of the National Education Association (NEA), and author of the widely disseminated text simply titled *School Supervision,* emphatically stated: "In every branch of human labor the importance of supervision has grown with the specialization of labor. The more minute the subdivision of labor, the greater the need for supervision."[14] Williard S. Elsbree, in his classic treatise, *The American Teacher,* observed that supervision as a function is an integral component of the American educational process. "Teachers in American schools financed partially or wholly at public expense have never been completely free from supervision and control."[15] Supervision, therefore, is viewed as an indispensable and vital responsibility that ensures the continued success of American schooling.

It is not surprising then that the function and role of supervision has played an important part in managing schools and improving instruction. This is readily apparent from an even superficial and cursory examination of American educational history. In the early nineteenth century, for example, supervision was carried out by selectmen, local clergy, and politicians under the aegis of ward boards. Later in the century, it was controlled by a group of schoolmen known as centralizers or superintendents. As the school system grew in size and complexity, the function of supervision was performed by an ever-increasing group of individuals collectively known as supervisors, but more specifically were principals, general supervisors, and/or special supervisors. Since the 1920s, supervision has been performed by assistant superintendents, principals, assistant principals, consultants, department heads, board of education officials, curriculum specialists, and very recently, by teachers. Due to the fact that supervision is a function carried out by a wide array of school officials, historians who have examined supervision have focused their discussion on the function of supervision without regard to title.[16] There are few studies that attempt to analyze the supervisory responsibilities of a particular group of individuals. Given the lack of specificity of function and multiplicity of officers engaging in supervision, it is clear that any analysis of the subject must necessarily encompass a broad spectrum in order to accurately assess the nature and character of public school supervision. This study, then, in addition to examining supervision from a broad function-oriented approach, will highlight groups of individuals, most often known as supervisors, whose primary responsibility was the promotion of pupil learning and the improvement of teaching in the public schools.

Who, then, is the supervisor? There are three distinct groups of individuals who merit discussion.

(1) THE SUPERINTENDENT OF THE LATE NINETEENTH CENTURY

In the late nineteenth century, education became synonymous with schooling and as such, the locus of authority shifted from home and parent to state and bureaucrat. The newly formed cadre of professionals who represented the growing corporate structure promulgated *standardization* and *efficiency* as watchwords of the day. It was during this period that schooling underwent previously unseen or unimaginable expansion and transformation that would set the framework for a centralized bureaucratic system that would remain the dominant mode of school governance throughout the coming century.

These urban reformers, or administrative progressives as David Tyack calls them, seized control of urban schooling in the late nineteenth century by arguing that the ward board system of organizing schools was corrupt, inefficient, and unprofessional.

Ellwood Cubberley, for example, called for a total school board reorganization and demanded that authority to make educational decisions should be placed in the hands of progressive business and professional leaders.[17] These leaders shared a common ideology arguing that a structured administrative hierarchy composed of professional school managers would bring order to an otherwise chaotic and corrupt system of education.

While this story has been told before, an important part of the story has not received adequate attention; that is, the importance of supervision in the attempt to gain control over urban education. Supervision was viewed as essential to coordinate and implement bureaucratic school management. During this era the superintendent of schools was the individual who performed supervision. William Howard Payne, for instance, conceived "supervision" as synonymous with the work of the superintendent.[18] Discovering who the supervisor was, necessarily entails, therefore, a description of the duties and responsibilities of the late nineteenth-century superintendent.

(2) THE PRINCIPAL AND THE GENERAL/SPECIAL SUPERVISORS OF THE EARLY TWENTIETH CENTURY

Schooling grew dramatically in the first two decades of the twentieth century. Between 1895 and 1920 total school enrollment increased from 14 to 21.5 million students. During the same period, the high school and above population grew from about 350,000 to 2,500,000 students. In 1895 there were slightly more than 398,000 teachers, earning an average annual salary of $286. The number of female teachers was more than double that of their male counterparts. By 1920, in comparison, the total number of teachers increased by more than 280,000 while their salary more than doubled. There were more than five times the number of female teachers as compared to male teachers. Significantly, the tally of principals and other supervisory personnel only began in 1920. Prior to this time, supervision was controlled chiefly by the superintendent, with little authority delegated to assistants and principals. After 1920, however, the number of principals and supervisors increased at significant rates.[19]

As the size and complexity of schools increased, greater administrative specialization was readily apparent. The principal as school leader and chief supervisor gained in stature and authority in the early twentieth century. Although present in the nineteenth century, the principalship did not wield any power. Nor did it significantly affect the nature and character of schooling. The principal in the nineteenth century was essentially relegated to the relatively noninfluential position of "head teacher." Not until after about 1920 was the principal relieved of teaching duties. As Willard S. Elsbree and E. Edmund Reutter point out, the principal, up until the 1920s, would "take over classes on occasion, and demonstrate to the teacher exactly how the job should be done."[20] Prior to this time, the principal's primary duties outside the classroom concentrated on offering assistance to less experienced teachers in areas such as instruction, curriculum, and general classroom management skills. In the late nineteenth century the principal was expected to obey the directives of city superintendents. In fact it was the superintendent who usually appointed an individual "principal" or head teacher. There were no fixed criteria for selection as a principal in the late nineteenth century. Selection as principal was based on presumed excellence in teaching and essentially was determined by the whim of the superintendent. The principal was given little authority to do more than complete attendance and other administrative reports. Supervisory authority to make decisions on teacher competence, for instance, rested solely with the superintendent. The situation changed dramatically after the turn of the century.

As schooling expanded so did the educational bureaucracy, with the number of principals doubling between 1920 and 1930. Educators accounted for this increase with industrial metaphors. Elsbree and Reutter explained the role and function of principals as follows: "The principal was looked upon as a kind of foreman who through close supervision helped to compensate for ignorance and lack of skill of his subordinates."[21] The principal's duties, however, broadened and became more comprehensive and complex after 1920. For example, principals became actively engaged in curriculum development, staff training, and school-community relations. As a result, the building principal assumed greater supervisory and inspectorial responsibilities. Due to increasing administrative duties, however, the principalship gradually shifted away from direct inspections, classroom supervision, and instructional development, and assumed a more managerial position. As a result, to focus solely on the principal will give a biased and provincial view of supervisory practice in the schools.

In addition to the building principal, a new cadre of administrative officers known as supervisors, emerged, who assumed the major responsibility for day-to-day classroom supervision. Two specific groups of supervisors were commonly found in schools. First, a "special supervisor," most often female and chosen by the building principal, was relieved of some teaching responsibilities to help assist less experienced teachers in subject-matter mastery. Larger schools, for example, had a number of special supervisors in each of the major subject areas. In the 1920s and 1930s, some schools even had special supervisors of music and art. Second, a "general supervisor," usually male, was selected to "assist" the principal in the more administrative, logistical operations of a school. The general supervisor, subsequently called assistant principal, would prepare attendance reports, collect data for evaluation purposes, and coordinate special school programs, among other duties.

After 1920, the general supervisor was chiefly responsible for supervising teachers and for maintaining school programming, usurping the role of special supervisors in the process. As the position of principal gradually, yet steadily, became more managerial, the general supervisor assumed greater responsibility for the improvement of teaching.[22]

While the general supervisor (assistant principal) and building principal were instrumental in maintaining supervisory control in each school, their tenuous position in the educational hierarchy limited their effectiveness in the schools. On the one hand, their major responsibility was to maintain control of the school organization by weeding out incompetent teachers, ensuring adherence to school regulations and policies, and evaluating overall personnel performance. In this sense, the supervisor and principal were system-oriented. On the other hand, supervisors wanted to assist teachers in solving classroom problems; in this sense, they were people-oriented. Herein lies the basic conflict that all who are engaged in supervision face; the unresolved dilemma between the demands of the system to evaluate and the desire of supervisors to genuinely assist teachers in instructional matters. The history of supervision indicates a desire by supervisors to resolve this conflict by minimizing administrative hierarchical pressures and maximizing professional engagement with teachers to improve the educational process. An examination of this second class of supervisor will reveal characteristic tensions that comprise the theme of this book; that is, the bureaucratic-professional dilemma experienced by public school supervisors in this country.

(3) EVERYONE AND ANYONE CONCERNED WITH IMPROVING TEACHING AND PROMOTING LEARNING

The year 1937 marked a turning point in the history of public school supervision. For a variety of reasons, which will be discussed later, supervisors and principals were unsuccessful in their attempts to resolve the basic conflict previously mentioned. Supervisors, in 1937 as well as in subsequent years, merged efforts with others in the attempt to gain greater professional autonomy and to mitigate bureaucratic constraints. In 1937, in particular, they convened with curriculum specialists in order to achieve heightened prestige and legitimation for their work in schools. This historic meeting between supervisors and curriculum specialists, which will be discussed in chapter 4, opened the floodgates for a host of others who would engage in the evaluation and supervision of teachers. Supervision, in effect, became a function usurped by a wide variety of school functionaries. In fact, since the 1940s there has been a proliferation of individuals with a variety of titles engaged in the function of supervision. Entertaining the question of who the supervisor is during this time frame must necessarily focus on the work of superintendents, their immediate assistants and directors, supervisors at both school and district levels, principals, curriculum directors and coordinators, department heads, subject specialists, and recently, even teachers themselves.

It is evident that to determine the role and function of the supervisor is a complicated task in which one must examine a great many historically determined variables and situations. Examination of the supervisory process does not fit into an easily definable package or formula; it involves factors that have changed considerably with the passage of time. While much historical inquiry is needed, this book will attempt to establish a theoretical framework from which future analysis into more minute details of supervisory practice may be more easily possible.

III
Applying the Bureaucratic/Professional Model to Public School Supervision

Bureaucracy and professionalism are important concepts if one wants to understand changes in the division of labor within schools. Bureaucracy affected the underlying structure and form of schooling by creating a centralized, standardized, hierarchical administrative structure. Professionalization affected schooling by enabling some occupational groups to achieve a dominant, and at times nearly monopolistic, status within the division of labor. Seen in this light, bureaucracy and professionalism are not two entirely separate and contradictory frames of reference, but rather complementary processes influencing American education. The bureaucratic form of governance was indeed compatible with the efforts of professionalism and in fact was adopted into the internal operations of most professional groups.[23]

In particular, the evolution of supervision as an occupation reflects the influence of bureaucracy and professionalism. This book tells the story of the emergence of supervision as a distinct occupational category within schools; it also discusses the efforts of supervisors to clearly delineate their work in order to legitimize their claims of professional status. The leitmotif of this story is that the professionalization of supervisors was thwarted at several historical junctures. While there are a number of reasons why supervisors were unable to achieve professional autonomy, the primary cause centers on what can be termed a *bureaucratic-professional tension* or *conflict*. Andrew Abbott makes the point that bureaucratization "may have affected [certain] professions' ability to provide services." Supervisors did in fact have difficulty in providing services to their clients due to certain bureaucratic constraints. Abbott explains that professionals have lost control of their work because of organizational constraints. He gives an example based on teachers' loss of control over "curriculum planning to supervisory personnel." Similarly, supervisors have "lost their work" to administrators in higher levels of the administrative hierarchy."[24]

The bureaucratization and professionalization of public school supervision must be understood and viewed within the larger context of urban schooling as a whole. What is meant, though, by the bureaucratization and professionalization of supervision? How does this help explain the evolution of public school supervision? How do the two processes then interact, and how were they uniquely manifested in the history of supervision?

Traditional conceptions of bureaucracy portray it as a cruel, dehumanizing institution limiting individual autonomy and compromising human potential and integrity.[25] Bel Kaufman's recently rereleased best-seller *Up the Down Staircase,* for example, portrays the anguish of the teacher Sylvia Barrett, as she valiantly muddles through bureaucratic hurdles of the New York City public school system in a hopeless attempt to "reach" her students. Kaufman tells of the mindless bureaucratic routines that thwart, at every opportunity, the ability of a teacher to effectively carry out his daily tasks and responsibilities. The excessive paperwork, closed lines of communication between teacher and principal, and the monotony of administrative chores make "life" in a school bureaucracy unbearable.[26] To many, the mere mention of the word *bureaucracy* conjures up all sorts of negative connotations.

In the literature of modern sociology, however, *bureaucracy* is used in a neutral context as one of several types of social organization, deliberately conceived, so that officially designated offices and roles are functionally aimed at fulfilling specifically prescribed ends or results. Robert K. Merton defines *bureaucracy* as an "integrated series of offices, of hierarchical statuses, in which inhere a number of obligations and privileges closely defined by limited and specific rules. . . . Each of these offices, contains an area of imputed competence and responsibility." Authority in a bureaucracy is derived "in the office and not in the particular person who performs the official role." Formal rules of behavior serve "to minimize friction by largely restricting (official) contact to modes which are previously defined by the rules of the organization." The entire system, concludes Merton, fosters "objectivity." Merton, in sum, explains that "the chief merit of bureaucracy is its technical efficiency, with a premium placed on precision, speed, expert control, continuity, discretion, and optimal returns on input."[27]

Any discussion, however, of bureaucracy must necessarily include the pioneering work of Max Weber.[28] His analysis of bureaucracy helps to more clearly focus the developments occurring in late nineteenth-century American education. Schools never even came close to Weber's "ideal type" bureaucracy, but his theory went far toward giving us a clearer idea of what administrative reformers tried to accomplish in terms of establishing a system for centralized authority and decision-making in urban education.

Weber outlined in great detail the various characteristics of his ideal type bureaucracy. In short, a bureaucratic-governed organization, according to Weber, maintained a precise "hierarchy" with "levels of graded authority" in which "a system of super[ordination] and subordination" would rule the conduct of each member of the organization. That the "top" gives the orders and the "bottom" carries them out was axiomatic to Weber. An organization without "fixed and official jurisdictional areas" along with detailed, prescribed rules of conduct lacked a rational means of administration.[29]

Despite his firm belief that bureaucracy was necessary for

modern society, Weber acknowledged that excessive bureaucratization could lead to severe problems. He realized that bureaucratic governance, with its emphasis on fixed rules of conduct, could stifle individual autonomy and free expression of will and purpose. Weber never did satisfactorily reconcile individual autonomy and bureaucratic governance. Adherence to fixed rules, said Weber, was the mainstay of bureaucracy and necessary for its survival. Any deviation or mitigation of these firmly established rules of behavior would seriously undermine the effectiveness of the organization. This problem, as we shall see, presented serious conflicts for public school supervisors.[30]

The emergence of school bureaucracy did not occur, however, in isolation of other processes affecting American urban education. Schooling also achieved a degree of dominance and monopoly within its sphere of influence, which suggests that professionalization, not just bureaucratization, occurred.[31] While historians have explored the nature and character of the professionalization of schooling, another important aspect of this process has been neglected; that is, an analysis of the particular professional efforts of various members of the school organization, especially teachers and supervisors. This particular strain of professionalization took quite a different course than what occurred in schooling as a whole. The evidence will demonstrate serious conflicts between the two processes for public school supervisors. Supervisors clamored for greater organizational recognition in their pursuit of professionalism. Before examining the bureaucratic-professional conflict however, we need to know what the *professionalization of supervision* means.

The term *profession* is often used in a variety of ways in the field of education. Certain characteristics, however, have been identified by scholars in the field.[32] The term often refers to a group of people who possess high levels of skill, commitment, and trustworthiness.[33] According to Eliot Freidson, in his seminal study of the medical profession, a "profession," as distinct from other "occupations," enjoys a "preeminence" in the division of labor. In Freidson's words, "A profession has assumed a dominant position in the division of labor, so that it gains control over the determination of the substance of its own work." Given this superior position within a particular organization, members of a profession have the ability to define parameters of their work, to establish standards, and to carry out their own evaluation. Freidson explains that doctors, for instance, "have an officially approved monopoly of the right to define health and illness and to treat illness." As a consequence of their ability to define their own destiny, a profession, according to Freidson, is free from major competition and from direct control by other groups within the organization.[34]

According to Ronald Corwin, professionals achieve autonomy and control over their work because they establish well-defined procedures for "recruiting and policing members and for maximizing control over a body of theoretical knowledge and apply it to the solution of social problems." It is not, continues Corwin, that professionals are necessarily more skillful than nonprofessionals, but that they have based their skill upon "theoretical knowledge and research." Since their knowledge is soundly based upon research and theory, the clients of professionals are more likely to "rely upon the professionals' judgment about their needs. . . . Professions have more legal control over their membership than other occupations through accrediting and licensing procedures and a code of ethics enforceable by law." Additionally, while certain groups may clamor for greater recognition and claim technical superiority, they are not given "professional" status unless they are perceived by others, either members of the same organization or the general public, as having worth and importance. Legitimacy by others is an important factor for professional recognition. The public, for example, believes that doctors serve a valued purpose in society and that they possess technical competence. Professionals, therefore, are a group of individuals who are recognized as having a unique position in the division of labor and who organize their work by establishing formal networks for decision-making, training and research centers, and a highly specialized knowledge base.[35]

This "power" model of professions can be contrasted with the "trait" model. To explore professional efforts by supervisors on a "trait" model, which focuses on general characteristics shared by a variety of professions and then attributing commonly held traits to supervisors, gives an incomplete and inadequate picture of occupational life in school organizations. Among other criticisms of the trait model of professions and professional control, is the fact that to define supervision based on common traits of those occupations recognized as professions is to "ignore the particular social and economic conditions that allowed one occupational group to achieve professional status while another did not."[36] The history of supervision is unique in its own right and defies any attempt to attribute preconceived notions of professional behavior. An analysis of supervision, therefore, requires an examination of how and why supervisors sought to become professionals. The power model, which focuses on the unique circumstances of how professions came to be, provides a more productive and accurate assessment of the evolution of public school supervision.

With this in mind, two factors can be associated with the professionalization of an occupation and of supervisors, in particular: dominance and recognition. These ideas are reflected in Corwin's definition of *professionalism*. "Professionalism represents the efforts of a vocation to gain full control over its work and to enhance its social and economic position in society."[37] A profession assumes a central posture in the decision-making process affecting the organization and is perceived by others as possessing skill, competence, and serving a useful function. It is in this light that the professional model will be used as an analytical and interpretive framework for exploring public school supervision. In other words, to what degree have supervisors achieved dominance within their sphere of influence and to what extent have they been recognized as professionally competent? I will argue that supervisors after the turn of the century became aware of their tenuous position in the educational hierarchy. Concerned about their obscure status in schools as well as mounting criticism leveled against them by teachers, supervisors attempted to deemphasize bureaucratic methods and autocratic role relationships. Supervisors, in effect, sought to achieve dominance and professional recognition for their work within the school system.

The function of supervision in the public schools has been influenced by two factors that have created enormous problems for supervisors. On the one hand, supervisors, by the very nature of their position in schools, are empowered to maintain and enforce organizational mandates and ensure administrative efficiency. They are, in other words, compelled by bureaucratic influences. On the other hand, they are chiefly responsible for the promotion of teacher effectiveness and student learning. The professional conduct of supervisors is dependent on sustaining individual interests and pursuits. Individual objectives, however, are often diametrically opposed to organizational interests. Supervisors experienced these tensions in rather significant ways in their pursuit of professional recognition. The literature is replete with examples of teacher disapproval of invasive supervision and evaluative measures. Teachers perceive supervisors as bureaucratic functionaries whose chief purpose is ensuring organizational security. Despite numerous attempts to dispel these notions throughout its history, supervision still represents an overseeing, controlling, and bureaucratic function.

Corwin finds clear-cut differences between bureaucratic and professional constructs. First, bureaucracy, by its very nature, requires a high degree of standardization with a stress on uniformity in both rules and conduct. Next, decision-making is highly centralized in a bureaucracy. Little, if any, responsibility for decision-making is given to members in low ends of the hierarchy. A third characteristic of bureaucracy is that organizational specialization is highly task-oriented. He includes three subcategories of task-oriented specialization: (a) depends on practice or experience, (b) involves the acceptance of a set of prescribed tasks, and (c) stresses efficiency and technical competence. Professionalism, on the other hand, is marked by a rather low degree of standardization. Corwin explains that stress is placed upon the uniqueness and individuality of a client/member without reference to highly detailed and prescriptive rules of conduct. Second, decision-making is decentralized and responsibility for decision-making is placed in the hands of employees/members. Primary loyalty is to the client rather than to the organization, explains Corwin. Third, specialization within a profession is client-oriented in that knowledge is based primarily on theory and research rather than on experience or practice. Efficiency, explains Corwin, is not a primary objective within a professionally dominated organization. Effectiveness and the pursuit of excellence are the utmost considerations.[38]

According to Corwin, then, professionalism as compared to bureaucracy is less standardized, less centralized, and more specialized with emphasis on the individual. Seen in this light, professional interests and objectives may be antithetical to bureaucratic concerns. Corwin explains these differences regarding teachers as professionals and bureaucratic organizations. He sees a "fundamental contradiction between the subordinate status of teachers in the system and their rights and obligations as professional persons responsible for improving the quality of education." Teachers must exercise "a great deal of latitude," discretion, and initiative in coping with students' problems and in dealing with important issues of school policy, says Corwin. These ideas, he continues, are at once "inconsistent with the fact that teachers are hired and evaluated by administrators to do a specific job; they also are inconsistent with many of the standardized requirements, a centralized decision-making system, close supervision, and task-oriented rules under which schools operate." Corwin suggests that teachers' interests and responsibilities may be inimical to bureaucratic goals and objectives. In schools, he claims, the organization is set up so as to create tensions between bureaucratic functionaries. The conflict centers primarily "between teachers and administrators over the control of work particularly over institutional and curricular matters." This "consistent pattern of conflict," which explains why educational bureaucracies have attracted so much criticism, is a principal topic of discussion in this book.[39]

Bureaucracy
and Professionalism

Part One
The Bureaucratization of Supervision

1
Bureaucracy and School Supervision: Antecedents for Current Practice

Throughout most of the nineteenth century, schools were controlled by loosely structured, decentralized ward boards. Beginning in the late nineteenth century, educational reformers sought to transform schools into a tightly organized and efficiently operated centralized system. Reformers attempted to persuade the American people that a highly complex system of schooling would best serve the interests of all. Bureaucracy, a byproduct of these reform efforts, brought order and organization to an otherwise chaotic, corrupt, and inefficient school environment. While the emergence of bureaucracy and the battles waged in the late nineteenth century over the control of urban schooling are now familiar stories, an important theme has either been ignored or underemphasized; that is, the important role played by the function of supervision amid the upheavals and conflicts over the control of schooling. Supervision, as an integral component of the school bureaucracy, served to perpetuate bureaucratic mandates such as standardization of curriculum and control of teacher behavior. The primary purpose of supervision was the attainment of obedience and compliance to hierarchical sources of authority. As such, supervision reflected the larger, more encompassing bureaucratic phenomenon. In other words, the bureaucratization of supervision occurred within the context of the bureaucratization of urban schooling. This chapter explores the role and function of supervision in the struggle to gain control over urban education. Some of the questions addressed are as follows: Who was the supervisor in the late nineteenth century? What role did the supervisor play in schools? What supervisory methods were employed? What was the overriding purpose or concern of the supervisor? How did the supervisor achieve his stated objectives? What problems did the supervisor of the late nineteenth century face? And, finally: What is meant by the bureaucratization of supervision? An analysis of supervisory practice during this period is important because the nature and character of supervison changed little over the next eighty or so years. Supervision is still important in preserving bureaucratic role relationships within schools.

Superintendent as Supervisor

In 1890, the director of the U.S. Census reported that the country "has been so broken into by isolated bodies of settlement that there can hardly be said to be a frontier line."[1] The significance of this statement was not immediately recognized. For many years, westward expansion meant increased opportunity and prosperity for many. The curtailment of this growth demonstrated the need for the American people to consolidate their accomplishments and formulate new goals. The events in the years to follow would reveal the gradual emergence of modern America.

In general, the second half of the nineteenth century was characterized by unprecedented growth and expansion, the disappearance of the frontier, and the emergence of a nation. This phase of American development was characterized by an unquestioning faith and confidence in the continued maturation of a country and an optimistic and spirited individualism that would pave the way for the future. Andrew Carnegie, in 1886, expressed the sentiments of citizens of a growing nation only beginning to realize its potential by stating that the "United States has already reached the foremost rank among nations and is destined soon to outdistance all others in the race." He continued, "In population, in wealth, . . . in agriculture, America already leads the civilized world."[2]

This phenomenal rate of change was accompanied by industrial expansion, economic growth, increased and concentrated wealth, higher national income, and intensified production of agricultural goods. Every aspect of society was affected. This was especially evident in the growth of urban populations in New York, Boston, St. Louis, and Philadelphia. Innovations in technology, transportation, and communication were rampant. Progress was indeed the motto. The Darwinian and Spencerian doctrines were readily adopted by the Carnegies, Rockefellers, and Vanderbilts and provided the philosophical rationales for competitive individualism and laissez-faire business practices.

Although these doctrines did not go unchallenged, affluence and prosperity prevailed amid the pockets of urban poverty and overcrowded pathogenic tenements. Thus, the American paradox of progress and poverty was fully apparent well before the close of the century.

The effects of national growth and urbanization and other dynamic changes occurring in American society were intensified after 1900. The years marking the latter part of the nineteenth century, however, can be viewed as crucial to the development of America, in general, and to the cities, in particular. The period can best be characterized as one of diverse attitudes, fervent ideas, and strident criticism. One cannot describe the changing political, economic, social, and intellectual patterns of life in the nineteenth century without giving considerable attention to the growth of education and schooling in the United States. In the year 1896, for example, the average daily attendance was nearly ten million pupils (grades kindergarten through 12), double the number of pupils who attended school only twenty years earlier.[3] Undoubtedly, the American faith in schooling as a prime agency in educating the young was unwavering. F. Louis Soldan, a superintendent from St. Louis commenting near the close of the century, stated that "the progress of public education, as far as external growth is concerned, has been stupendous during the last fifty years."[4] William A. Mowry, one of the nineteenth-century patriarchs, commenting on the progress made in education stated that "no sane student of American history can be a pessimist, . . . we need have no fear of the future."[5]

The struggle for the growth of American education, starting in the days of Horace Mann and Francis Parker, continued and assumed a new dimension in the latter decades of the nineteenth century. The schoolmen, specifically superintendents, began shaping schools in large cities into organized networks.[6] Organization was the rallying cry nationally and locally. There was a firm belief that highly organized and efficient schools would meet the demands of a newly developed industrialized age.

During this period, faith in public education increased, transformations in the family, cities, population, and economy took place, and political and social reform were pervasive. In effect, urbanization, industrialization, and institutionalization, along with concomitant forms of rationality and increased efficiency, served to reorganize the socioeconomic, political order. This order would inevitably influence the character of education, in general, and supervision, in particular, in American schools. It should not be surprising, then, that the bureaucratic form of organization found likely justification within the upheavals of the late nineteenth and early twentieth centuries. It was not that bureaucracy was inevitable; rather, the differentiation of roles, reliance upon autonomous, rational, efficient implementation of specific goals and dependence on predictable levels of authority, control and supervision were "peculiarly suited to the fluidity and impersonality of an urban-industrial world."[7] Bureaucratic organization, then, with its hierarchical forms of control, developed in response to a change in the socioeconomic order.

The reform movement in education in the late nineteenth century was reflective of the larger, more encompassing changes that were occurring societally. Although the nineteenth century was characterized by rapid economic growth, reformers realized that there were serious problems in the nation's schools. In the battle that ensued to reorganize the nation's schools, sources of authority and responsibility were transformed to such a degree that the face of education was permanently altered.[8] By the end of the nineteenth century, reformers concerned with undermining inefficiency and corruption transformed schools into streamlined, central administrative bureaucracies. Supervision would play an important role in this transformation.

The story begins within this volatile and decisive period during which a nation was rapidly changing from agrarianism to urbanism. This was not only a dramatic time for urban education, but for society as a whole. Social and political unrest laid the foundation for crusading ideals in education. A battle was raging in late nineteenth-century urban America. The lines were clearly drawn. On the one side stood local control of the schools by a corrupt ward trustee system made up of lay officials and politicians. On the other side was the "reformer" who offered the public a system of schooling that would be at once centralized, professionalized, efficient, and honest. This conflict over the control of the schools in urban settings reached national prominence as a result of a series of muckraking articles appearing in *The Forum*. In a series of nine issues, Joseph Mayer Rice outlined in detail the results of a systematic survey of public schools encompassing thirty-six cities and twenty teacher-training institutions. The study would reveal the condition of America's schools in the late nineteenth century.

The study was undertaken between January 7 and June 25, 1892. Rice, a pediatrician, became interested in child study in the 1880s and studied in the universities of Jena and Leipsig, then the intellectual meccas of the world. Upon his return, he spent six months studying the American city school system, primarily in the East and Midwest. "In undertaking this journey it was my aim not only to learn what methods of instruction were commonly followed in our country, and the general condition of our schools," wrote Rice in 1893, "but also to investigate the manner in which the schools of different cities were managed." He believed that he could not rely on "reports published by school officials regarding the condition of their schools" because these reports were frequently "no more than purely political documents, and consequently, as a rule, entirely misleading." Therefore, said Rice, "I relied, in studying the condition of schools, only on personal observation of class-room instruction."[9]

Although his views were subject to criticism,[10] Rice presented an accurate account of public school life in the late nineteenth century. He disclosed the poor conditions of urban schools and called for greater parental involvement; the depoliticalization of boards of education; and the need to secure competent, efficient teachers. He revealed that schools were run by inefficient and unprofessional ward boards. Many educators joined Rice in his condemnation of local control of schools by "corrupt and incapable ward politicians." William Mowry, in 1895, was mournful of the fact that ward boards control the schools without the assistance of "competent superintendents. . . . With a large and able supervisory force the committee still holds all power in their hands, and neither the superintendent nor his six experienced supervisors make any move until they are ordered by the board."[11] Similarly, William George Bruce, editor of the *American School Board Journal* as well as a school board member, in 1895, made a plea to remove the politician from the schools. He stated that the schools must "weed out" the corrupt politician. Bruce continued his tirade by urging school people to "shirk no duty in carrying out the best interests of your school system. Meet the demands of your community fearlessly and honestly. Rebuke the politician."[12]

Not more than a year and a half later, Lewis H. Jones, a prominent school superintendent who had previously received acclaim from Rice, described the political influence in the schools. In an article published in the *Atlantic Monthly* entitled "The Politician and the Public School," Jones claimed that the "unscrupulous politician is the greatest enemy, . . . in public education." Jones said that the problem would not be so bad if it were only that the "public treasury" was "plundered." The problem, he continued, was that "the men and women who teach in schools, who are infinitely superior to the political bosses, must submit to the most galling indignities." The effect on children was even more striking. These "political tricksters," charged Jones, were responsible for hiring incompetent teachers who would ultimately lead to the "spiritual death of the children." Jones concluded his denunciation of political corruption in the schools by stating that "the modern politician murders the children for mere gain, . . . partisan politics is the most horrible curse that ever spread its blighting influence over the public schools."[13]

The *Atlantic Monthly* continued to publish accounts of political dominance in the management of public schools. In July 1896, an article entitled "Confessions of Public School Teachers" decried the dominance of lay influence in the schools.[14] Again, in November 1898, the same publication ran an article entitled "Confessions of Three School Superintendents," in which three anonymous superintendents related their experiences regarding politics in the schools. "The low moral tone" of the schools, they charged was due to the "damaging influence of the ward board. . . . The favoritism and corruption is rampant." To ameliorate this situation "there must be more concentration of responsibility, and consequently of authority, in the administration of school affairs. . . . There is probably no other public official, of equal ability, intelligence, and character, who has so little real legal authority as a superintendent of schools." The authors of this article concluded that in order for schools to improve, there must be greater authority placed with the superintendent, by making him "strictly responsible for results."[15]

However, it was Rice, more than anyone else, who spelled out in concrete terms what needed to be done to change the system of education in America. Rice was not politically naive. He knew that the corruption in education could only be eliminated by a complete transformation in the locus of control and management of the schools. The power and authority to make educational decisions, said Rice, must be placed in the competent hands of professional educators whose chief concern is "the welfare of our nation's youth." Superintendents, contended Rice, were professional educators who would apply the latest scientific supervisory principles and at the same time would support "more humane" efforts in education.[16]

It was, however, Rice's discussion of supervision that reveals how superintendents could achieve their goal of transforming urban education. He called for more professional management of the schools and placed much importance on the supervisory functions of city superintendents. Transformations of the urban school environment could not take place, thought Rice, without competent, scientific supervision as performed by the superintendent. Perhaps more than anyone else, Rice argued for greater supervision of the schools in order for superintendents to gain control over urban education. Rice advocated the use of "efficient and professional" supervision, by superintendents, to accomplish their objectives. Rice lamented the "antiquated system of supervision" that was prevalent throughout American schools. "Supervision that aims simply to secure results by a periodical examination of classes" is simply poor supervision. He decried supervision solely based on "visitation, inspection or examination. . . . Our problems are a result of misdirected and incompetent supervision. . . . Teachers are as a rule too weak to stand alone, and therefore need constantly to be propped up by the supervisory staff. . . . Properly directed supervision" could "elevate our nation's schools to the highest of degrees." While supervision was necessary to raise the standards of teaching, Rice, a shrewd and perceptive reformer, realized that the first duty of the superintendent was to take command so as to be able, at some later time, institute a program to improve instruction in urban schools.[17]

Rice, in sum, proposed that the schools be organized efficiently and that power should rest in the hands of professional experts, thereby divorcing the school from politics. He also stressed that closer supervision should be maintained so as to enable superintendents to control the schools thereby raising the standard of teaching. Rice, albeit drawing a bleak picture of America's primary schools, was optimistic. He believed, as did other late nineteenth-century urban school reformers, that the extension of a universal system of free schooling in America was imperative. He stated that "the general educational spirit of the country is progressive," and "the schools of a large number of our cities [are] now laboring in the right direction."[18]

Rice's proclamations in *The Forum* received wide publicity. However, it cannot be concluded that his recommendations single-handedly transformed urban education. To be sure, many of Rice's criticisms had been discussed by leading educators for many years preceding the publication of the articles in *The Forum*. For example, one of the earliest educators to recognize the problems of city schools and the need for an efficient plan for urban school organization was John D. Philbrick, a prominent superintendent from Boston. In 1885, he presented an influential report entitled *City School Systems in the United States*. It was introduced by John Eaton, who was the commissioner of the Bureau of Education, as the most "valuable study of city school systems of public instruction" to date. Philbrick explained that since the "American school system is largely founded on the idea of local competency in the management of educational affairs," the school board represented an important factor in the "success of city systems." He believed that "securing competent school boards" was one of the most critical problems facing city systems, and which was difficult to achieve because "everywhere there are unscrupulous politicians who do not hesitate to improve every opportunity to sacrifice the interests of the schools to the purposes of the political machine." The political influence and "excessive decentralization," thought Philbrick, were "evils of our city systems," which must be confronted and expunged.[19]

Philbrick discussed in detail the enormity of the problems the schools faced, but yet envisioned progress for the future. This success was dependent on the degree to which educators would organize and centralize authority. "Organization," wrote Philbrick, "is nothing more than a system of arrangements whereby means are adapted to ends for the production of desired results. . . . City schools must organize in the most efficient manner possible. . . . Problems of imperfections and mismanagement," warned Philbrick, will occur. However, these defects "are not due to the excessive perfection of the organization, the adoption of means to ends, but to precisely the opposite cause, namely, the need of still further improvement in these organizations." It was quite evident to Philbrick that "in the matter of administration the tendency is towards a greater centralization and permanency of authority and that this tendency is in the direction of progress and improvement."[20]

It is obvious then that sentiments for increased centralization and close supervision were echoed by schoolmen of the day. The significance, however, of the Rice study was that it consolidated thought regarding the organization of city schools and provided a rallying point from which superintendents and other leading school figures would be able to justify their demand for control of the schools. Sentiments of centralization and increased efficiency in schools gained considerable momentum immediately following Rice's study. Not coincidentally the superintendent assumed a position of greater authority in educational decision-making. Superintendents advanced the idea that improvements in urban education could only be attained through close supervision. The superintendent, of course, would oversee school facilities and supervise instruction, thereby ensuring excellence in urban education. Indeed, the role of the superintendent was intimately entwined with the function of supervision. The superintendent as supervisor received wide discussion in educational circles.

The authority of the superintendent as supervisor was axiomatic. "The superintendent must have unlimited authority to manage the schools."[21] Aaron Estellus Gove, an eminent superintendent from Denver, concurred with the idea of "superintendent authority," but warned that the placement of "unlimited authority in the hands of one man" would raise suspicions and, inevitably, provoke opposition.[22] The idea that centralization might be viewed as a usurpation of authority was hotly debated in 1890 at the annual meeting of the NEA. Emerson E. White, a distinguished superintendent from Cincinnati, took the floor and reacted sharply to the idea of equating centralization with dictatorship. "The term dictator is objectionable, . . . A dictator is one who usurps authority. Those who employ official position for the public disadvantage do so under the prescribed forms of law." White claimed that "the issue is not one between democracy and monarchy. Our people are not dreaming of monarchy."[23] It is, at the same time, interesting to note White's ideal for a superintendent. "A school superintendent should be a Caesar, a Solomon, and an angel, all in one person!"[24]

"Centralization as a plan for urban school organization" was advantageous, stated Andrew Draper, one of the foremost superintendents/supervisors of the period, because it "confers authority, . . . centralizes responsibility, . . . involves close supervision, . . . and harmonizes and solidifies the force. . . ."[25] I am not in favor of limiting the authority of city superintendents. If I could, I would confer upon them much broader authority than they now have." Draper explained that he would give superintendents "almost autocratic powers within their sphere of duty and action, and then I would hold them responsible for results."[26] I am a firm believer in one-man power," claimed Israel H. Peres, a former president of the Memphis, Tennessee, school board. "The superintendent should be superior to the teacher in mental power, culture, and experience; if the reverse is true, there is a maladministration of forces which works a positive injury to the public-school system and tends toward regress instead of progress. . . . The superintendent is the life-blood of the school system. He is the main-spring; he is the fountain. From him come energy, ambition, progress, life and success," concluded Peres.[27] A. E. Winship, the editor of the *Journal of Education,* in an address before the NEA in 1899 said, "You are a conductor, . . . nor a baggagemaster."[28] The reformer of the late nineteenth-century maintained that superintendents must be given carte-blanche to effect desired changes in the educational system. To achieve their stated objectives, supervision, it was believed, was the primary means by which the superintendent would gain control of public education. That the function of supervision was of great importance was beyond doubt, as an editorial in *Education* declared. "No educational question now before the public is of more vital importance than that of supervision. All branches of industry have a responsible head, the directing, adjusting, and controlling power."[29] According to William Maxwell, a superintendent of schools in Brooklyn, "A school reaches its highest efficiency" when there is "one directing mind" who supervises and "coordinates the work of teachers and pupils."[30] "We must have supervision," stated J. P. Wickersham. "Hence, we must have superintendents."[31] Supervision, then, became synonymous with the work of the superintendent.

Perhaps the most important statement regarding the organization of city schools and the role of the superintendent as supervisor was published in 1895, three years after the Rice study, by the Committee of Fifteen. The subcommittee on the organization of city school systems was chaired by Andrew S. Draper, formerly superintendent in Cleveland, Ohio, and at that time president of the University of Illinois. The committee recommended that the superintendent of schools "should be charged with no duty save the supervision of the instruction." Furthermore, the superintendent of instruction "should be charged with the responsibility of making" supervision "professional and scientific." The committee recommended that the superintendent "be given the position and authority to accomplish that end." In this way, the committee believed the schools could be most efficiently organized to secure the desired results. In effect, the committee recommended the diminution of lay influence in the schools, increased authority in the hands of a professional expert, namely the superintendent, and increased attention to the importance of supervision. To this last point, the committee realized that the work in the schools "must be reduced to a system and the workers brought into harmonious relations," a job supervision would perform.³² Reformers during this period argued thus: schools were run by incompetent nonprofessionals. If positive changes were to occur, then control must be given to competent, professionals who would use efficient, modern techniques of supervision. Supervision in the late nineteenth century served a dual function: (1) it was hailed, in a propagandist sense, as a modern, innovative strategy to bring order to a chaotic system of schooling; and (2) became a chief means whereby superintendents could control all aspects of the school environment and thereby inculcate bureaucratic values such as uniformity and obedience to authority.

A review of the literature indicates unmistakably that, in the years following Rice's observations of the "deplorable" conditions of America's schools, there was an overwhelming impetus in large cities throughout the country to centralize decision-making. The superintendent as supervisor would be the central figure in urban education in the late nineteenth century. Reformers maintained that a strong superintendency, equipped with professional and efficient supervisory strategies, would serve the best interests of urban schooling. But what were the techniques and strategies used by superintendents? Did they in fact serve the best interests of urban schooling? One of the major ways superintendents legitimized their control over the schools was by promulgating the notion that supervision by educational experts would improve urban-school conditions. Reformers in the late nineteenth century tried to persuade the American public that the function of supervision, as performed by the superintendent, would bring order to a school system that heretofore was characterized by chaos and teacher incompetence. Supervision, in fact, was a convenient mechanism by which school reformers could justify their control over urban education and proved to be an effective means to control the activities of teachers, thereby achieving a certain degree of stability and uniformity in school operations. Superintendents, in the late nineteenth century, based their activities more on school control than on educational improvement. This is evident based on an examination of supervisory practice in the schools. The evidence supports the view that superintendents utilized autocratic methods not solely for improving teaching, but of equal, if not greater importance for constraining teachers to obey the rules and regulations of the school bureaucracy. All this was accomplished under the guise of promoting the superintendent as a "teacher of teachers." By examining supervisory methods in the late nineteenth century it will become obvious what superintendents intended to accomplish.

The function of supervision, as carried out by the superintendent of schools, was synonymous with inspection and visitation. John Prince, in his widely read book on school administration, stated that the most important supervisory duties were those concerned with "inspecting, examining, advising, and directing."[33] Attesting to this fact, F. Louis Soldan, a noteworthy superintendent from St. Louis, stated in his annual report that the efficiency of schools was maintained by constant supervision "by a number of officers who spend their whole time in visiting and inspecting schools."[34] Many supervisors believed that a large part of their duty was to inspect the physical facilities of schools, manage the increasing number of pupils, and administer school programs. Andrew Draper, in a little book entitled *The Supervision of Country Schools,* stated that "school supervision has come to be a kind which requires a frequent visitation of the schools by an official who is specially prepared for it. . . . The purpose of visitation is to discover the spirit of the school."[35] Visitation and inspection, to Draper and other superintendents, were important to ensure compliance to the various administrative rules and regulations imposed by newly created central offices. Supervision, in this light, served two functions: one, to inspect the overall management and condition of school buildings, and two, to visit and inspect classrooms in order to, as the famous school superintendent James Greenwood stated, "diagnose the malady" and provide the proper "prescription."[36] Supervision, during this time, assumed a rather perfunctory and administrative quality.

Yet, it is unmistakable that many educators advocated that much of the superintendent's time should be devoted to the "teaching of teachers." A. W. Edson, a county supervisor in Massachusetts, stated that "a superintendent should be, first of all, a teacher of teachers, an expert critic teacher of large and successful experience. . . . This implies that he should have a broad and deep scholarship, . . . be a reader and a thinker. . . . As professional head to the whole educational system he should be thoroughly acquainted with modern education at its best, be in thorough sympathy with it, and be able to inspire his whole teaching force with a true professional spirit." Edson believed that supervisory visits should be frequent in order to "train teachers to do better work."[37] Edson, as did other superintendents, believed that teachers were weak and "needed assistance. . . . Many teachers lack training and education. . . . Professional supervision," said Edson, is the only way to improve teacher training in schools. "The superintendent, as an inspirational force, is needed, and should be frequently in every schoolroom" all across the nation.[38] T. M. Balliet of Massachusetts was another leading superintendent who did not favorably view the competency of most teachers. In 1894, he insisted that there were only two types of teachers: the efficient and the inefficient.[39] The only way to reform the schools, thought Balliet, was to "secure a competent superintendent; second, to let him "reform" all the teachers who are incompetent and can be "reformed"; third, to bury the dead."[40] Characteristic of the remedies applied to "improve teaching" was this suggestion: "weak teachers should place themselves in such a position in the room that every pupil's face may be seen without turning the head."[41] Similar suggestions to these were offered by many other leading superintendents. All superintendents believed that teachers were weak and therefore needed the assistance of a supervisor. "The greatest problem facing our schools today is the professional weakness of teachers," stated E. Cates.[42]

William Torrey Harris, considered by many as the most prestigious and influential "centralizer" of the time, also regarded teachers as weak and ineffectual. Teachers who are "weak in discipline," said Harris in explaining his remedy to cope with ineffective teachers, should be placed "on the 'substitutes' list and let them fill vacancies here and there as they occur through the temporary absence of the regular teacher. . . . I have known teachers that had become chronic failures in discipline entirely reformed by a few weeks of such experience."[43] The attitudes and practices of this foremost "scholar of centralization" leads one to conclude that autocratic supervisory methods found justification in the public schools. Autocratic methods in supervision were prevalent for essentially two reasons. One, superintendents did not favorably view the competency of teachers. They believed that immediate and stringent remedies were necessary to improve teaching in order to demonstrate their "professional expertise" in running the schools. Two, reformers realized that "bureaucracy" and "centralized control" were the only solutions for the problems of urban education in America. In regard to the first reason just noted, it is interesting to point out that the attitudes of these superintendents/supervisors about teacher competency were shaped in part by patriarchical ideologies, as briefly noted in the Introduction, and will also be alluded to later in the chapter. The fact that superintendents and centralizers were mostly male while most teachers were female was certainly not coincidental but reflective of economic interests and patriarchical relations that were fundamentally reinforced by the dominant ideology in the larger society. The sexual division of labor was also consistent with the increasing formalization (bureaucratization) of the educational system that supported a segregated workforce in consonance with a growing administrative hierarchy composed chiefly of men. The views of superintendents/supervisors about the competence of the teaching force is indicative of this sexual bias.

In a revealing address delivered before the NEA in 1888, James M. Greenwood, a prominent superintendent, described the typical affairs of a superintendent performing the function of supervision.

> Going into a school I try to put aside everything like authority, or superiority, and to approach the teacher in a proper spirit of helpfulness. Then, I endeavor to see the school from the teacher's standpoint, and if necessary, to have the teacher see her school as it appears to me.
>
> What to Do?
>
> 1. I go in quietly. 2. I watch the teacher and pupils awhile, usually until the novelty wears off. 3. Sometimes I conduct a recitation, with the teacher's permission, and thus bring out points in which she may be deficient; or, simply to test the knowledge that the pupils have of the subject. 4. If suggestions should be made to the teacher, I do so privately, or request her to call after school. 5. Depending on the peculiarities of the teacher, the conversation must be directed in such a way as to benefit her. If the teacher be "heady," frequently the most efficacious remedy is to let her alone a few days, and when her room is badly demoralized, help her straighten it out. Of a dozen teachers in a building, no two can be precisely alike. I think the question may be put in this form: Given the teacher, the school, the defects; how to improve them?
>
> Signs To Look For
>
> 1. Common sense. 2. Good heatlh. 3. General scholarship. 4. Critical knowledge of the branches. 5. Order. 6. Ability to manage hard cases. 7. Power to teach. 8. Power to develop thought in the pupils. 9. Routine teaching. 10. "Reciting-post" teaching. 11. Skill in questioning. 12. Skill in fertility of resources. 13. Energy and vigilance properly directed. 14. Pleasant voice. 15. Disposition to antagonize pupils. 16. Power to gain the good-will of children without spoiling them. 17. Disposition to scold and to grumble. 18. Attention to pupils reciting and also to those at their seats. 19. Neatness and cleanliness of room,

desks, etc. 20. Ability to secure cheerful and thorough work by the pupils. 21. The tendency to waste time doing nothing laboriously. 22. Variableness teaching. 23. Steadfastness of purpose in teaching. 24. Disposition to take care of school property. 25. Ventilation of schoolroom, and looking after the children's health. 26. Tact and skill in adapting new methods in teaching. 27. Originality in management and in methods.

Sometimes I jot down items that need attention and hand them to the teacher.

Very much of my time is devoting to visiting schools and inspecting the work.[44]

In 1888 centralization was only just beginning to take hold across the nation. Superintendents would soon realize that due to the increasing population and overall complexity of urban education, they would not be able to supervise the schools as closely as they would have preferred. Case in point: note Greenwood's change in posture only three years later. The skilled superintendent, said Greenwood, should simply walk into the classroom and "judge from a compound sensation of the disease at work among the inmates."[45] There is much evidence to conclude that Greenwood's supervisory methods, which relied on experience and intuition rather than technical or scientific knowledge, were adhered to widely.

In an address in 1891, Aaron Gove outlined the limitations of "supervisory inspections." He claimed that "inspection lacked method and precision. . . . I do not know how to test the quality of a teacher's work; you don't. If we could do this, we would make our schools efficient as they should be."[46] The paper presented by Gove opened a lively and heated discussion which, in the end, reaffirmed visitation and control as primary supervisory duties of the superintendent. W. W. Chalmers, a city superintendent in Michigan, rationalized his use of "inspection for controlling the schools in my jurisdiction" in the following way: "Of the 1,000 hours of school in the year, we must be able to judge of the 999 by seeing the one, . . . our knowledge of a teacher's work must come through these hasty visits." Chalmers explained that he was able to save valuable time by using a "mechanical device of monthly reports." Teachers would complete detailed reports and return them to the clerk. "My clerk reads them carefully, . . . notes all irregularities, . . . and hands them to me." Chalmers claimed that he could spend a couple of minutes perusing the reports and would be able to determine the quality of the school. "I then write letters to principals and teachers, suggesting changes that I deem wise."[47] Superintendents, like Chalmers, believed that it was impossible to closely supervise classrooms as it once was. Therefore, superficial inspection using statistical methods for accumulating data was the best alternative.

Greenwood then arose to defend his supervisory methods. He claimed that the methods used in supervision had to come from experience and intuition. He described an interesting case of "a young medical student" who once had difficulty diagnosing a particular ailment. He asked his mentor to accompany him to check the patient. "No sooner was the door of the sick room opened than the old practitioner gave the young doctor a nudge and whispered, "Smallpox!" The novice asked," continues Greenwood: " 'How could you so quickly, without seeing the patient, tell that it was smallpox?' The physician answered, 'By the smell and the feeling which this disease always creates in me.' " Greenwood explained to his audience, "So the skilled superintendent, often by merely entering the room, can judge from a compound sensation of the disease at work among the inmates."[48]

John Burke, a superintendent from Kentucky, rose to defend the methods employed by Greenwood by stating that these methods are the "only practical methods of testing the quality of a teacher's work." Burke continued by explaining his own methods for observing and improving the "quality of the teacher's work. . . . I do not like, as a rule, to see bare blackboards, even though they may be clean. . . . If the boards are covered with neat work, and show that a number of pupils have been demonstrating their knowledge on them, this is a good sign. He continued to explain that a teacher should not feel nervous by the superintendent's presence because the visitor is really "a friend and sympathizer, as well as an expert and critic."[49]

As noted, supervision in the late nineteenth century became an important function of the superintendent in his attempt to organize and gain control of urban city schools. The superintendent, in the role of inspector, supervisor, educational expert, scholar, man of high moral integrity, and teacher of teachers, envisioned the improvement of American schools by means of one central, efficient source: himself. In other words, the chief source for his authority was not technical competence or specialized training, but rooted in hierarchical sources of power. Under the guise of "modern or scientific supervision," superintendents sought to legitimize their control over schools. Unfortunately, in their zeal to gain control and increase efficiency in American education, supervision became little more than an institutionalized, perfunctory mechanism by which the superintendent would manage and maintain control over schools. A school system based on bureaucratic organization, with supervision as the primary means to oversee school operations, they thought, would serve the best interests of American education. The fallacy of such an argument would soon be clearly evident; however, relief would fall short of expectation.

Managing the Urban Schools: Influence of the Bureaucrats

In the late nineteenth-century, the theme of bureaucracy was ubiquitous. Bureaucratic rules and regulations were necessary to accomplish the purposes of centralization. It is not surprising that autocratic tendencies dominated public school supervision in the late nineteenth century. While it is evident that the impulse toward bureaucratic school governance and autocratic supervision can be explained in terms of the socioeconomic-political conditions of the time, the values and ideas of influential men, which encouraged authoritarian rule in urban education, finds relevance here. It was men like William Payne, William Harris, and William Chancellor, as progenitors, who articulated the ideas of order, control, and autocratic supervision. These men were neither self-serving nor altruistic. Rather, bureaucracy was perceived as a phenomenon *sui generis* (self-regulating); that is, it confronted supervisors with a reality that appeared unalterable and inevitable. Exploring the views of these men who supported the continuation and maintenance of bureaucracy in the urban setting will provide insights not only into what schools were like, but how supervision was carried out.

William T. Harris, a U.S. commissioner of education, speaking in 1891 before the NEA, stated that "the rapid growth of American education would continue well into the new century." Harris fervently believed that the school was the foremost institution in American society and that its continued success "is of utmost importance."[50] Harris, however, was not unmindful of the fact that serious problems confronted public education that needed prompt attention. Harris maintained that schools must promote "punctuality, regularity, attention and silence, as habits necessary through life for successful combination with one's fellowman in an industrial and commercial civilization." To Harris, supervision would be invaluable in order to inculcate these values in schools.⁵¹ Many supervisors in the late nineteenth century similarly asserted that the only way to promote "efficiency" is through structured school governance. "Without question, the greatest problem today is how best to administer the public school interests of a city," affirmed Aaron Gove, a superintendent from Denver. Gove urged his fellow supervisors to support the efforts of reformers to establish "an efficient school management."⁵² A strongly supervised and centralized school system, it was thought, would promote what was known as "the Seven School Virtues": regularity, punctuality, neatness, accuracy, silence, industry and obedience."⁵³ These ideas of "regularity" and "obedience" were advocated by many other educational reformers. Many supervisors, in particular, discussed the need to endorse "discipline" in the schools. "Discipline, the power to control which produces and sustains order is necessary to eradicate existing evils. . . ."⁵⁴ Discipline and control alone are better than spontaneity," wrote J. L. Hughes in 1892.⁵⁵ In an address given before the National Herbart Society, William Torrey Harris, a superintendent of schools in St. Louis and later U.S. commissioner of education, focused attention on school discipline by insisting that "lax discipline in a school saps the moral character of the pupil." Harris believed that the lack of discipline allowed the pupil to do "as he pleases" without the reinforcement of "regularity, punctuality, and systematic industry." Harris continued to charge that the lack of discipline in schools allowed the individual to grow up with poor habits, such as "whispering" and "intermeddling." Harris stated that the individual, "never having subdued himself," would be unable to cope with the "world of chaos" and inevitably "will have to be subdued by external constraint on the part of his fellow men."⁵⁶

The lack of discipline and absence of obedience, which characterized education before centralization, were anathema to the reformer. A revealing account of actual school practice in the 1870s and early 1880s was described by John Trainer in a book titled *How to Grade and Teach a Country School*. Trainer's observations were made as a result of a survey of schools he conducted under the auspices of the NEA. "The discipline was all that could be desired by the most inveterate scold!" Teachers, explained Trainer, complained of the lack of discipline and lack of obedience of pupils. "There was no regularity or system in calling or dismissing the classes, . . . pupils came in as they passed out—as they pleased and when they pleased." Trainer continued, "The whispering was intolerable; pupils talked loudly and constantly about everything except their school work; pupils of all grades passed promiscuously and with freedom to all parts of the room for different purposes." During one of his visits, Trainer observed that when "two boys were sent to Mr. Green's for a bucket of water, . . . they did not get back until the dismissal for recess at 2:30, and then the bucket was but half filled with water, and that contained many broken pieces of glass stalks and pieces of weeds." Trainer continues describing what he observed. "The children crowded around the bucket and soon consumed the water, leaving the floor wet and muddy where they trampled. During the recess hour the pupils lounged upon the tops of the desks in ungainly positions, and chatted very loudly about the neighborhood news." Trainer admitted that "we found a few schools in worse condition than this one."[57]

Given the values and beliefs of nineteenth-century reformers like Trainer, it is not surprising that many educators advocated the implementation of the Lancasterian Monitoral System. Joseph Lancaster brought his uniform system of education to America from England in the nineteenth century. The Lancasterian method offered a structured system whereby anywhere from 500 to 1,000 children could be "monitored" at once. Children would be seated in a large auditorium and monitors would be assigned at each end of the row to ensure that they were "obedient and silent."[58] David MacRae, a Scottish writer who observed the Ward School No. 50 in New York City, reported that at the morning assembly the auditorium was filled with about 600 students between the ages of 5 and 12. MacRae was impressed with the efficiency by which the lesson was carried out by the principal. "Pupils replied in unison" and when the lesson was completed they "rose and moved off with military precision."[59] Similar findings were reported by a group of concerned citizens after visiting the public schools in Philadelphia. Like MacRae, they were impressed with the precision and discipline exhibited by the pupils in a Lancasterian-type setting. "The regularity of movement in so large a number of children, all well dressed, and many of them tastefully attired was truly interesting." The visitors were also delighted to hear students recite their lessons in "simultaneous enunciation" and the way in which "a thousand little forms are as erect in their seats, as though they were rivetted there by some process of mechanism."[60]

In order to achieve this systematization of schooling Trainer recommended that schools be strictly supervised and that educators cultivate respect for order, discipline, and control. "GIVE

THE SCHOOLS A THOROUGH SYSTEM OF SUPERVISION THAT SHALL TEST THE WORK OF ALL CONNECTED THEREWITH, FROM THE STATE OFFICER TO THE CHILDREN, INCLUSIVE, AND THE BEST OF RESULTS MUST FOLLOW."[61] In fact, many reformers stressed the importance of supervision for "bringing order to a chaotic and backward school system."[62] Supervision was the primary means by which reformers would ensure adherence to "punctuality," and "silence," and "obedience." As such, supervision was the chief mechanism used by superintendents to inculcate certain bureaucratic values and ideas into the schools. Supervision perpetuated and sustained autocratic influences in order to safeguard centralization and bureaucracy in urban education.

"School discipline must be assured in our schools," pronounced Larkin Dutton, a superintendent, in 1892. Dutton pointed out that the attainment of "discipline" in schools can "only be assured through the judicious use of supervision." The superintendent, performing the function of supervision, must ensure that "no pupil is to do what will disturb and distract the attention of others." "There is to be no moving about the room or even raising a hand to ask a question or do anything else which will interrupt the progress of the class," explained Dutton. "Answering pupils' questions wastes valuable time. . . . Nothing is more disturbing to a class, and few things are more irritating to studious pupils than the incesssant interruptions and the everlasting prattle of a loquacious teacher."[63]

"Supervision is valuable," declared the prominent school superintendent James Greenwood from Kansas, because "it directs obedience and constituted authority." Supervision, for Greenwood, was necessary so as to "infuse a school with the proper amount of discipline and respect for authority." Greenwood advocated strict guidelines for behavior; supervision would be responsible for monitoring this conduct. For example, a supervisor should carefully inspect a classroom because "whispering in school under the teacher's sanction is a dangerous experiment, and leads straight to demoralization."[64]

The imposition of values such as "discipline," "neatness," "punctuality," "order," and "obedience" was the mainstay of supervisory practice during the late nineteenth-century. Although these ideas were certainly not new goals among American educators, they found new meaning in the educational milieu of late nineteenth-century America. Homer Seeley, a superintendent from Iowa, stated that the superintendent, as supervisor, "must be an effective disciplinarian, capable of securing order, obedience." He must," continued Seeley, "instill discipline among all the patrons of the school, . . . and they must conform to his plans, . . . if true discipline exists. . . ."[65] The greatest fault of our American schools is lack of reverence for properly constituted authority."[66] Supervision, it was argued, would restore reverence throughout America's schools.

One of the most prominent people who, almost more than anyone else, changed the character of public school supervision in the late nineteenth century was William Harold Payne. Payne was the prominent author of the first text written on school supervision, *Chapters on School Supervision, A Practical Treatise on Superintendence; Grading; Arranging Courses of Study; The Preparation and Use of Blanks, Records, and Reports, Examinations for Promotion, etc.* which was published in 1875.[67] Payne was a prolific writer and was in attendance at most of the meetings and conventions held nationally and locally. According to G. C. Poret, Payne's biographer, the latter knew intimately and corresponded with, the leading schoolmen of his day, including William Torrey Harris and Louis Soldan.[68] Although not a superintendent in one of the large cities of the country, Payne's ideas received considerable national attention and were applied by such reputable superintendents as Harris of St. Louis, Maxwell of New York, Draper of Ohio, and Gove of Denver.

Payne was born on May 12, 1836, in Ontario County, New York. Being slight in build, he was urged by his mother to study, and was sent to Macedon Academy in 1852. Interestingly, Payne, an excellent student, did not receive his training from formal institutions; rather, he systematically taught himself psychology, philosophy, and related sciences. He began his teaching career in 1856, in a small rural school in Michigan. Two years later, he was made principal of Three Rivers Union School; two other principalships were to follow. Finally, he became superintendent of schools in Adrian, Michigan, and held that position for ten years. From 1864 to 1869, he was editor of the *Michigan Teacher.* In 1879, he was called to head the Department of Education at the University of Michigan. He was then elected president of Peabody College and remained there for fourteen years. In 1901, he returned to the University of Michigan. He died in Ann Arbor on June 18, 1907, at the age of seventy-one.

Among Payne's works were *Contributions to the Science of Education* and *Education of Teachers,* as well as translations of Rousseau's *Emile,* and Compayre's *Psychology Applied to Education.* Payne was an ardent supporter of popular education. He believed that a successful, well-managed school could only be achieved through "competent administration and supervision." The superintendent, said Payne, would be chiefly concerned with the "supervision of teachers. . . . Teachers need external aid, . . . they need to be told in definite terms, by some authority considered competent, both the quality and the quantity of work that can reasonably be undertaken." Payne asserted that teachers, in instructional matters, did "not know where to begin and how to proceed." As a result, continued Payne, their work was poor and ineffective." Payne believed that the superintendent must instill in the teacher "sound scholarship, a knowledge of the art and science of teaching and a love for teaching."[69]

Payne's belief of the superiority of the superintendent in managing schools and instructing teachers were informed by his philosophy of society in general. "Human society," said Payne,

> is a hierarchy of forces. Organization implies subordination. If there is to be a plan, some one must devise it, while others must execute it, . . . in human society the many must follow the direction of the few. . . . It is not possible to conceive a state of society in which there are not inequalities based on gradations in the ability to govern, . . . Human society is organized on the principle that the weak are to be protected by the strong, . . . the masses of mankind must voluntarily submit to the guidance of those who have the faculty of directing.[70]

Payne translated his notions of a "hierarchy of forces" in society to the situation in schools. The schools, said Payne, must "follow the law which prevails in all other industries—differentiation, classification, system." The teacher must be "held responsible" for the work he does in the classroom. The superintendent, continued Payne, "should be a responsible head, able to devise plans in general and in detail, and vested with sufficient authority to keep all subordinates in their proper places, and at their assigned tasks. . . . A graded-school of a thousand pupils and twenty teachers involves a system of great complexity, and requires the nicest adjustments in order to work with harmony and efficiency." Payne noted the specific areas that need prompt attention by the "directing official." "The arrangement of courses of study, the examination and classification of pupils, their discipline and correction, the oversight of teachers, the compilation of records—these are some of the items on which depends the success of the system and which require the attention of a single responsible head."[71]

The extent to which Payne's ideas concerning "the necessary hierarchy of the school system" were communicated to and accepted by other reformers can be well documented. Josiah Little Pickard, the first president of the NEA, was an eminent school superintendent and college president. Pickard delineated his views on the emerging school hierarchy and the role that supervision plays in a school system in a book simply entitled *School Supervision*. As did Payne, Pickard believed in the inevitability of hierarchical school control. In his introductory chapter, Pickard explains that supervision of school operations, as a "branch of human industry," plays an important part in "the specialization of labor." "The more minute the subdivision of labor, the greater the need of supervision," writes Pickard. Pickard, explaining the role of the individual in a school, states that "each laborer is by practice perfected in the work to which he is assigned, and is confined to a narrow field." The worker, says Pickard, realizes that his employer has certain expectations regarding the results to be attained and that "his work is only a part, a small part, in the great plan." Pickard reminded his readers that "over the worker" there stands "one whose special work it is to adjust the parts, himself familiar with each, but freed from active work in any part. He is the overseer, the superintendent."[72]

Supervisors reminded the public that "a great school system" is "entirely analogous, . . . to a great army which has its general, its colonels, its captains, and its privates."[73] Albert Marble, president of the NEA and a superintendent from Massachusetts, informed his audience that the endurance of a school system is dependent on the maintenance of "superior and subordinate" role relationships. "We find," said Marble, "the authority and duty of the teacher by subtraction, . . . and the authority of school officers by addition."[74] The development of a hierarchical school system was proceeding at a rapid pace.

Similarly, Norman Allison Calkins, a prominent and highly respected assistant superintendent from New York City, explained that "during all ages of the world, in every country, among all races, nations, tribes, and communities, the many must follow the directions of the few . . . condition represents an essential principle in the organizations of society, whether military, civil, scientific, benevolent, or religious." Calkins was not concerned about the method by which "the head" takes charge. "It matters not how it comes about that the few direct the many; whether it be through physical, intellectual, or moral power; or whether the position be an inherited, assumed, or elective one, the fact remains the same." Calkins concludes: "In all matters where numbers act together for a common purpose, there is and must be supervision and direction to attain the end sought. By this means the greatest good is secured; without it, no real progress could be made." Calkins, as did other reformers throughout this period, emphatically stated that the superintendent must be the "overseer and inspector" of a school system. "He is an examiner, . . . an inspector, . . . a supervisor, that oversees carefully, advises wisely, . . . organizes and directs. A real superintendent must be more than a teacher,—more even than a merely skilled teacher."[75] Payne and his colleagues firmly maintained that there must be a hierarchical school system with the superintendent in charge.

Payne and others clearly delineated the primary job responsibility of a school superintendent. "The most important task of a superintendent is that of supervising and maintaining control." Payne believed that supervision was necessary for the survival of the school system. According to Payne, one of the most important supervisory tasks was "that of the inspection of a school." Payne insisted that if school inspection was to "serve any valuable purpose," it would embody three essential elements. First, school inspection, must determine the condition or quality of the school under observation. "Out of ten inspectors of the average mould, not more than five are competent for the first duty." Second, if the school is categorized as poor, then the inspector must "locate the trouble, or . . . assign a cause for the failure." Of the remaining five inspectors who were competent to perform the first duty of school inspection, "not more than three can locate the difficulty." Third, school inspection, to serve a useful purpose, must "provide an adequate remedy."[76]

A large part of the work of a supervisor, according to Payne, is concerned with "record keeping." One of the most efficient ways to "consolidate work in schools" is through the use of rather "extensive reports." Payne's book on supervision contains at least two dozen types of reports that the superintendent was required to file. One of the more important reports, according to Payne, had to do with "inspection of classroom procedures." Figure 1 indicates the imprecise and subjective appraisal of "teacher efficiency," as assessed by the school superintendent. The supervisor would assign points, 1 through 10, for each category based on his

Figure 1
AN EXAMPLE OF A SUPERINTENDENT'S RATING SHEET

SUPERINTENDENT'S REGISTER

NAMES OF TEACHERS	ORDER	POWER OF HOLDING ATTENTION	SKILL IN INSTRUCTION	SKILL IN DISCIPLINE	MANNER	GENERAL IMPRESSION	AVERAGE STANDING
Miss F. A.	9	8	7	8	8	8	8 1/3
	9	9	8	8	9	9	
Miss B. M.	7	7	6	7	7	6	7 3/4
	8	8	8	7	8	8	
Miss A. C.	10	9	8	8	7	8	8 1/2
	9	9	8	9	8	9	

observations in the classroom. Payne maintained that this "scientific method of classroom inspection" would gain respect "from all quarters" for the work of the superintendent.[77]

These forms, which were in fact "rating devices," were widely used all across the nation. A widely disseminated "rating" form developed by William Estabrook Chancellor, a leading superintendent, is presented in figure 2. This rating form, said Chancellor, is an approved version of the one originally developed by Payne. Chancellor felt that the use of points in Payne's scale was "not very scientific" and therefore, "My form incorporates the use of descriptive words such as 'excellent,' 'good,' 'poor,' etc." These forms, Chancellor believed, were a vast improvement over the "lengthy inspection reports of the past."[78]

The intuitive and experiential approach to "supervision" was not uncommon and indeed characterized the work of school superintendents in the late nineteenth century. These reports, and others like them, served three related purposes: one, superintendents demonstrated their "superiority" over teachers by indicating, in rather graphic terms, the "inefficiency and incompetence" of teachers' work. Two, they could now legitimize their work by demonstrating to the public the "professional and efficient methods at work in the schools"; a far cry from the incompetence and corruption of ward politicians. Three, the methods employed by superintendents would serve to control teachers and students. "Control" of urban education in general was a primary objective of the school superintendent, therefore "control" and "management" of teachers in schools merely reflected this larger goal.

Without doubt, the most influential educator of the late nineteenth century was William Torrey Harris. This foremost Hegelian scholar, born in 1835, more than any other person influenced the direction of urban education in the late nineteenth century. His views would influence school supervision well into the twentieth century as well. Harris's impact was due to the significant posts he held throughout his illustrious career. As a superintendent of public schools in a large urban city for twelve years, chairman of a subcommittee of the Committees of Twelve and Fifteen, and U.S. commissioner of education from 1889 to 1906, Harris's ideas received national attention.

Harris was a noted philosopher as well as a prominent educator. He founded a journal in 1867 called the *Journal of Speculative Philosophy* in which he proclaimed, "Philosophy can bake no bread but it can give us God, Freedom, and Immortality."

Figure 2
SUPERINTENDENT'S RATING FORM

Date: _____

Name: _____ School No.: _____ Grade: _____

Teacher Principal Supervisor Specialist Subjects: _____

Certificate held: _____

Date of Appointment: _____ Salary this date: _____

Graduate: _____

Marks: A, admirable. E, excellent. V.G., very good. G, good. F, fair. T, tolerable. P, poor. V.P., very poor. C, complete failure. O, no preparation whatever. H, highly commendable. S, satisfactory. D, deficient. I, improving.

V.G. is the highest mark given until the fourth half year here, and G. the highest until the second. X, no opinion. Z, opinion unnecessary.

Instructing ....

Methods	_____	Voice	_____
Questioning	_____	Manner	_____
Blackboard	_____	Handwriting	_____
Results	_____	Fitness in scholarship for position	_____

Controlling ....

Self-control	_____	Willingness to receive suggestions	_____
Class control	_____	Ability to carry out suggestions	_____
Methods	_____	Ability to see what is going on	_____

Educating ....

Tact	_____	Scientific knowledge of children	_____
Executive qualities	_____	General scholarship and culture	_____
Disposition and character	_____	Apparent native ability	_____

Special strength _____

Special weakness _____

Specialties: ....

Music _____ Drawing _____ Physical Culture _____

Remarks: Total rating _____

Signed _____

Position _____

Every rating is with reference exclusively to the position now held. A duplicate is to be kept on file. The original may or may not be seen by the teacher at his option

ILLUSTRATION: Manner, F, I, means fair but improving

His Hegelian emphasis on organization and institutions inevitably affected his views concerning the administration and supervision of the public schools. Like other supervisors of his time, Harris believed that "the first prerequisite of the school is order."[79] That nonconformity and disorganization were anathema would be assented to by Harris, Payne, and Pickard. Payne, for example, emphatically stated in 1875 that "nonconformity . . . can not be tolerated without great danger to the system. . . . Ceaseless vigilance should be exercised against the encroachments" of the "evil," which he termed, *nonconformity.* Payne warned that "two things should be absolutely forbidden: the use of any textbook not in the prescribed list, and the study of any subject not included in the prescribed course." "To allow either of these things to be done," continued Payne, "is to sanction the gradual disorganization of a graded-school."[80] Harris accepted these ideas as being vital to the continuation of the urban school system.

Harris believed that the superintendent must be the foremost educational expert maintaining "supervisory control in the management of the schools. . . . The superintendent is the pilot for the whole system, and must watch the rocks and breakers, and winds and clouds, and look often from them to the eternal stars to ascertain the drift of his course." The control of a superintendent, said Harris, must be manifested not only over matters concerning mechanical aspects of the schools, such as heating, ventilation, lighting, and the construction of buildings, but also in school visitation. "School visitation," claimed Harris, "was an important responsibility of a superintendent. . . . Teachers," he maintained, "must accept the authority of the overseer, the expert, . . . the superintendent." Freedom, according to Harris, was not a viable option for teachers. Teachers need to be told in rather definite terms "what is acceptable practice and what is not."[81]

Harris's autocratic methods in school supervision were widely adopted by schoolmen of the day. Harris was known for his "supervisory devices," which were to be used by the superintendent to improve "the method of instruction" so that "a teacher's manner of discipline could be made milder and less tinged with petulance." One device in particular could have a "wholesome influence on the parent and the teacher" and at the same time correct the "waywardness" of the pupil. "This device," explained Harris, "is the suspension of the pupil for repeated and inexcusable absence or tardiness, or for persistent and willful violation of the order of the school." A pupil's suspension or transfer would be indicative of the lack of classroom control on the part of the teacher, thought Harris. This suspension or transfer "is a gentle suggestion to the teacher to correct his or her own petulance."[82]

A second device advocated by Harris, which was mentioned earlier, was considered quite effective "in strengthening the power of governing a school." This device, said Harris, "is the practice of placing teachers weak in discipline on the 'substitutes' list and letting them fill vacancies here and there as there as they occur through the temporary absence of the regular teacher. . . . I have known teachers that had become chronic failures in discipline entirely reformed by a few weeks of such experience," stated Harris.[83] The nineteenth-century superintendent as supervisor believed employing such supervisory methods would beneficially affect instruction and teaching in the schools. More important, he knew that employing such supervisory methods would be effective in controlling behavior in the schools.

Another leading superintendent who was respected and whose views received wide acceptance was William Estrabrook Chancellor. Chancellor maintained that a hierarchical school system was a necessity and would "afford the superintendent greater prestige and authority that he formerly had." He tried to allay the apprehensions that apparently some people had concerning the incipient hierarchy by stating that there was little difference between teachers and supervisors. However, a close examination of his ideas belies this view of equality or democracy. Chancellor explained that supervising officers "are not necessarily higher in character, ability, energy or scholarship" than teachers, "though they usually receive more money." He admitted using the words "superior" and "subordinate," because there was "no other way to express the relation of a superintendent, principal and class teacher." But, he continued, they were related in one way: "administrative and supervisory, not necessarily intellectual and moral. . . . There is equality of relation one to another in opportunity, but there is no equality in knowledge and power." According to Chancellor, administrative and supervisory ability were more highly valued than teaching.[84]

Bureaucracy meant that the "top" gives the orders and the "bottom" carries them out. That men should occupy the "top" was axiomatic. Note Payne's opinion on the matter. "No; women can not do man's work in the schools; and one of the greatest dangers which threaten our public school system is the gradual displacement of men from the higher departments, where their influence is especially needed." Payne explained the role of men and women in the schools by saying that "children up to the age of nine years should be instructed and governed almost exclusively by women; from nine to fourteen, they may still be instructed by women, but should be subject, in case of need, to government by men; while from the age of fourteen, they should be taught by both men and women, and should be subject still more to government by men." "With respect to instruction," said Payne, "pupils may be taught by women exclusively till the end of the grammar grade; but beyond this there are some branches, as physics, chemistry, and mathematics, which are best taught by men."[85] Note Chancellor's remarks about women in administrative positions. "That men make better administrators I have already said. As a general proposition, women make the better supervisors. They are more interested in details. They do not make as good associate or assistant superintendents, however.[86]

The evidence overwhelmingly suggests that the opinions and values of late nineteenth-century reformers supported the establishment of a highly standardized and bureaucratized school system. These schoolmen, reformers, muckrakers, if you wish, placed a great deal of emphasis on the supervision of urban schools as an effective means to gain control of the schools and to thereby wrestle control away from corrupt ward-boards. These reformers realized that in order to attain standardization and regulation in curriculum and teaching, the superintendent must be in total control of the management of urban education. Affected in part by the prevailing mood of the time toward urbanization, industrialism, and organization, as well as by his own particular values and priorities, the superintendent/supervisor inexorably moved toward bureaucracy as the primary means of managing urban schools. It was not until well into the new century that the effects of these nineteenth-century developments would be realized.

Authority versus Freedom: An Intractable Problem for School Supervision

Superintendents in the late nineteenth century were not blind to the fact that consolidation and centralization of authority might have certain negative consequences. The evidence suggests that these supervisors were aware of the fact that the growth of bureaucratization might very well lead to a diminution of individual rights and freedom. The problem of bureaucracy, then, was the degree to which they would be successful in harmonizing individuality with the development of a hierarchical school organization. How in fact could individual initiative and professional autonomy be maintained and nurtured in a centralized, bureaucratic organization? What would happen in the event of a clash between "individual interests" and "organizational mandates"? The resolution of these issues was crucial to the future success of the public school system. Superintendents attempted to deal with this dilemma between the "individual" and the "system," but increasingly became aware that this might be an intractable problem not easily resolved.

"Human society is a hierarchy of forces. Organization implies subordination," asserted Payne. "The many must follow the direction of the few . . . the weak are to be protected by the strong."[87] Payne wholeheartedly advocated hierarchical school organization and did not acknowledge any significant problems resulting from "superintendent supremacy" and centralized authority. E. C. Warriner stated the matter quite succinctly. "I see no reason for giving a teacher any choice as to what is taught . . . the superintendent's first function is to say what shall be taught, his second, to see that it is taught. As is the superintendent, so is the school."[88] William H. Maxwell, a well-known superintendent from New York City, reaffirmed the widely held view that order and authority could not be compromised in running a school system. Writing in 1894, Maxwell proclaimed that "an army of teachers can no more be managed without rules and orders than an army of soldiers."[89] It was not that Maxwell and others did not envision the possibility of some degree of curtailment of individual liberties; rather they believed that the benefits of centralization and bureaucracy would greatly outweigh any deleterious effects.

Teachers, in contrast, had sharply divergent opinions regarding the emerging hierarchical school system. Although acknowledging the necessity for some sort of structured organization, they believed that the most essential elements in any school system are freedom and individual initiative. To this group, the organization must meet the demands and needs of the individual. Albert B. Hart, writing in the *School Review* in 1893, advocated this position. "Do not insist on uniformity, the great bane of American education. Do not make a solar system of our schools, with superintendents as force-giving suns, masters as light-reflecting planets, and teachers as automatic satellites or asteroids!"

Hart demanded that those in control of the schools should "give us the opportunity to think, to suggest and to criticize, without our heads rolling off! . . . give us more freedom."[90]

There was a third view regarding individual initiative versus organizational regulations. In the previous two views, each group sharply sided with either "freedom" or "authority." In this third category, it was maintained that a reconciliation between the two potentially conflicting principles could and should be made. Both elements were necessary for the continued success of the school system. It was believed that the superintendent, for example, should be in complete charge of the schools but must administer fairly and expeditiously. Josiah L. Pickard, a superintendent from Chicago and later named president of the University of Iowa, speaking in 1872, felt that a superintendent's "ideas must imperceptibly permeate all below him. But he must not crush out individuality in his subordinates, or he defeats himself."[91] In a similar vein, Louis J. Block, a principal of a school in Chicago, contended that "supervision ought to be a benignant and healthful activity, its business is to build up and not to destroy." Speaking in rather idealistic terms, Block maintained that "supervision, . . . has its fountains in a just and lofty understanding, which communicates its fervor and wisdom to all who come within the radius of its influence."[92]

Numerous writers and speakers throughout the late nineteenth and early twentieth-centuries referred to this issue of "freedom" versus "authority." One of the earliest statements was made by Emerson Elbridge White in 1871. White was president of Purdue University as well as an eminent school superintendent in Cincinnati. He was a tall, commanding figure who attended almost every convention across the country and was a leading voice second only to William Torrey Harris. White asked: "How can a corps of teachers be subjected to efficient supervision without reducing them to operatives?" White understood very well the problem at hand for the late nineteenth-century reformer. He told his audience that "the difficulty lies in the fact that success involves the adjustment of two apparently antagonistic principles." White explained that in order to have "system there must be a good degree of uniformity in instruction and management . . . and at the same time in order that the teacher may do true work, he must have freedom."[93]

White clarified and expanded on this theme in greater detail three years later in a paper he read before the Elementary Department of the NEA, which was subsequently published in the

National Teacher. White charged that many supervisors looked disparagingly upon teachers. "The prime fact in every school is the teacher." At the same time, he continued, the "system" must be sustained. The ultimate question that must be answered, continued White, was: "How can requisite uniformity be secured and, at the same time, the teacher have necessary professional freedom?" White, along with other reformers of the time, were not able to adequately answer this important question.[94]

The dilemma was rephrased rather uniquely by Burke Aaron Hinsdale, a noted college president, professor, and school superintendent in a paper read before the North Eastern Ohio Teachers Association in 1877. "We must accept the system," said Hinsdale, "as a man accepts his wife, 'for better or worse.'" Hinsdale acknowledged "that the graded-school system is exceedingly rigid and inelastic," and that there is a "tendency to stretch all the pupils on the same bedspread." He admitted that "you cannot have the greatest personal intrepidity and the best organization, . . . the question is, how shall we combine both elements most wisely?"[95] Like White, Hinsdale was unable to proffer a solution.

Over forty years later, Franklin Bobbitt, in a piece written in the National Society for the Study of Education yearbook, indicated that "efficiency implies centralization of authority and definite direction by the superintendent of all processes performed." Still, said Bobbitt, "Efficiency demands that the individuality of the teacher be respected; that initiative and professional alertness be not stifled; and that the whole work be alive with spontaneity." Bobbitt now comes to the crux of the matter by saying that "one of the difficult supervisory problems is to centralize direction and yet keep the total organization fully alive in every unit of its being."[96] Although realizing the importance of balancing individual initiative and organizational demands, Bobbitt did not resolve this troublesome issue.

"There is no democracy in our school system today," charged Sallie Hill, president of the League of Teachers Association in Denver. "Democracy," she explained, "cannot exist with the present system which gives so much power to those who supervise."[97] Francis E. Harden, a teacher from Illinois, agreed. "We will never have fundamental democracy in our nation until it is first established [sic] in our public schools." Harden, in an impassioned speech before the Department of Classroom Teachers of the NEA, lamented the fact that "a small group of the top decides all questions of courses of study, textbooks, and general policies, while the great group below follows unquestioningly and often blindly." If perchance anyone would "question the absolutism of those in authority they would usually be made to suffer." What is needed, concluded Harden, is "more democracy . . . and less autocracy."[98]

"Autocracy and despotism" are necessary in order to maintain an efficient public school system, claimed Aaron Estellus Gove, a noted superintendent in Denver and one of the founders of the National Council of Education of the NEA. Those who think "that a public school system should be a democratic institution have a false conception of true democracy." Although Gove realized that "the placement of unlimited authority in the hands of one person" will inevitably "provoke much opposition," he clearly was in favor of centralized control in public education. On the issue of freedom Gove was exact. "The teacher has independence . . . like that of a man in the shoe factory who is told tomorrow morning to make a pair of No. 6 boots. The independence of that workman consists in the fact that he can sew four stitches in a minute or forty, can work rapidly or slowly, as he chooses or as he is able; but his dependence is that the boots must be made and made exactly."[99]

The battle lines were drawn: bureaucracy and autocracy versus democracy and individualism. The issue was hotly debated well into the twentieth century. Educators from a wide array of pedagogical points of view offered their own perspectives on the issue. One of the more outspoken personalities against bureaucracy and centralization was Margaret A. Haley, the president of the Chicago Teachers Federation. In 1904 she urged teachers to organize in order to restore the "true ideals of democracy" into a school system beset by misdirected goals and unsatisfactory administration and supervision. The system, continued Haley, destroyed the "individuality of the teacher and her power of initiative." She asserted that there was a "lack of recognition of the teacher as an educator in the school system due to the increased tendency toward 'factoryizing education', making the teacher an automaton, a mere factoryhand, whose duty it is to carry out mechanically and unquestioningly the ideas and orders of those clothed with the authority of position." Haley bemoaned the fact that "authority was valued more than the freedom of the teacher."[100] Many teachers who felt as strongly as Haley maintained that unless school personnel reorient their thinking about "work in the schools," very little will be accomplished along the lines of accentuating democratic role relationships in schools. If, for example, an administrator's philosophical bent is toward viewing a school much like running a factory, then he is more likely, if not inevitably, to see teachers as "cogs in the machinery." As such, he is not very likely to be concerned with "teacher choice" and professional autonomy. The paramount factor, rather, is the maintenance of a smooth-running, efficiently operated factory. In other words, individuality will always be subordinate to the demands of the organization as long as one's value system supports such an outlook.[101] Supervisors undoubtedly valued authoritarian rule.

"Why there is no such thing as absolute freedom in this world!" charged Oscar T. Corson in 1906. He told his audience of school administrators that "I am inclined to think today that the teacher who is worthy of freedom in the true sense is the one who rarely mentions it."[102] Jesse H. Newlon, an influential and well-known superintendent from Denver, believed that teachers who complain about freedom "are a menace to our profession and their numbers should be eliminated."[103] The nineteenth-century reformer believed that individual autonomy was a threat to the centralization of control and social efficiency in urban education.

There were some supervisors, however, who entertained the idea that "authority" and "freedom" could be somehow combined into what one writer called "sympathetic authority." Henry Sabin, a state superintendent in Iowa, was one of the few administrators who openly advocated this position. Sabin feared "that to place all this power in the hands of one man will lead the people to distrust the schools and will bring the entire school system eventually in disrepute." He maintained that a school system is not analogous to a "military system." "The teacher is not a private, whose only duty is to obey and ask no questions." Sabin accused many supervisors of relying too heavily on "rules" regulations, and restrictions." "The martinet," continued Sabin, "is unjust, inhuman, and in some cases amounts to an absolute tyranny. We do not want this." Sabin believed that a central figure must be present to assume responsibility. However, he must be "wise, intelligent and rational."[104] Sarah L. Arnold, a supervisor in Boston, insisted that supervisors are capable of maintaining their authoritative status and at the same time being helpful and understanding. Supervisors, she insisted, should not be depicted as "Argus-eyed and many-tongued, . . . the supervisor is no such ogre. He has but one function, to help his fellows." She asserted that teachers welcome the coming of this sort of supervisor "like the coming of sunshine on a cloudy day."[105]

"Will you have meat *or* bread? Why not meat *and* bread? What we need most," said Charles W. Bardeen of New York, "is system *and* individuality."[106] A review of the literature reveals that, unfortunately, only a handful of supervisors advocated this consolidation of "freedom" *and* "authority." But even among these supervisors there was a belief that the single greatest factor for the survival of urban education was not individualism but, rather, the maintenance of a centralized bureaucracy. When a clash between "system" and "individuality" occurred, it was the system that was more highly valued. Pay close attention to the words of Charles Bardeen, a supervisor in New York, who advocated "system *and* individuality." "Our schools are for the bestowal of the greatest good to the greatest number and that can exist only when there is a harmony throughout," continued Bardeen in a discussion following an address made by Henry Sabin entitled "Organization and System vs. Originality and Individuality on the Part of Teacher and Pupil." He continues, "If, as superintendent of a school, I had suspended a boy, and if, without consulting me, the teacher had assumed to restore him, that teacher would go, or I would. . . . No benefit to the individual pupil would atone for the injury to the school from such a conflict of authority."[107]

While Bardeen saw the necessity of both organization and freedom, when a choice had to be made between the two, as was often the case, he stated, "I must rejoice that our individuality is subordinate to a system."[108] W. H. Anderson of West Virginia arose to conclude this important discussion session held in 1890, by admonishing the audience that "organization and system should always be found, but applied in such a manner as to gently repress but not to suppress originality in both teacher and pupil."[109] In practice, however, "repress" and "suppress" were often confused.

Throughout the era in which the "authority" versus "freedom" debate ensued, one curious point needs emphasis; namely, the fact that almost all the participants in the debate had an ingrained belief that centralization and a hierarchical school system would best serve the needs of urban education in the late nineteenth and early twentieth centuries. The debate never centered on creating structural changes or finding alternatives to bureaucratic school governance. Educators during this critical period in the development of urban schooling had an unwavering belief that bureaucracy would reverse pupil absenteeism, pupil illiteracy, teacher incompetence, and unscrupulous political influence in the schools. It is perhaps unfair to assume that supervisors during this era could develop alternatives to the fundamental structural characteristics only recently acquired. Much effort was geared to administrative and organizational reform. The evidence demonstrates that bureaucracy was viewed as the only viable alternative for American urban education. A reconciliation between authority and freedom was never accomplished. The issue that apparently troubled educators in the late nineteenth century would continue to be equally intractable in the coming century.

The persistence of bureaucratic administration had a significant impact on all aspects of schooling; supervision was only one of many areas of public education affected. Insofar as bureaucracy pervaded all facets of urban education, it is not very surprising to find that supervisory behavior in schools was characterized as autocratic. Bureaucracy, as the major form of school organization, and autocratic supervision would go unchallenged for many years to come.

The Bureaucratization of Supervision

The purpose of this chapter has been to demonstrate that the bureaucratization of public school supervision occurred in the late nineteenth century. It was during this period that supervision was shaped and influenced by both educational and noneducational factors. These developments affected supervision in such an encompassing, indelible way that both the theory and practice of supervision were established for the next half century.

The late nineteenth century was a time in which urbanization reached new levels of growth. Small towns, like Chicago, became a metropolis between 1820 and 1860. A perusal of the statistics demonstrates the frenetic pace of urban development all over America.[110] Urbanization was perhaps the single greatest factor that created the bureaucratization of urban education. The older decentralized village schools were no longer prolific; they were rapidly replaced by centralized urban centers. Organization and bureaucracy were the inevitable consequences of the sheer increase of numbers in the cities. Albert P. Marble, a superintendent in Worcester, Massachusetts, explained that "organization becomes necessary in the crowded schools in congested districts."[111]

The movement toward centralization in large urban cities gained considerable momentum as a result of increasing urbanization. Professional educators, namely superintendents, sought to gain command over urban schools in order to eliminate the deplorable conditions caused by decentralization and lay control. It was argued in this chapter that supervision, as a function performed by the school superintendent, emerged as an important tool by which centralization could be accomplished. Superintendents legitimized their control over the schools by claiming that "professional and efficient" supervision would bring order to a chaotic system and improve education. Although basing their activities more on school control, superintendents did, at times, support the use of supervision for educational improvement.

Supervision, as was pointed out, reflected the general tendency toward bureaucratization. Supervision, as such, was characterized by autocratic methods and procedures. Henry Warren Button, in a fine descriptive history of supervision, observed "that acceptance of an autocratic theory of supervision occurred because supervisors found themselves in a situation in which such a theory was highly workable."[112] Supervisors did much to preserve and expand bureaucratic role relationships in schools. Bureaucracy, as Michael B. Katz has pointed out, "is the crystallization of particular values."[113] Supervisors and educators in general placed more value on authority, direction, and control than on freedom and individual initiative. Superintendents had an unwavering conviction that centralized, bureaucratic control would have an unprecedented positive influence on urban education.

The bureaucratization of public school supervision was established as a result of a number of interrelated factors. First, it was buttressed by Rice's suggestions, in 1893, that supervision should be the major function used by superintendents to gain jurisdiction over urban schools. Through the use of "scientific and efficient" supervision, their influence in schools would gain greater legitimacy. The autocratic methods employed by supervisors would bring order to a school system beset by confusion and incompetence. The bureaucratization of supervision took place within the larger campaign to bureaucratize schooling.

Second, the bureaucratization of supervision was furthered by the replacement of decentralized control over the schools with centralization and social efficiency. Supervision, within this context, would assume much importance in order to accomplish the goals and directives of the newly established administrative organization.

Third, the idea that supervision must be performed by a central authority, possessing special training and expertise, contributed to autocratic methods of supervision. As mentioned, supervisors did not favorably view the competence of most teachers. As such, they believed that the utilization of some rather drastic supervisory strategies was urgently required to reverse the ill-effects of teacher incompetence.

Fourth, the bureaucratization of supervision was supported by the ideas and philosophies of influential men, such as William Payne, William Harris, Andrew Draper, and William Maxwell. These men maintained that in order to accomplish the objectives of bureaucracy, certain dogmatic and restrictive techniques of supervision were necessary. These men fervently believed that these methods would improve educational standards in the nation's school system.

Reformers in the late nineteenth century tried, in the Weberian sense, to establish a "most efficient form of administrative organization."[114] However, bureaucracy as conceived and executed by the nineteenth-century reformer did not approach the Weberian "ideal type." In many ways the newly formed school system mirrored and perpetuated the very conditions that existed before the advent of this "new reform." "The more things change, the more they remain the same" may be aptly stated in this context. The evidence suggests that while many reformers were aware of this problem, more, not less, bureaucracy was applied. Supervisors wanted to perfect bureaucracy by establishing a "stringent hierarchy of higher and lower levels of authority in such a way that each lower level is subject to control and supervision of the one immediately above it."[115]

Due to the exigencies of a society rapidly changing from agrarianism to urbanism, bureaucracy was cast as the only viable option for the educational system in urban America. Supervisors, at the time, did not understand that bureaucracy was inimical to the goals of free inquiry and individual initiative, necessary ingredients for the survival and effective operation of a school. They did not imagine that bureaucracy and education, in the words of David S. Seeley, "are like oil and water-they do not mix."[116] It is unfair to hurl accusations at these reformers for not seeking alternatives to bureaucracy. History, however, has shown us that bureaucracy turned out not to be the "one best system," as hoped by supervisors in the late nineteenth century, but probably was, in the words of Seeley, the "one worst system" for education.[117] If we are to learn from our past mistakes then we must remain vigilant in our conviction that bureaucracy, while offering administrative stability, is essentially anti-educational and a detriment to good pedagogy. It is for this very reason that today we must reexamine bureaucracy, and at the very least, discover ways to accentuate democracy and individuality.

It was not until well into the twentieth century that supervisors realized the adverse effects of bureaucratic school organization and would decide to take affirmative steps to combat the curtailment of individual liberties. The "democratization" of supervision was in its infancy in the early years of the new century. As a result of the publication of John Dewey's *Democracy and Education* and James F. Hosic's article, "The Democratization of Supervision" appearing in *School and Society,* "democratic supervision" would gain greater voice in the schools.[118] In perhaps a prophetic statement, Samuel T. Dutton, a shrewd observer at the time, stated that "the efficacy of a centralized school management will be tested by the degree by which the superintendent succeeds in controlling the huge forces under his command without excessive red tape. If centralization of power, should mean such a refinement of rules, and such curtailment of individual freedom, and such exasperating espionage as to depress the spirits and cripple the free action of teachers, there would certainly be a reaction in favor of the earlier and more democratic methods."[119]

It was in direct response to bureaucracy, supported, as will be shown, by teachers who were against the bureaucratization of supervision, that the supervisor in the twentieth century directed his drive toward professional autonomy and democratic methods. The next chapter will be devoted to examining the beginnings of the democratization of school supervision.

Part Two
The Drive Toward Professionalism

2

From Cautious Optimism to Confirmed Despair: The Supervisor's Newly Found Status within the School Organization

At the turn of the century, bureaucracy was undeniably the dominant form of school organization across the nation. The bureaucratization of supervision, in particular, occurred as a result of the efforts of reformers to standardize, control, and restore order to an urban school system beset by incompetency, inefficiency, and political influence. This chapter will explain the effects of bureaucracy on supervisors. Supervisors during the first two decades of the twentieth century realized the tenuous position they occupied in the hierarchical school organization. They became aware of the fact that they were caught up in apparently unresolved conflict: as middle-management personnel their responsibility was to preserve and maintain organizational goals (e.g., ensuring the competency of teachers through evaluative/rating measures) and at the same time their efficacy was determined, in large measure, by the degree to which they could assist teachers in solving classroom problems (by providing in-service education which, to be effective, must be unevaluative). This long-standing, inherent supervisory conflict was reflected, early on, in the kind of evaluative tools used by supervisors. This chapter makes the point that supervisors succumbed to this basic conflict by favoring rating over a more potentially nonjudgmental evaluative technique. Supervisors, it will be argued, viewed rating as a rhetorical tool in the struggle for professional status. Rating was wholly consistent with the rise of bureaucracy in schools. In fact, the drive toward professionalism, initiated by supervisors, was taken in direct response to the rapid spread of bureaucracy in the public schools. To explore the specific factors that led supervisors toward a concerted effort to professionalize is a task that this chapter will undertake.

Progressivism, Educational Growth, and the School Supervisor

It was the dawn of a new age marked by numerous and sweeping economic, political, and technological changes. The nation approached the new century with confidence and anticipation. America's imperialistic venture in the Spanish-American War of 1898, albeit an easy victory, catapulted her into a world power with possessions in the Caribbean and the Pacific. During this time, there was some organized opposition to America's new role in world affairs. William Jennings Bryan warned that U.S. imperialism would lead to corruption and poor administration. However, his defeat in the presidential election of 1900 demonstrated that the American people generally acknowledged and welcomed America's newfound international prestige.

Monumental transformations occurred in modern American society as a result of industrial and urban development. These transformations had promising benefits for business, industry, science, labor, agriculture, and education. The talk of progress in 1900 meant urban development, materialistic concerns, a literate populace, accentuated differences between the rich and poor, the extension of educational opportunity, and the promise of new abundance. To a large extent, nineteenth-century changes and reforms were consolidated with twentieth-century societal advancements to reach a new level of expectancy.

The nation, however, was shocked on September 6, 1901, when President McKinley, attending the Pan-American Exposition at Buffalo, was assassinated only six months after his second inauguration. With McKinley's death, Theodore Roosevelt became the youngest president to enter the White House. Roosevelt was a Harvard graduate, former Rough Rider, governor of New York, and vice president of the United States at the time of McKinley's death. Historians generally associate Roosevelt's activities and policies in office with an era marked by political, economic, and social reform known as the progressive movement. Although incorrectly labeled as the founder of this movement, Roosevelt supported many of its reforms, such as protecting the rights of consumers, farmers, and factory workers, and eradicating governmental corruption, institutional regimentation, and bureaucracy. As most progressives, he cast "the school as a fundamental lever of social and political regeneration."[1] In a period marked by tremendous social and intellectual upheaval, the early years of the new century witnessed a breed of reformers not unlike, in many respects, those of a decade earlier. In the tradition of muckrakers, such as Henry George, Henry Demarest Lloyd, and Jacob Riis, the twentieth-century progressive reformer resolutely tried to improve American life by extending democracy and working for economic and social justice.

The progressives were hopeful and optimistic. Writers such as Upton Sinclair, Frank Norris, Jack London, Ida Tarbell, and Lincoln Steffens, although presenting scathing critiques of American society, were nevertheless confident that America would realize its potential and obligation to democratic principles. These and other progressives believed that "old" provincial America was no longer a reality due to increasing urbanization and industrialism. While accepting the precepts generally associated with industrialism, reformers sought to eradicate the evils wrought by modernization and its concomitant processes. They were hopeful that the American industrial system could be preserved from its own injustices and defects. The way to eliminate the maleficence of a democratic-industrial state was, according to the progressive thinker, to be more democratic. "The remedy of the partial evils of democracy," wrote John Dewey, the leading spokesman of progressive reform, "is in appeal to a more thoroughgoing democracy."[2]

To be sure, progressivism, a broad social and intellectual movement, had its beginning in the 1890s. Lawrence A. Cremin, a noted historian of progressive education, stated that progressivism

> arose during the 1890s as a many-sided protest against pedagogical narrowness and inequity. . . . In the universities, it appeared as part of a spirited revolt against formalism in philosophy, psychology, and the social sciences. In the cities it emerged as one facet of a larger program of social alleviation and municipal reform. . . . Among farmers it became the crux of a moderate, liberal alternative to radical agrarianism.[3]

In other words, progressivism was all-encompassing. As such, progressivism in education also took on special significance. Progressives realized that social progress was impossible without attention to reform in education. "I believe that education is the fundamental method of social progress and reform," wrote Dewey.[4]

Charles E. Merriam, a professor of political science at the University of Chicago, in his comprehensive examination of civic education in the U.S. stated that "of all the agencies of social training, the school emerges as by far the most important in our time and country." The school's primary task, he said, was "to prepare the next generation for participation in social life. The church, the family, the group or gang, the culture system in the broadest sense of the term, all contribute to the training of the oncoming generation, but the heaviest burden is laid increasingly upon the educational institutions of the land."[5] Beset by the magnitude of industrial growth, tremendous waves of immigrants, and perplexing problems of poverty in the cities, urban reformers turned to the schools for relief. Schools were seen as vital agents for eradicating inequities within society. Irrefutable experiential and statistical evidence of the success of schools in American society buttressed their belief that reforms through schooling would reestablish justice, hope, and prosperity.

Thaddeus Stevens, Horace Mann, Henry Barnard, Francis W. Parker, James Carter, William McGuffey, Calvin Stowe, and other nineteenth-century school reformers laid the foundations for the conviction that the public school experience would succeed. It was people like William Torrey Harris, William H. Payne, and Nicholas Murray Butler who helped standardize and systematize public education in the U.S. in the late nineteenth century. With numerous technological changes and the increased authority of the school superintendent to expertly administer the ever-growing hierarchical system of education, *progress* was indeed the watchword at the turn of the century.

However, the overall picture was not a rosy one. A profound value conflict arose at the turn of the century, which represented a serious source of agitation to the progressive reformer. The inheritors of the school system, shaped by nineteenth-century educators like Harris and Maxwell, witnessed a system troubled by the increased mechanization and regimentation of school practices. Many of the regimented practices that reformers in the nineteenth century sought to eradicate persisted and even at times, grew worse in the early twentieth century. The organizational reforms of the late nineteenth century did not solve all the problems of American education, as reformers hoped for. Although not ill-intentioned, educators in the late nineteenth century formed, in essence, what we would term today a *bureaucracy*.[6] It would now be the task of twentieth-century educators to redefine, as each new generation must, the purposes, roles, and organizational framework of schooling within society.

Reform in the nineteenth century meant uniformity. Would reform in the twentieth century take a similar stand? The problem confronting the twentieth-century reformer was whether to transform the bureaucratic school organization into a vehicle for change and democracy, or maintain stability and authoritarian governance. The solution seemed apparent, yet, strikingly elusive.

It is my contention that rather than confronting the problem directly, the twentieth-century progressive reformer attempted to circumvent the crucial and fundamental issues involved in modern industrial society by not attacking the cause of the problem. In other words, progressive optimism did not challenge the viability or suitability of "bureaucracy" as a form of school organization. While this question needs further analysis, suffice it to say that the bureaucratic organizational tendency continued to permeate and influence American institutions, and the schools in particular, in the new century. It is not surprising then that educators, aware of the problems confronting schools, such as the lack of professional guidance for teachers, inefficient school maintenance, and underdeveloped instructional methods, sought a nostrum that provided for more bureaucracy, more school officers to supervise an already elaborate school system. Reformers at the turn of the century realized, perhaps even to a greater extent than before, that the problems in education can be resolved, by expanding and intensifying supervisory efforts. Thus, the increase in supervisory officers after 1900 is not very surprising.

The growth of supervisory officers was already occurring in the nineteenth century. For the most part, however, supervision remained the primary responsibility of the superintendent. For example, prior to 1988, "supervision" was indexed in the Annual Report of the U.S. Commissioner of Education under the title of the "superintendent." However, beginning in the 1890s, as schools were becoming more populated and as authority was centralized, the superintendent could no longer personally supervise schools as he once did. Therefore, he delegated responsibility to his assistants. The increase of supervisory personnel was marked. In 1888–89, the U.S. commissioner of education, in his annual report, stated that "the quest of supervision is an important one and is receiving increased attention." It is noted in the commissioner's annual report that "484 cities report 1,928 supervisors, or an average of four to each city—supervisory staff about 2,300." For the period 1895–96, the commissioner said that "it is plain that supervisory officers are becoming yearly more numerous. . . . The supervisory force has grown more rapidly than teachers or pupils," reported the commissioner.[7] Analyzing these statistics alone, however, does not provide an accurate account of public school supervision during these years. Although the school system was growing, the superintendent was not aloof from the day-to-day operations; he, in fact, remained very much in charge of supervising schools. The supervisors who were appointed by the superintendent were merely involved in collecting data, reading reports, and the like.[8] The activities of these early supervisors were quite limited and closely monitored by the superintendent. Therefore, the term *supervisor*, when used prior to 1900, was really synonymous with the superintendency.

However, after 1900, as urbanization intensified and as the school system was growing more complex, the superintendent lost contact with the day-to-day operations of the schools. As a result, due to these exigencies he had to establish certain administrative and supervisory positions. In other words, supervision of schools after 1900 was the responsibility of someone other than the superintendent. There is much statistical evidence to illustrate this increase of supervisory personnel after 1900. In the period 1900–1901, the U.S. commissioner of education said that "the total number of supervisory officers reported is 4,733, . . . raising the number [in proportion] of teachers to supervisors from 17.6 to 18.5." In 1905, it was reported that during the period 1903–5, the increase of male and female supervisory officers was significant. The total number of supervisors during this period went from 5,119 to 5,729, an increase of 4.69 percent. In contrast, the total number of teachers went from 96,624 to 100,186, an increase of 3.69 percent. In 1911, the commissioner of education stated that for the year 1906, the Bureau of Education reported 6,600 supervisory officers and 106,026 teachers in cities of 8,000 population and over. For the years 1909–10, continued the commissioner, the corresponding numbers were 11,144 and 125,246. Thus, said the commissioner, during a period of five years, the increase of supervisory personnel was 68.8 percent, while that of teachers was only 18.1 percent. "The ratio of teachers to supervisors in 1906 was 16.6; in 1910, it was only 11.2." These figures and statistics, said the commissioner, represented a "tendency towards a closer professional supervision of the schools."[9]

Who were these supervisors? These individuals were often former teachers who moved up the ranks into supervisory positions. Sometimes they were outside people who had influence in the community or business. There was no formal examination for becoming a supervisor; you were generally recognized by the superintendent or his immediate assistants and then made a "supervisor." It was of course assumed that you were qualified to handle administrative and instructional details. There was no formalized and special training for a supervisor beyond the teaching degree. The school superintendent in all cases officially appointed these individuals to their respective positions. Basically, there were two categories of supervisors after 1900, as was described in the Introduction: special and general supervisors and principals. Special supervisors were those individuals who aided teachers in various subject areas such as penmanship, music, drawing, and spelling. These supervisors, usually female, received no formal training and were selected from the ranks based on presumed excellence in the classroom. General supervisors, almost always male, dealt with the more general subjects (mathematics and science) and certain administrative duties. Apparently, the prevalent nineteenth-century notions of male-female role relationships persisted into the early twentieth century. Note the remarks made by a prominent nineteenth-century superintendent, William E. Chancellor. "That men make better administrators I have already said. As a general proposition, women make the better special supervisors. They are more interested in details. They do not make as good general or assistant superintendents, however."[10] It is also interesting to note that special supervisors were more readily accepted by the ranks of teachers than were general supervisors. Special supervisors played a very useful and helpful role by assisting teachers in such practical areas as spelling and art. In addition, as will be mentioned shortly, these special supervisors really did not have any independent authority and did not serve in an evaluative capacity as did, for example, the building principal or the school superintendent. Therefore, teachers were not likely to be threatened by their appearance in the classroom. The general supervisor, on the other hand, was concerned with more administrative matters and were consequently viewed as more menacing to the classroom teacher. Special supervisors also probably gained more acceptance by teachers, most of whom were female, because they too were female. General supervisors were all male and perhaps were perceived differently as a result. Frank E. Spaulding, in his analysis of this period, concurs and states that general supervisors "were quite generally looked upon, not as helpers, but as critics bent on the discovery and revelation of teachers weaknesses and failures, . . . they were dubbed Snoopervisors."[11]

It is important to note that the position of special supervisor did not endure for a very long period in the public schools. The duties and responsibilities of the position were gradually yet steadily usurped by general supervisors. While in-depth analysis of this trend certainly is needed, upon scrutiny of the matter it seems likely that special supervisors were phased out for three related reasons. First, special supervisors never succeeded in forming an organization or union to bolster their efforts and concerns. No leader emerged voicing support for special supervisors. In most cases, these supervisors, when terminated by principals usually without the consent of school boards and superintendents, either returned to the classroom or were prematurely retired. Second, there was an effort after 1922 to streamline the supervisory positions in the school system. In 1920 there were 6,583 supervisors, excluding principals. Two years later, the number almost doubled. By 1924 the number of supervisors dropped to 7,924. This significant reduction in supervisory staff was largely due to the streamlining of primarily special supervisors. The duties of special supervisors could, it was thought, be assumed by general supervisors and principals. The streamlining of supervisory officers was in consonance with the tendency to make the schools more efficient and to eliminate waste. But as to the reason why special supervisors, in particular, were expendable, a third factor needs analysis.[12] The relative obscurity of special supervisors after 1922 can be attributed to discrimination based on gender. Consisting of an overwhelming number of females, special supervisors were not perceived in the same light as were general supervisors, principals, assistant superintendents, and superintendents, who were mostly male. Frankly stated, females were not afforded equal access and opportunities for managerial positions in school systems due to prevalent sexist and discriminatory practices. The subject of gender and the sexual division of labor has recently received wide attention.[13] Foregoing a complicated analysis of gender relations in education, suffice it to say in this context that an ideological bias of sex role stereotypes in education as a whole was commonplace and in consonance with bureaucratic school governance. Not only were curriculum and instruction standardized, but hiring, promotion, and salary scales were also routinized. Along with the newly emerging bureaucracy came the expansion of managerial positions, which were filled almost always by men. This is not very surprising given the views of women held by leading urban school reformers of the day. Certainly representative of the bias against women in the educational workplace were the notions espoused by William H. Payne on the school hierarchy and the sexual division of labor. "Women," asserted Payne, in 1875, "cannot do man's work in the schools."[14] Payne, like many of his colleagues, believed that men were better suited for the more prestigious and lucrative job opportunities. This widely held view of patriarchal dominance in the educational milieu is consistent with structured forms of control highly valued by urban school reformers. Myra Strober and David Tyack explain this relationship between gender and social control as follows:

> By structuring jobs to take advantage of sex role stereotypes about women's responsiveness to rules and male authority, and men's presumed ability to manage women, urban school boards were able to enhance their ability to control curricula, students and personnel. ... Rules were highly prescriptive.... With few alternative occupations and accustomed to patriarchal authority they mostly did what their male superiors ordered.... Difference of gender provided an important form of social control.[15]

In short, general supervisors gained wider acceptance simply because they were men.

The distinction between the supervisor and principal is interesting and revealing. The principal[16] was the first and only person who was required to have specialized training. The principal's primary duties involved "helping" teachers and administering his particular school. Principals, who were by and large male, were directly responsible to the local superintendent. General and special supervisors, on the other hand, were subordinate to the building principal. The supervisor was seen as an advisor with no independent authority. The supervisor was often warned "not to forget that the superintendent runs the whole system and the principal runs his school, and you are merely an expert whose duty it is to assist improving instruction."[17] Interestingly, while the duties of general supervisors and principal were concerned to some extent with the supervision of teachers, it was the assistant superintendent who had direct contact with the superintendent to administer the system on a large scale. The assistant superintendent, being handpicked by the superintendent, had much wider authority than did either the general supervisor or the building principal.[18]

The discussion in this part of the book focuses on special and general supervisors as middle-management personnel, who somehow were caught between teachers on the one hand and principals on the other. These middle-management specialists (later called asssistant principals, educational assistants and/or district office personnel) attempted to bolster their vulnerable position in schools by organizing and gaining support for their plight. However, these middle-management supervisors were severely restricted and limited in terms of their sphere of influence and authority. The evidence clearly suggests that the job specifications for these supervisors remained nebulously defined. In the early twenties, for example, it was admitted that "the present status of supervision is one of confusion, not to say of chaos. We have a multiplicity of names that plague us just as our unscientific alphabet does; the same function is called by different names and each name stands for a variety of functions."[19]

An irony was thus crystallizing. Although many agreed that supervision was important, relatively little attention was given to the supervisor after 1900. There are a number of explanations. First, it was a time when the "superintendency" was emerging as a specialized profession and field of study. Influential men, such as Frank Spaulding, George Strayer, William Chancellor, and Ellwood Cubberley and their ideas of business and management helped formulate the basic theories of the emerging field. Administration, not supervision, was the prime concern. Supervision, if anything, was seen as an extension of school administration, or as one authority states. "Supervision was merely the arm of administration."[20]

Second, supervision did not dominate thought and discussion because there was no voice or advocate for the twentieth-century supervisor. The days of Harris's enormous influence had passed. Administering and managing a school system were of utmost concern, not the supervision and improvement of instruction in schools. Interestingly, Franklin Bobbitt, whose views will be discussed shortly, was a prominent educator who was very committed to school supervision in the early 1900s. His views regarding supervision, which were widely disseminated, could have elevated supervision to a prominent position and field of study in its own right. Yet, as will be shown, his views were criticized by many and even Bobbitt, after 1920, shifted his emphasis to curriculum development and away from school supervision.[21]

Supervisors during the first two decades of the twentieth century realized the tenuous position they occupied in schools. The ill-defined nature of supervision and the indefinite and obscure status of supervisors within schools contributed to the attempt to find institutional legitimacy for their work. As a result, after 1910, there was a concerted effort by these supervisors to clarify their role and function in schools.[22]

The professionalization of supervision began as an effort to gain legitimacy in the eyes of teachers. They thought that the way to accomplish this was to devise objective, scientific methods for promoting "teacher efficiency." Supervisors were greatly influenced by Bobbitt's ideas of school management and particularly his call for teacher efficiency. Supervisors, at this point in time, were not unaware of the problems they faced. They hoped that Bobbitt's ideas would revitalize interest in supervision; they proceeded, however, with cautious optimism.

Bobbitt and School Supervision

American education after 1900 was greatly affected by numerous technological advances. During this time the "efficiency movement" gained considerable momentum throughout American industry.[23] This movement also had important consequences for education. Throughout urban cities the curtailment of excessive expenditures, elimination of waste, and inefficiency were priorities. As a result of the work of Frederick Winslow Taylor, who published a book in 1911 titled *The Principles of Scientific Management, efficiency* became the watchword of the day. Taylor's book stressed scientific management and efficiency in the workplace. The worker, according to Taylor, was merely a cog in the business machinery and the main purpose of management was to promote worker efficiency. Within a relatively short period of time, Taylorism and efficiency became household words and ultimately had a profound impact on administrative and supervisory practices in schools.[24] The principle person who attempted to adopt Taylor's ideas in the schools was Bobbitt. Bobbitt's work, particularly his discussion of supervision, is significant because his ideas shaped the character and nature of supervision for many years. Bobbitt's ideas appeared, on the surface, to advance professional supervision but in reality were the antithesis of professionalism. What he called "scientific and professional supervisory methods" were in fact scientistic and bureaucratic methods of supervision aimed not at professionalizing, but at finding a legitimate and secure niche for control-oriented supervision within the school bureaucracy.

Bobbitt, then a professor of educational administration at the University of Chicago, tried to apply the ideas espoused by Taylor, to the "problems of educational management and supervision." In 1913 he published a work sponsored by the *National Society for the Study of Education* entitled, "Some General Principles of Management Applied to the Problems of City-School Systems." Of particular concern, Bobbitt firmly held that management, direction, and supervision of schools were necessary in order to achieve "organizational goals." Bobbitt maintained that supervision was an essential function "to coordinate school affairs. . . . Supervisory members must co-ordinate the labors of all, . . . find the best methods of work and enforce the use of these methods on the part of the workers."[25]

Bobbitt, who took his Ph.D. at Clark University only four years prior to the publication of his article in the *Twelfth Yearbook of the National Society for the Study of Education,* focused much attention on supervising and managing schools. He felt that our field is backward, . . . in the recognition and development of scientific principles." He said that it was feasible to apply these principles even though, at present, most administrators are unaware of its importance. "Our profession must advance along the same road as that already traversed by the best of the industrial world." The employment of scientific principles in supervision, said Bobbitt, is a necessity for the continued progress of our school system.[26]

Bobbitt divided his presentation into eight sections in which eleven major principles of scientific management were discussed. The first two principles were concerned with the establishment of "definite qualitative and quantitative standards" for each product. He realized the necessity for developing "scales and methods for measuring the educational product so as to determine with at least reasonable accuracy whether the product rises to standard." He was impressed with the work of T. W. Stone and S. A. Courtis and their attempts to develop "scales of measurement" for teachers. "Ordinarily, the teacher, if asked whether his eighth-grade pupils could add at the rate of 65 combinations per minute with an accuracy of 94 per cent, could not answer the question; nor would he know how to go about finding out," explained Bobbitt. "He needs a measuring scale that will serve him in measuring his product as well as the scale of feet and inches serves in measuring the product of the steel plant." He praised the efforts of Stone and Courtis in developing "practical usable measuring scales for arithmetical ability." These scales are so important, said Bobbitt, because "each teacher can know accurately what is expected of her." The teacher, continued Bobbitt, can then know whether or not she is in fact, a good teacher.

The establishment of "definite scales of measurement" also had important uses for administrators and supervisors, said Bobbitt. A superintendent, for example, could glance over the records of a particular school and be able to discern "weaknesses and deficiencies." He can "locate instantly the strong, the mediocre, and the weak teachers." He could also "see at a glance whether building principals are doing a superior grade of work or relatively poor work." In this way, continued Bobbitt, the superintendent would be "able to tell at once where his strong subordinates are and where his weak ones are." Supervisors also benefit from these methods, maintained Bobbitt. Special supervisors may, for example, "by glancing over student records would know whether the teacher is securing the full results expected, . . . and whether in doing so she is handling the normal number of pupils." For Bobbitt, the teacher who would be able to bring a greater number of pupils up to the standard in a minimum amount of time would be a good teacher. In other words, these "scientific methods" would enable supervisors to categorize "good" and "bad" teachers and then be "able to provide appropriate methods to remedy the deficiency."[28]

Bobbitt's third principle dealt with the discovery of the best methods "which are the most efficient for actual service under actual conditions, and secures their use on the part of the workers." It was the responsibility of those who "direct the work" in schools to find the best methods. "The primary functions of educational directors and supervisors, as relating to methods, are," said Bobbitt, "first, the discovery of the best methods of procedures in the performance of any particular educational task; and second, the giving of these discovered best methods over to the teachers for their guidance in securing a maximum product." Teachers, maintained Bobbitt, could not be given "complete freedom in the way of methods used. . . . This tends to paralyze his efforts toward using his authority in the direction of methods, even in the case of the younger and weaker teachers. . . . The situation creates a system of privileges and immunities claimed by all the teachers in the matter of freedom to go wrong as much as they please in the selection of their methods."[29]

Bobbitt's fourth principle was particularly relevant for supervision. It focused on the qualifications of teachers and the attempt to raise their efficiency. Bobbitt considered "teachers weak" and in need of assistance. He declared, "One of the large problems of the supervisor is the treatment of weak teachers." Bobbitt insisted that teachers were poorly trained and that teacher training institutions were not producing "efficient" teachers. Therefore, it is the responsibility of the supervisor to "bring them up to maximum efficiency." However, Bobbitt decried the "subjective character" of supervision based on "frequently mistaken, and always quantitatively indefinite" judgments. Supervisors, he continued, must be equipped with scientific and objective means to measure the efficiency of teachers. "The way to eliminate the personal element from administration and supervision is to introduce impersonal method [sic] of scientific administration and supervision." The rating of teachers, thought Bobbitt, according to the latest principles of science, would raise supervision to the "lofty status it deserved."[30] I will return to Bobbitt's advocacy of "teacher rating" shortly.

Bobbitt, in his remaining principles, elaborated on many other important facets of scientific methods as applied to education. One of the more relevant areas of discussion was that of "hierarchy in the organization." The position of supervision in schools, thought Bobbitt, "must be safeguarded" and respected. He maintained that a hierarchy is necessary in order for a factory or school to operate efficiently. He made it very clear that teachers have no decision-making authority in schools and that it was the supervisor who would have the final say. "The teacher's freedom is necessarily narrowly limited, but the limitations are those of law and not the limitations of personal arbitrary authority." Supervisors, however, must give "definite directions as to what is to be done and how it is to be done." This is imperative, said Bobbitt, because teachers cannot "direct this work from within.... Supervisors must take the initiative."[31] It is clear that the persistence of hierarchy in education can be attributed, at least in part, to the infiltration of the business-industrial ideology.

Many supervisors were eager to adopt Bobbitt's ideas of scientific management to be applied within the school system. However, there were some, although in the minority, who did not readily accept his views.³² One of the most vociferous opponents of Bobbitt's ideas was James F. Hosic, a professor of education at Teachers College, Columbia University. Hosic contended that Bobbitt's "analogy is largely false. . . . Teaching cannot be 'directed' in the same way as bricklaying. . . . In education the supervisor's function is not to devise all plans and work out all standards and merely inform his co-workers as to what they are." The supervisor, held Hosic, "should not so much give orders as hold conferences. . . . His prototype is not a captain, lieutenant, or officer of the guard in industry, but chairman of committee or consulting expert."³³ Despite Hosic's criticism, schoolmen of the day readily adopted the business model. Note what William McAndrew said about his role as supervisor in the school. "I am the captain of big business."³⁴

Alvin S. Barr and William H. Burton, well-known professors of education, argued that teachers are reluctant to accept Bobbitt's methods. "The absence of the modern conception of cooperation" has led teachers not to comply "with the directions handed down from experts of the planning room above." They also did not believe that the establishment of "definite qualitative and quantitative standards would improve instruction in the schools.³⁵ Bobbitt was well aware of the fact that some of his ideas might be criticized. He therefore called for a more persistent and determined effort to apply scientific ideas in the schools. If "an objection will be made to scientific direction and supervision," then educators must remain vigilant in their pursuit of 'science in education.' . . . The business world knows that it cannot afford to neglect" science. Educators likewise, warned Bobbitt, must realize the importance of achieving "efficiency" of school operations.³⁶

The criticisms directed against Bobbitt's methods, nonetheless, accurately stressed a number of disturbing ideas. First and foremost was the ill-conceived notion that "education in a school" is analogous to "production in a factory." Bobbitt claimed that "education is a shaping process as much as the manufacture of steel rails."³⁷ Supervisors in the early twentieth century were becoming aware of the fallacy of this logic, and also realized the negative effects of bureaucracy in education. Bobbitt's "scientific management and supervision" found justification within a school organization that was bureaucratically organized. Bobbitt said he did not hope for autocracy in school management, but rather emphasized that "democracy is to be employed because it stimulates a far greater amount of thinking and unlocks greater stores of energy."[38] He did, however, later comment that "if autocracy in the long run could be more efficient, it should probably be employed."[39] It is not surprising, then, that educators in the early twentieth century were attracted to efficiency and scientific methods, as described by Bobbitt. These ideas were wholly consistent and compatible with bureaucracy.

It is clear that supervisors realized that hierarchy and bureaucratic control might be inimical to the interests of education. One prominent fact, however, must be kept in mind throughout the early history of supervision: what supervisors did and how it was done was based on their goals of professionalization. The rhetoric of scientific management, efficiency, rating, and later democracy were significant only to the extent that they helped supervisors establish a firm professional base. Supervisors were not motivated by any particular value about "interests of education," as much as they were concerned about ensuring and maintaining professionalization.

Still, it remains clear that the significance of Bobbitt's work was his advocacy of scientific and professional supervisory methods. Supervisors thought that their work in schools would be more clearly defined and accepted by adopting Bobbitt's principles of "scientific management." Supervisors believed, as did Bobbitt, that "the way to eliminate the personal element from administration and supervision is to introduce impersonal methods of scientific administration and supervision."[40] Supervisors looked to Bobbitt's ideas of scientific management and teacher efficiency as a means to accomplish their goal of heightened professionalism and legitimacy in the schools. As a result of Bobbitt's work a number of "rating scales" were advocated and developed by supervisors. The nature and use of these rating devices, which were a direct outgrowth of Bobbitt's work, will now be discussed.

Teacher Rating as a Function of Supervision

As a result of Frederick Taylor's rise to national prominence *efficiency* and *scientific management* became the watchwords of the day. Taylor's work inspired Bobbitt to apply the business model to the nation's schools. Within a relatively short period of time, educational efficiency experts emerged with their own agenda for promoting better schools. Chief among the techniques that would be employed in the schools was the use of "scientific rating scales." Supervisors in the early twentieth century were very much interested in utilizing and devising "rating schemes" to measure "teacher efficiency." Their expectation was that the application of Bobbitt's scientific methods would elevate their status in schools. One of the early attempts to apply Taylor's model to rate teachers was carried out in 1912 by Joseph S. Taylor, a superintendent from New York City. He explained that the measurement of teacher efficiency was essential in New York City schools. He indicated the benefits of a rating scale for teachers. "Every teacher who accomplishes the task receives a bonus, not in money, but in the form of a rating which may have money value." Teachers, later on, would viciously attack this idea of basing salary or differentials on results of rating. Taylor also conveyed quite clearly what would result from unfavorable ratings. "Those who are unable to do the work are eliminated." He explained that supervisors are in a unique position to improve instruction through the use of rating schemes. If, warned Taylor, the teacher is inefficient, the supervisor has every right to say, "Take my way or find a better one."[41]

Many other educators in the early twentieth century sought to apply business principles of scientific management to the problems of the school. Clyde C. Green, a superintendent from Pennsylvania, explained in 1915 that "the desire to apply business principles has prompted the administrative authorities of most large cities and many small ones to adopt some form of the merit system of promoting teachers and fixing their salaries."[42] The use of rating scales was considered to be of enormous benefit. In 1913, William M. Davidson, a superintendent from Washington, D.C., stated that "it is obvious that, as the tree is to be judged by its fruits, so the teacher is to be judged by the effects he produces in the pupils of his class." Davidson argued that "the worth of a system of rating is to be determined not merely in terms of its accuracy in stating the facts, but almost as importantly in terms of its tendency to improve the quality of the teachers rated." Davidson contended that systems of rating and criticism "cannot effect the impossible; they cannot re-create the teacher. But much they may do in the direction of stimulating cultural and professional growth."[43]

Charles J. Dalthorp, a superintendent from South Dakota, concurred that rating is an invaluable aid in supervision. Dalthorp contended that rating is useful for improving education by keeping teachers alert and growing. "It is the duty of the supervisor and executive in the modern progressive school to do everything possible to help the teacher rise to her highest level of efficiency."[44] However, to be effective, rating scales had to scientifically developed and applied. "We possess nothing which the great body of teachers is willing to accept as either just, reliable, or workable," said Henry D. Hervey, a superintendent from New York. If rating is to be successful, Hervey thought it "must be raised out of the realm of mere guesswork and personal opinion and placed upon a genuinely scientific basis, which shall be recognized as such not only by teachers who are to be rated, but also by their friends and by the general public."[45]

Several different versions of rating scales appeared in the early twentieth century.[46] One of the early methods for rating "teacher efficiency" was initiated by Edward C. Elliott, of the University of Wisconsin. "The chief purpose of any teaching efficiency scheme," stated Elliott, "is to serve as the means of promoting development and improvement of the individual teacher." He had hoped to eliminate the rating of teachers based on personal and biased accounts. "The science of education has allowed us to devise objective methods for rating teachers." His scale included categories ranging from physical and moral efficiency to social efficiency. Points, from 0 to 10, would be awarded for each category based on the "observations" of the supervisor.[47] Another significant attempt to devise a "teacher efficiency rating scale" and one that was widely disseminated throughout the schools was made by Arthur Clifton Boyce, working as a student in the Department of Education at the University of Illinois, and later at the University of Chicago, in 1915. Boyce, in devising his method, first conducted a study of 350 cities over 10,000 in population, asking schools to report their methods of rating teacher efficiency. Boyce discovered that most, if not all schools, relied on what he called the "impression method" of supervision. This method included rather impressionistic and subjective conclusions after a brief visitation in the classroom. One administrator in Newburgh, New York, stated that "we have 70 teachers, and our means of judging them is by visiting their classrooms and observing their work." Boyce concluded that this "impression method" used by many schools in rating teacher efficiency was inadequate for a number of reasons. "The weakness of these schemes," charged Boyce, was that they "result from (1) inadequate analysis . . . (2) a lack of definition of terms, resulting in vagueness and indefiniteness, and (3) the method of recording judgments, which is frequently wasteful of time or inaccurate or uncontrolled." Boyce claimed that his "scheme" would "overcome to some extent these difficulties by incorporating a comprehensive list of qualities, careful definition of terms, and the graphical method of recording judgments." His scale was composed of forty-five different items, grouped in five main headings, as follows: "personal equipment, social and professional equipment, school management, technique of teaching, and results." His scale, like many others during this period, ranked teachers in each of these categories using value judgments such as very poor, poor, medium, good, or excellent.[48]

The evidence indicates that these scales were used quite extensively in many schools across the nation. Supervisors, again, hoped that these "latest scientific methods" of rating teacher efficiency would give legitimacy and acceptance to their work. Unfortunately, criticism of these scales emerged shortly after their implementation in the schools. Writing in 1920, H. O. Rugg, then of the Lincoln School at Columbia University, stated that "the movement to rate teachers . . . needs a new impetus and a new emphasis." Rugg claimed that these "schemes" were "nearly always opposed by the teachers themselves and frequently the [supervisors] have been skeptical of their value." Rugg identified three shortcomings of rating schemes. First, the rating cards in practice "are not aimed at self-improvement," and have frequently been "an administrative scheme superimposed from above." Second, rating schemes, according to Rugg, were biased and abstract. "Rarely have such schemes been made concrete enough so that two or more rating officers rating the work of the same teacher could visualize precisely the same group of qualities." Third, concluded Rugg, the classification of traits themselves was ambiguous and ill-defined.[49]

Rugg's dissatisfaction with existing rating scales prompted him to devise a scheme of his own. He divided his rating card into five headings: skill in teaching, skill in the mechanics of managing a class, teamwork qualities, qualities of growth and keeping up-to-date, and personal and social qualities. Rugg used terms such as *low, medium,* or *high,* to classify teachers. Rugg warned educators that no matter what scale is used, ratings should always be conducted a number of times in order to get an accurate picture of the teacher's efficiency. "No single rating on teachers should be used as a measure of that teacher's efficiency. Conditions should be found by which at least two administrative officers can rate each teacher. If not," continued Rugg, *"the final rating on a teacher should certainly be the average of several independent ratings of the same officer."*[50]

A committee of Southern educators surveying various rating schemes, published their findings in the *American School Board Journal* in 1921, under the title, "The Rating of Teachers." They concluded that many rating schemes "now in use around the country" had serious defects and deficiencies. However, they stated that despite the defects, "rating must go on. . . . Defects are to be found in every score card, in order to secure the best results in rating teachers, some mechanical device must be used."[51] Writing in 1922, Franklin W. Johnson, of Teachers College, Columbia University, criticized rating scales "because of their emphasis on qualities of teaching rather than on the results of teaching." He, as well as other educators, decried the use of rating scales as autocratic devices used "to judge and assume to measure the fitness of their teachers for retention or for earning promotion."[52]

A number of other educators criticized rating scales as well. In 1920, Leroy A. King stated quite emphatically that there was no available evidence as to the value of "teacher rating scales."[53] L. J. Brueckner, a noted writer in the field of school supervision, explained the unreliability of the rating of teachers by supervisory and administrative officers. "In the first place," said Brueckner, "there are lacking any objective standards by which the work of the teacher may be rated, . . . In the second place, ratings are unreliable because they usually consist in a composite rating based on ratings of specific factors which are unweighted as to their importance. . . . They are evaluated almost entirely in terms of the subjective judgment of the rater. . . . This results in merely compounding the error of the rating."[54] Willard S. Elsbree, an associate professor of education at Teachers College, Columbia University, stated that "the refinement of our measuring instruments and the development of a clearer concept of what constitutes good teaching," would mean that "the time may not yet come when we can measure teaching efficiency with an accuracy which approaches our present measurements of intelligence. . . . In the meantime, there is little if anything to be gained by employing the crude rating devices which are now available."[55]

Despite these criticisms, rating schemes were widely used in schools throughout the first twenty-five years of the twentieth century. During this time, many supervisors and professors of educational administration attempted to promulgate their own scales of rating. However, the proliferation of rating devices contributed to much confusion. No agreement was reached regarding uniform standards for measuring teacher efficiency. It was possible and often commonplace for a teacher to be rated unsatisfactorily with one scale, yet competent with another. With no agreed upon criteria for excellent teaching, college professors and supervisors began to question the efficacy of rating schemes. Criticism also mounted against rating scales because in many instances they were not used to offer any constructive advice as to how to improve teaching. Rating scales were merely seen as ways of categorizing, stigmatizing, and controlling teacher behavior. Teachers argued that rating scales were not consistent with the ideals of democratic schooling and only mirrored bureaucratic and autocratic methods of the nineteenth century. The next section discusses the mounting dissatisfaction, primarily among teachers, to autocratic methods in supervision.

The Attack on School Supervision

Many teachers were troubled about increasing antidemocratic practices in schools, which resulted primarily from the extended use of rating scales. J. W. Crabtree, in an address before the Department of Classroom Teachers in 1915, told his audience what they wanted to hear. "Any system of rating teachers, in order to have my support, must not only give classroom teachers a squarer deal than any I have studied, but it must actually promote their educational and financial welfare in a more pronounced manner than any I have yet seen in operation." Crabtree, who at the time was a principal at the State Normal School in River Falls, Wisconsin, told his audience, mainly comprised of teachers, that he was not in favor of any current rating scheme that "is used for promotions and salary increases, . . . I shall not attempt to thrust on you a scheme that attempts to control your promotions and your salary increases." He concluded his address by stating: "Why not apply the [rating] scheme to superintendents and supervisors before applying it to the teachers under their supervision?"[56]

Teachers in particular did not favorably view rating scales. Ava L. Parrott, a teacher, speaking before the Department of Classroom Teachers in 1915, charged that rating scales were pernicious and bureaucratic devices. They are "fundamentally wrong . . . entirely unnecessary, a detriment to good pedagogy." She warned that as long as "teachers are rated by a superior officer, . . . the public and other professions will refuse to call teaching a profession." She decried the use of rating scales as "artificial, arbitrary, perfunctory and superficial." Responding to a statement made by a superintendent that physicians and lawyers were also rated, Parrott insisted that "a teacher's work cannot be measured, . . . therefore rating schemes must be abolished." Parrott offered two reasons for abolishing rating scales. First, she said, rating scales do not provide a consistent and reliable measure of a teacher's performance. "To illustrate further: Superior Merit, or an A, under one principal or district superintendent, might be a B under another. B under one might be a C under another, . . . This is too self-evident to dwell upon longer." A second reason for abrogating rating, according to Parrott, "is that it gives those who rate too great power and places them in a position in which they are open to temptation. Let's rid ourselves of supervision of this sort." Parrott claimed that rating had several "injurious pedagogical effects" such as turning teachers into "rate slaves." Teachers, charged Parrott, "are afraid to voice their opinions" in opposition to rating. It is unnecessary to do more than simply state that teachers controlled by fear, or under a system which inculcates fear tending toward cowardice, are not the most desirable teachers for the children of our future generations." Parrott concluded her tirade against rating by stating that the simple reason why rating schemes are used by supervisors is that "teachers are not trusted as are other professions."[57]

Jesse H. Newlon, a well-known superintendent from Denver, in 1922 presented quite a different outlook. He asserted that supervision and rating were necessary because teachers were inexperienced and ill-trained. He insisted that teachers wanted more, not less, supervision. In response, perhaps to teachers like Parrott, Newlon charged that "there are many teachers [who] resent supervision of any kind and quite often these are the poorest and most talkative teachers in the school system." Newlon lamented the fact that these teachers were "accorded places of leadership in teachers organizations." Newlon believed that these teachers "are a menace to our profession and their numbers should be eliminated."[58] Similarly, H. C. Storm, in 1923, insisted that those who were supervised were overly sensitive and merely stressed "the destructive nature of supervision. . . . We have classroom teachers who think themselves so perfect and so wonderfully professional that they need no supervision. These teachers would do away with all supervision and would sink all supervisors to the bottom of the deep blue sea. If they ever succeed," warned Storm, "our public schools will go to the bow wows."[59]

Supervisors maintained that a successful school system is dependent on authoritarian rule. Ensuring that curricula met uniform standards, that teachers conformed to acceptable behavior, and that the instructional process as a whole was under the close control of a supervisor, were the primary objectives of public school supervision. Teachers, for example, who were generally considered incompetent and inexperienced, needed close supervision and had to be kept under the thumb of a supervisor. Teachers were particularly sensitive to this close scrutiny and viewed the supervisor with distrust and fear. In a revealing account of the traditional views of supervisors toward teachers, Angelo Patri, a principal in New York City in the early years of the twentieth century, relates how suspicious and fearful teachers were of supervisors. He relates, in his book, *A Schoolmaster of the Great City,* that as a new principal he was impressed with the order of the school and the sympathetic relationship between teacher and student. "I passed the open door of a classroom and saw a teacher smiling down at a little boy . . . I was glad and walked towards the teacher. Instantly the smile disappeared, her body grew tense, the little boy sat down and all the other little boys sat up stiff and straight and put their hands behind them. . . . I tried to say something pleasant but I saw they were afraid of me and I went away." Discouraged and restless, Patri sought counsel from the previous school principal. Patri explains: "I've tried to have the teachers and children feel that I'm their friend, that I'm eager to help them but I don't seem to be able to get them to speak or act freely in my presence. They are afraid of me!" The former principal responded in astonishment: "Afraid of you? Of course they are and they ought to be. The teachers and children are all right. You'll find them well trained. Take my advice if you want any peace of mind, keep them under your thumb." Patri bemoaned authoritarian supervision that encouraged "blind obedience." "Obedience," writes Patri, "the loyal obedience that was school tradition."[60] Traditional supervision, based especially on critical appraisal of teacher performance, was the mainstay of supervisory practice in the late nineteenth century. Supervisors, like Newlon and Storm, defended their authoritarian position and posited that supervisory rating was necessary for the survival of public education.

Despite these defenses, the criticism against rating was virulent. In 1912, an editorial appearing in the *American Teacher,* the journal of the American Federation of Teachers (AFT), stated that "there is probably nothing, not even meager salaries, that frets and worries teachers more than supervision does."[61] Other teacher associations took the lead from the AFT and also vehemently criticized supervision. In September 1924, the Brooklyn Teachers Association, in its fiftieth annual report, stated, "Brooklyn teachers have consistently fought centralization and excessive supervision." The report continued to explain that teachers vigorously protested "the one man power set up" of centralization because it "sacrifices the rights of teachers."[62]

In 1913, an anonymous writer in the *American Teacher* reacted to what was termed the "master-servant" thesis in relation to the supervisor and teacher. The writer urged that "teachers especially should actively repudiate this pernicious doctrine that there is virtue in the humility of the servant. . . . We must refuse to bend the knee, and to look to the men and women higher up as the bootlack looks to the patron thru the corner of his eye. . . . We are not in schools to serve the principals and superintendents, although we are under their direction. We are in school to serve the public and the children of the public, in co-operation with the supervisors."[63] Similarly, in 1915, Frank J. Keller of De Witt Clinton High School in New York City portrayed the supervisor as a "sleuth." He criticized the "overbearing attitude" of the supervisor who "only looks for defects." This makes "the supervisor play the role of a sleuth with the teacher as the possible miscreant!"[64] "The bane of the teaching profession is the unthinking and unquestioned obedience to the authority of official supervisors," stated Abraham Lefkowitz, a New York City teacher in 1920. Lefkowitz explained that autocratic domination by supervisors had to be eradicated in order for teachers to achieve their goals of professional autonomy. "Our schools breed servants and autocrats but not democrats; followers, but not leaders; improvers, not inventors, imitators, not innovators; men fattened by the gratification of desire and not those consumed by the fire of great ideas; spineless followers, not fearless and independent thinkers. . . . Freedom from molestation from superiors," charged Lefkowitz, is an ideal that every organization should work to accomplish.[65]

Research indicates that many teachers considered supervisory rating as anti-democratic and unprofessional. One of the most scathing critiques against supervision came from Sallie Hill, a teacher, in 1918. In referring specifically to rating, Hill charged, "There is no democracy in our schools. . . . Here let me say that I do not want to give the impression that we are sensitive. No person who has remained a teacher for ten years can be sensitive. She is either dead or has gone into some other business," stated

Hill. She particularly disliked supervisors who were inadequately trained and incompetent. "It is humiliating and tends to neither cheerfulness nor hopefulness," said Hill, "to have to submit one's work to the criticisms of those whose lack of training and experience has not fitted them for their positions." She concluded by saying that there are "too many supervisors with big salaries and undue rating powers."[66]

Criticism was also advanced by distinguished college professors. For example, W. C. Bagley of Teachers College, Columbia University, speaking before the Department of Classroom Teachers in 1918, complained about the "factory" plan of school administration and its tendency to conceptualize teachers in industrial terms.

> I mean by this very frankly that the status of the classroom teacher is becoming more and more akin to that of the "hands" in a factory, working under foremen and superintendents who assume the real responsibility. . . . More and more frequently too these foremen and superintendents in our school are being recruited from a group which never has served an apprenticeship in the actual work of teaching boys and girls.[67]

Thus, supervisors found themselves in a vulnerable position in the school hierarchy. They sought to legitimize their existence in schools by devising methods for rating teachers hoping that this would alleviate many of their problems. However, despite good intentions, they encountered much opposition. Teachers and other educators were dissatisfied with bureaucratic school governance that placed the teacher at the low end of the hierarchy. They were also disenchanted with emphasis placed on business ideology and "factory-type" education. Particular criticism was aimed at "rating schemes" that were used by supervisors primarily for decisions regarding promotions and salary. This was a period of time in which cautious optimism slowly turned into confirmed despair for supervisors. As a result, supervisors in the 1920s began to search for new methods and conceptions in supervision.

The Dubious Attempt to Improve Instruction

As previously stated, supervisors wanted to justify their position in schools by attempting to improve instruction and to help teachers.[68] They used rating scales to achieve these goals. When opposition began to mount against rating, supervisors, rather than abandoning their methods, sought to improve them and to broaden their use in schools.[69] Their attempts ultimately met with resounding failure because they did not understand that "rating," as conceived and carried out in schools, only measured and classified, but did not improve and assist. As one visionary stated in 1917, "The principal object of supervision should be the improvement of teaching. . . . Rating cannot achieve this objective."[70]

That the proliferation of rating schemes is a natural consequence of bureaucratic role relationships and that it is essentially inimical to democratic interests in schools was understood in 1933 by the renowned educator and college professor, Orville Brim. He charged that "the rating scale is wrongly conceived, unreliable and destructive of teacher efficiency in the larger sense." Brim clearly stated that "rating scales" were an outgrowth of bureaucracy. "Rating," said Brim, allowed "autocratic administrators" to maintain a firm hold over teachers. Rating serves as a "crutch for weak supervisors, supervisors who do not of their own knowledge know the qualities of a good teacher. . . . Good teaching is an art and defies this nice quantitative distribution of traits."[71]

If, in fact, supervisors were desirous of improving teaching and that they were simply misdirected in their attempts to utilize rating to attain this end, then the question of whether or not they had an alternative to rating becomes interesting. The evidence, indeed, suggests that there was an alternative that could possibly avoid unproductive and autocratic evaluation and measurement of teacher efficiency. This alternative appears to be found in the use of "stenographic reports." The use of stenographic accounts, which began in 1910, the same year that the first rating scheme was devised, was the "brainchild" of Romiett Stevens, a professor of education at Teachers College, Columbia University. Stevens thought that the best way to improve instruction was to record verbatim accounts of actual lessons, "without criticism or comment. . . . The stenographic lesson report soon reveals the actual strength or weakness in the content of the lesson and in the psychology of its presentation. . . . It gives, the *facts* of the lesson for analysis and study." The teacher would then be able to make proper adjustments based on the evidence gathered.[72] According to two recent authorities, Stevens's stenographic account was "the first major systematic study of classroom behavior."[73]

Several others also urged that these "reports" be used as supervisory tools to improve instruction.[74] In 1924, John D. Rossman, an assistant superintendent in Gary, Indiana, encouraged the use of "stenographic records" by supervisors, although he preferred to call it the "case method" of supervision. "Constructive supervision," maintained Rossman, involves an "efficient stenographer who notes every spoken word during the period, transcribes these and supplies a copy both to the supervisor and to the teacher visited."[75] Similarly, Walter D. Cocking of the George Peabody College for Teachers, advocated the use of stenographic accounts as one very effective method by which to achieve "objective means to improve instruction." Cocking maintained that any type of supervision that relies on rating or evaluation is likely to be resented by teachers. On the other hand, he felt that teachers would "endorse stenographic records."[76]

Advocates of stenographic reports did recognize certain deficiencies with its use. Stevens explained that there "were certain drawbacks with the use of stenographic records. . . . At best the conditions under which teachers and pupils appear in all such lessons cannot be considered normal. . . . The mere presence of stenographers, is sufficient in itself to destroy utterly the natural relations of a good classroom." He urged that teachers be made fully comfortable before actual use of stenographic records in the classroom.[77] Rossman also pointed out that the idea "seems to be failing because of unsatisfactory results and the great cost involved." He explained that many supervisors did not like to take notes while observing a classroom teacher because they were unable to get the whole picture of what was happening in the room. Thus, they were forced to rely on events from memory. "As a result the teacher frequently comes to the conference with fear and trembling or with a hostile attitude."[78]

It appears that some supervisors misused stenographic reports by not following the prescriptions outlined by Stevens. Indeed, stenographic accounts have the potential to become as autocratic and arbitrary as rating if used incorrectly. In an interview this writer had with the late Florence B. Stratemeyer, Professor Emeritus of Education at Teachers College, Columbia University, she explained that many supervisors whom she interviewed claimed they were using stenographic accounts, but "upon closer observation they in fact were observing teachers in the familiar autocratic ways of the past." However, when properly conceived, Stratemeyer claimed, stenographic reports have the ability to effectively influence instruction by offering teachers objective, running accounts of actual classroom interaction so that teachers can choose with the guidance of, let's say, a "master teacher" certain areas of the lesson that need strengthening.[79]

The distinction between rating and stenographic accounts is instructive. The aim of rating scales is to make distinctions between good and bad or competent and incompetent, whereas stenographic reports observe and record, but do not criticize or comment. Many of its detractors claimed that stenographic accounts were too expensive and time-consuming and as such their practical use in the schools was unrealistic and unworkable. It is my contention that rating was viewed more favorably, not due to the deficiencies of stenographic records, but because it accomplished the objectives of the school bureaucracy; that is, control and classification. Stenographic accounts were more likely to foster cooperation and democracy between school personnel. Of course even stenographic accounts are tools that have the potential to be misused. However, they did not gain acceptance as a method of observation in the public schools because rating devices, with their reliance on quantitative distinctions, were more readily consistent with the objectives of bureaucratic school management. It is not surprising that rating scales were widely used in schools in the early twentieth century. It would not be for many years later, with the advent of clinical supervision, that stenographic reports would resurface and gain much wider acceptance in the schools.[80]

So it was, that the supervisor entered the third decade of the twentieth century with inappropriate methods for improving instruction. Rating, not improving teaching, was highly valued. This effort met much opposition. The supervisor's quest for professional status to gain legitimation in the eyes of teachers and to distinguish himself from administrators, would assume unprecedented importance after about 1925.

3
The Fall of Autocracy and the Emergence of Efficient, Cooperative, Democratic Methods and Scientific Supervision: The Supervisor's Dream

The early history of public school supervision indicates the prevalence of bureaucracy as the main focus for practice. Supervisors in the early twentieth-century tried to disassociate themselves from bureaucratic role relationships. However, the first two decades of the new century proved to be a difficult time for supervisors. They realized the precarious position they occupied in the school hierarchy. Somehow, as middle-management personnel, they were caught between teachers on the one hand, and administrators on the other. They understood very well that their successful existence in schools was dependent on finding justification for their work. The drive for professional autonomy by supervisors was a direct consequence of their efforts to gain greater recognition. To fully understand the efforts of supervisors to professionalize and the difficulties they encountered, the reader must view the evolution of supervision, as explained in the Introduction, in light of a "power" model of professionalism, which seeks to understand how and why an occupational group achieves professional status. An analysis of supervision in this way provides an accurate view of the professional efforts of supervisors.

As noted in the Introduction, education and schooling have been a bureaucratically controlled, state-supervised enterprise since the nineteenth century. As the hierarchical structure of schooling was being set in place along with increased specialization and differentiation of roles and responsibilities, decisions about who bears authority and how power is distributed became a bureaucratic rather than professional function. What occurred in American education at the turn of the century was not a transformation from a loosely connected ward system to some sort of professional bureaucracy with high standards, technical rationality, and the like. Instead, what happened was a transformation from school as cottage industry to school as factory. The practice of supervision in schools reflected this bureaucratic inclination. The increase in supervisory offices in the early twentieth century is not an indication of greater professionalism but of putting into place a bureaucratic factory system of supervision. The professionalization of supervision was merely a label captured by the bureaucracy and used to further its own ends. Bureaucratic governance has a vested interest in ensuring strict adherence to supervisory mandates. Supervision perpetuates bureaucratic ideals and values; hence, supervisors fulfill similar ends.

Why did supervisors have difficulty in securing professional recognition for their work in schools? The answer, it seems to me, has much to do with an inherent conflict, which by definition, is not easily resolved. Supervisors functions within the school bureaucracy to oversee, inspect, and ensure efficient operation and management of the organization. As such, they are actively and continually involved in evaluating performance of teachers. Ross L. Neagley and N. Dean Evans, in their *Handbook for Effective Supervision of Instruction,* explain that one of the supervisor's major responsibilities is to "assist the principals in a staff capacity in evaluating the quality of teaching and learning."[1] The function of evaluation, according to Arthur Costa and Charles Guditus, while necessary to remove "incompetent teachers," tends "to interfere with the helping relationship needed to work productively with other staff members."[2] As a result, teachers may be reluctant to ask for assistance fearing a negative evaluation. Supervision, in the eyes of many teachers, is closely linked to this evaluation function. Teachers may eschew assistance and in-service education despite efforts by supervisors to allay teacher fear and distrust of autocratic supervision. Supervisors encountered problems in professional identification in large measure due to the fact that they were perceived, principally by teachers, as intrusionary functionaries whose chief purpose was to evaluate, not improve, instruction.

The supervisor's quest for professional autonomy to eradicate the ill-defined status in schools, to gain legitimacy in the eyes of teachers, and to distinguish their work from administration would assume unprecedented importance after 1920. Professionalism as a process affecting supervisors represented, especially during the twenties and thirties, a concerted effort to achieve some sort of internal organization, guidelines for expertise, professional training, a strong political power base, and control over their work. The advocated theme for supervision in the post-1920 period was "the improvement of instruction," not rating efficiency. The attitudes, concerns, and aspirations of supervisors during this period can best be summed up by the following anonymous poem found in *Playground and Recreation* in 1929 titled "The Snoopervisor, the Whoopervisor, and the Supervisor":

> With keenly peering eyes and snooping nose,
> From room to room the Snoopervisor goes.
> He notes each slip, each fault with lofty frown,
> And on his rating card he writes it down;
> His duty done, when he has brought to light,
> The things the teachers do that are not right.
>
> With cheering words and most infectious grin,
> The peppy Whoopervisor breezes in.
> "Let every boy and girl keep right with me!
> One, two, three, four!
> That's fine! Miss Smith I see.
> These pupils all write well. This is his plan.
> Keep everybody happy if you can."
>
> The supervisor enters quietly,
> "What do you need? How can I help today?
> John, let me show you. Mary, try this way."
> He aims to help, encourage and suggest,
> That teachers, pupils all may do their best.[3]

This new emphasis on "democratic supervision" gained popularity among supervisors after 1920. Supervisors during this period tried to alter the perception of supervision away from "snoopervision" to a more humane and democratic function. This advocacy of professionalism and democratic supervision manifested itself in a number of ways after 1920.[4]

Supervisors used democracy as legitimizing rhetoric in an effort to align themselves with teachers who wanted autonomy, rather than higher-level administrators who wanted efficiency and rationality. Supervisors, in other words, did not become more democratic in order to advance schooling, but envisioned democratic ideas and principles as advantageous to their occupational/professional goals within the educational bureaucracy. The shift from "rating" to "democracy" was a shift in rhetoric demanded by the conflicts facing supervisors. So long as measurement and rating were their stock and trade, supervisors met unflinching opposition from teachers. Insofar as teachers were calling for autonomy and calling it democracy, supervisors needed to meet this challenge. Appeals to democracy, therefore, were part of an effort to achieve legitimacy in the eyes of teachers. Supervisors believed in democracy only to the extent to which it furthered their self-interests. Seen in this light, democracy served as a kind of rhetorical tool in the struggle for professional recognition.

The Professional Orientation

Supervisors sought professional autonomy and development through the formation of a new organization and journal, the first of its kind devoted exclusively to supervision. Dr. James Hosic, speaking in September 1921, lamented the fact that there was a dearth of literature in the field of supervision, while at the same time there was much written about administration. Hosic charged that there was a growing need for an organization dealing with the particular concerns related to supervisors and supervision. After all, continued Hosic, even the teachers had an organization in the Department of Classroom Teachers, founded in 1914.[5] Hence, there followed the birth of the National Conference on Educational Method. In May 1922, the editor of *The Journal of Educational Method* proclaimed, "Meanwhile, through every possible agency we shall do well to publish the fact that supervision is a distinct occupation in itself, worthy of life-long devotion and demanding peculiar training and fitness."[6] An examination of the publications, statements, and activities of this new supervisory organization indicates the desire by supervisors to redefine and reconceptualize supervision as a professional enterprise incorporating "democratic" methods to improve instruction in the schools.

In the afternoon of the first session of the newly formed organization, a constitution was adopted that stated that the "objective of the society is the improvement of supervision and teaching."[7] To support this goal the newly created organization placed significance on "method." As an editorial in 1921 explained, "Supervision if it is ever to come into its own must have 'methods' too." The editorial continued to urge that the "methods" of both supervision and teaching be in unison so that "the two functions should proceed side by side. . . . If supervision were merely scientific management or inspection or bossing the job, then truly it would have but little in common with the art of teaching." The editor concluded that "the term Educational Method is a fit one to designate the entire body of principles which underlie all modern school practice."[8]

Focusing on method, it was thought, would enable supervisors to attain professional recognition. An editorial in May 1922 of *The Journal of Educational Method* stated that in order for supervision to be considered a professional field of study it must provide "rigorous preparation, maintain definite standards, and give unmeasured service." Unfortunately, continued the editorial, supervision at present lacks "methodological direction." In order to foster this direction, the editorial proclaimed that the National Conference on Educational Method "must publish the fact that supervision is a field of study in its own right possessing distinct method in its work in schools."[9]

While the journal sought to promote supervision as a unique profession and supervisors as specially trained professionals, the evidence indicates that reality fell far short of expectation. Professional growth and development through special training and preparation was inadequate to say the least. Supervisors, prior to about 1930, were selected on the basis of a minimum of undergraduate and graduate preparation, success as classroom teachers, and skill in certain administrative duties. The special supervisor was selected by the building principal or assistant superintendent on the basis of presumed expertise in a particular subject. General supervisors and principals were selected by school superintendents based on "competence in teaching, theory of supervision, and the science of measurements," said W. G. Coburn, a superintendent from Michigan.[10] In an extensive survey conducted by J. M. Gwynn in thirty-one of the largest cities in the United States, it was found that the conditions for eligibility, qualifications, and appointment of supervisors were less than adequate. In a majority of cities surveyed, there existed no legal requirements or qualifications to be a supervisor. When stated in some cities, the legal requirements were vague and general. These requirements stated that the supervisor " 'must hold a teacher's certificate,' or 'must be a practical educator.' " In most cases, "the judgment of the superintendent is depended upon to determine the eligibility of supervisors."[11]

The subjective, nonscientific training of supervisors can be demonstrated by a reading of a book written by George C. Kyte, a professor of education and supervision at the University of Michigan. The book, widely used in "supervisor preparation courses," presents case studies describing problems that supervisors are likely to encounter. The student is asked to carefully read each case study and to "solve the problem."[12] The case study method was quite popular and considered effective in training supervisors. With little, if any, rigorous requirements for eligibility as a supervisor, however, supervisors quickly realized the importance of establishing more comprehensive programs for training recruits. A review of the literature after 1930 indicates that rigorous standards were established for supervisors.

Supervisors never abandoned their dreams of becoming accepted professionals within the school organization. One of the more prominent ways they hoped to accomplish their objective was to promote the idea that supervision was a "helping function," not an obtrusive or autocratic function. "Snoopervision" and "Whoopervision" were no longer considered acceptable supervisory behavior. Rather, the "Supervisor" as a "helper" was the paradigm. Ethel I. Salisbury, a special supervisor in Minnesota, claimed that besides being "progressive, open minded, patient, . . . and sympathetic," supervisors were professionals who cultivated democracy and cooperativeness in their relations with teachers.[13] In a similar being, F. E. Bamberger, a professor of education at John Hopkins University, asserted that supervisors were "helping professionals" and that the "older conception as bureaucrat" was no longer extant.[14] Note, in figure 3, the change in advocated theory as represented by Allen's typology, which contrasts "professional supervision" with "political and military supervision."[15]

Indeed, the promotion of democratic ideals was an important theme in supervision during this time. Note the choice of words used by Fannie W. Dunn in her address before the Department of Rural Education in 1923 when she maintained that supervision was "a highly professionalized, helping, coordinating, cooperating, inspiring function."[16] Similarly, inspired by the work of John Dewey, *Democracy and Education,* Hosic furthered the ideals of democratic supervision in an article appearing in *School and Society* in 1920. He stated that the supervisor, although "invested for the time being with a good deal of delegated authority does not justify him in playing the autocrat. . . . To do so, is neither humane, wise, nor expedient. . . . Supervision must be cooperative, creative, scientific, effective and democratic."[17]

Supervisors realized that democracy must govern their rela-

Figure 3

ALLEN'S TYPOLOGY OF SCHOOL SUPERVISION

Types of School Supervision

No individual supervisor is exclusively of any one type. In general, supervision is becoming more professional (Read both vertically and horizontally.)

	1. School supervision of the political type	2. School supervision of the military type	3. School supervision of the professional type
1. Aim	To hold his job and secure promotion	To get results	To serve individuals— teachers, pupils, and parents
2. Methods of operation	By building up personal following By personal friendship By conferring favors or promising them By keeping eye on next in rank above and below	By "putting on the screws" By discipline of both pupils and teachers By competition By putting pressure upon principal, teachers, pupils, and parents By keeping his eye on "results"	By building up teacher and pupil morale By cooperation By the spirit of service from bottom up: the pupils help each other, the teacher helps the teacher, etc. By keeping his eye on the task in hand
3. Methods of measuring the teacher	Rates the teacher on a basis of personal loyalty	Rates teacher according to class performance in grade work	Rates teacher on team-work, and on attitude and improvement of pupils
4. Methods of measuring the pupil	By subjective judgement	By subjective tests of grade work	By achievement quotient and growth By objective measure of progress in each student
5. Effects of the method of supervision	Distrust of superiors and associates, jealousy, neglect of professional requirements	Competition, fear, worry, overwork, failure, dissatisfaction on the part of principal, teacher, pupil, and parent	Cooperation, trust, team-work, mental health, success, joy in work on part of pupil, teacher, and principal
6. Reasons for its adoption	Tradition; lack of training; "necessity"	Only way he knows how "Necessity" "Efficiency"	Professional training, professional growth Produces best results for welfare of pupils

tionship with teachers if they were in fact going to be accepted as professionals. Orville G. Brim, a professor of education at Ohio State University, revealed the necessity for supervisors to continue their pursuit of democracy in schools. Admitting that early supervision was "inspectoral and autocratic," Brim explained the change in emphasis away from this conception due to the fact that "teachers grew critical, bitter, and antagonistic, so much so that the problem of good will became and today is a major supervisory issue." According to Brim, the idea of a "helping" supervisor emerged in direct response to autocratic supervision.[18]

Supervision tried to move away from bureaucratic practices, originating in the late nineteenth century, to a more democratic and cooperative function in order to attain a greater degree of professionalism. The principal vehicle for enhancing their goal of professionalization was the formation of a new organization, the National Conference on Education Method. Principally through their journal and related publications, supervisors demonstrated their desire to improve instruction and accentuate democratic role relationships in schools. It is curious to note that this newly formed organization, which attempted to promote the goals and objectives of supervisors in public schools and at the same time wanted to distinguish their work from administration, maintained a close affiliation with administrators and superintendents. In fact, the National Conference on Educational Method held its annual meeting under the auspices of the Department of Superintendence of the NEA.[19]

In February 1928, the organization changed its name to the National Conference of Supervisors and Directors of Instruction. A number of prestigious educators contributed to the organization's first yearbook. People like Alvin S. Barr of the University of Wisconsin, Orville Brim of Ohio State University, William H. Burton of the University of Chicago, and L. J. Brueckner of the University of Minnesota added prestige and impetus to their drive toward greater professional acknowledgment. About a year and a half later, the supervisory organization once again changed its name by dropping "National Conference" from its title. Becoming part of the NEA, the organization was now called the Department of Supervisors and the Directors of Instruction. Membership consisted primarily of people in local school systems throughout the country as well as in state departments of education. Perusal of the publications, statements, and activities of this association indicates a concerted effort to further the "professional orientation" of supervisors throughout the nation's schools.

Science and School Supervision

Supervisors realized that they could not attain their goal of professional status without a sound scientific and theoretical knowledge base informing their practice. The application of science to the study and practice of supervision was seen as indispensable for continued progress. "Such applications of the scientific method are what will make education a science and supervision a respected profession," maintained C. W. Stone.[20] Writing in 1925, W. E. Wiley, a superintendent from California, stated that "'Snoopervision' has to give way to real constructive supervision, ... the greatest improvements will be possible, ... through objective scientific methods."[21] In an address before the Department of Superintendence in 1922, E. E. Oberholtzer proposed that "the next step in school supervision is to establish scientific procedure and a proper organization for the evaluation of supervision as it relates to all phases of public education."[22]

One of the foremost proponents of science in education and supervision and a prolific writer, was Alvin S. Barr. He emphatically stated that the application of scientific principles "is a part of a general movement to place supervision on a professional basis." Barr explained the importance of science in supervision and education in his book, *An Introduction to the Scientific Study of Classroom Supervision,* published in 1931. In his preface, Barr noted that there was much confusion in "the field of supervision." Correspondingly, he said there was confusion regarding "supervision as a professional subject." Barr asserted that supervision could not rely solely, as many educators believed, on "existing subjects," such as philosophy, measurements, statistics, and methods of educational research. Rather, supervision must find its own methods in the "science of instructing teachers." Barr stated in precise terms what the supervisor needed to know.

Supervisors must have the ability to analyze teaching situations and to locate the probable causes for poor work with a certain degree of expertness; they must have the ability to use an array of data-gathering devices peculiar to the field of supervision itself; they must possess certain constructive skills for the development of new means, methods, and materials of instruction; they must know how teachers learn to teach; they must have the ability to teach teachers how to teach; and they must be able to evaluate.... In short, they must possess training in both the science of instructing pupils and the science of instructing teachers. Both are included in the science of supervision.[23]

Barr objected to the use of scientific method in supervision as wholly inadequate. He described in great detail seven proposals to improve instruction. Barr said the supervisor should first formulate objectives, followed by measurement surveys to determine the instructional status of schools. Then, probable causes of poor work should be explored through the use of tests, rating scales, and observational instruments. The results of supervision must be measured. Most important, according to Barr, the methods of science should be applied to the study and practice of supervision.[24] More concretely, he asserted that a scientific analysis of teaching is a necessary part of the training of a supervisor. "How can the scientific knowledge of the teaching process be brought to bear upon the study and improvement of teaching?" Barr contended that teaching could be broken down into its component parts, and that each part had to be studied scientifically. If good teaching procedures could be isolated, then specific standards could be established to guide the supervisor in judging the quality of instruction. He based his scientific approach to supervision "upon the success of the professional student of education in breaking up this complex mass into its innumerable elements and to study each objectively."[25]

Another noteworthy person who influenced the idea of scientific supervision was Charles H. Judd. In an address before the National Association of Secondary School Principals in 1920, Judd stated that "teachers must be supervised in a fashion which is at once direct and scientific." Judd criticized the manner in which supervisors were chosen without adequate training in the science of education. In the future, he said, "They will be selected because they are equipped by mental capacities and by careful scientific study for administrative and managerial functions." Judd further urged that "both the non-supervisory attitude and the attitude of excessive supervision ought to be replaced by scienific method of determining whether classroom work is efficient or not."[26]

Supervisors also had to be able to apply scientific principles to the measurement of pupil performance. E. E. Lewis, a superintendent in Rockford, Illinois, described three ways of measuring pupil accomplishment: through personal opinion, comparison with other pupils, and by standard units of accomplishment. Dismissing the first two rather quickly, Lewis favored IQ testing.

"It is much fairer and far more accurate to measure the general intelligence of a child in terms of an I.Q. (intelligence quotient) than it is to measure in terms of 'bright,' 'average,' or 'dull.'" Furthermore," continued Lewis, "an I.Q. means practically the same thing anywhere the child may happen to go, while 'bright,' 'average,' or 'dull' may change meaning when used by the same person a half hour later." Lewis also emphasized the importance of fair and just scientific comparisons between teachers. In sum, "Let us give this new movement in education our heartiest support and in time we will really have a science and a technique of measurement that will be a substitute for inaccurate opinion and comparison."[27]

It is clear that educators, in the twenties and thirties, urged for a more scientific approach applied to supervisory practice in schools and that the methods of the past were no longer viable. The early attempts to apply science via "rating cards" was now losing favor. William H. Burton, a distinguished professor and prolific writer in supervision, explained that the use of "rating schemes from our pre-scientific days, . . . would be wholly inadequate today." Burton, while recognizing the usefulness of rating in some instances, believed that "it is desirable and rapidly beocming possible to have more objectively determined items by means of which to evaluate the teacher's procedure." Burton mentioned the scientific and statistical work done by Barr, Gray, Brueckner, and himself as examples of "progressive development" in supervision."[28] Florence E. Bamberger also envisioned that "scientific supervision" would replace "conceptions of the past." "The old form of supervision, which regarded classroom visitation and supervision as synonymous, has passed away. Visitation serves its purpose but does not absorb all or even the greater part of the supervisor's time and energy." Supervisors, she continued, must now incorporate "the highest principles of science."[29]

Supervisors advocated a scientific approach toward their work in schools. The establishment of a rigorous scientific base, it was thought, would elevate supervision to the lofty status it so very much desired. In this sense, scientific supervision can be seen, as was rating and democracy, as legitimizing rhetoric to bolster their professional objectives. The reader must keep in mind that the ultimate objective of supervisors was the attainment of professional recognition within the educational bureaucracy. Rating, science, efficiency, and democracy were merely convenient and timely methods used by supervisors to accomplish their goals.

The current interest in scientific supervision served a similar purpose. Unfortunately, however, for reasons that will be discussed later, the attainment of scientific supervision remained largely illusory.

The Distinction between Supervision and Administration

Thus far, I have described the formation of a new supervisory organization, its attempts to achieve professional status for its members, and its advocacy of scientific principles as a basis for legitimizing its work in public schools. Another major theme expressed in *The Journal of Educational Method* was the desire to make a clear and definite distinction between supervision and administration. The major reason for this is in large measure due to the fact that supervisors in the thirties wanted to isolate themselves from practices that might be perceived by teachers and others as bureaucratic. The new conception of supervision during this time was aimed at democratic relationships between teachers and supervisors. That supervisors were professional educators whose primary aim is the improvement of instruction, and not administrative inspection, was widely advocated by writers of supervision.

Supervision, as previously explained, was a function of the school superintendent in the late nineteenth century. Supervision was an important function used by superintendents to carry out their objectives of standardization and centralization of authority. The primary emphasis of supervision, then, before 1900 was administrative, not instructional. The term *administrative supervision* is frequently found in the literature of the time. However, through the expansion of administrative and supervisory offices in the early twentieth century, some supervisors began to question the taken-for-granted notion that supervision must be equated with school administration. Increasingly, there was much discussion at local and national conventions of delineating supervisory practice from administration. As early as 1906, John T. Prince said, "When the duties of supervision become properly adjusted," then "the evolutionary lines of progress will no longer lie in methods of administration merely."[30] Supervisors realized that if they were to become professionals then they needed their own identity by establishing unique standards and specialized knowledge distinct from school administration.

In short, they argued that supervision was primarily concerned with instruction, not administration.

In the first volume of *The Journal of Educational Method,* in October 1921, Margaret Madden, a supervisor in Chicago, contended that supervision is a field of study distinct from administration. "It is significant that the card index of a public library in a very large city shows one card only on the subject of school supervision. It bears the legend, 'See School Administration.'" "This does not mean that the library is ill equipped or that is is badly catalogued; it simply indicates that there is not a clear conception of the nature of supervision, . . . *school supervision is not school administration; it is not school management.* . . . It is a field in itself or should be, directly concerned with questions of classroom instruction."[31] Charles A. Wagner maintained that there was a clear difference between supervision and administration. He said, "Arranging the budget of expenditure is an administrative duty, but arranging the course of study is a supervisory duty; purchasing textbooks is an administrative job but selecting textbooks for use is a supervisory job."[32] In a similar tone, John M. Foote, a state supervisor in Louisiana, explained that "administrative supervision, old as American education, provides the facilities of teaching, controls the school system, is more obvious and spectacular and has well-developed standards of excellence." On the other hand, Foote continued, "supervision of instruction, yet in infancy, is concerned with the teaching performance, aims to improve instruction, requires more intensive study and greater technical skill."[33] Even the Department of Superintendence, in its eighth yearbook published in 1930, devoted an entire chapter to the relationship between supervision and administration. The authors observed that there was much confusion regarding this issue, and insisted that the term *supervisor* be restricted to mean the "supervision of instruction." The authors continued by explaining that there is a clear demarcation between the two functions. "The administration is responsible, through the provision of plant, equipment, and personnel, for the organization of schools and of classes in which a variety of opportunity is provided," while they continued, "good supervision seeks to promote improvement in instruction through constructive changes."[34]

Although educators did not accept the view that there was a difference between supervision and administration,[35] most leaders concurred that a clarification of the two functions was necessary. Unmistakably, during the twenties and thirties, there was an urgent appeal to recognize supervision not only as separate from administration, but on equal footing with it. As E. O. Melby wrote in 1932, "During the last two decades supervision has sought to differentiate itself from administration and to secure recognition as a branch of our educational machinery coordinate with administration."[36]

The Democratic Impulse

Supervisors knew that the ancestral legacy of administration was rooted in authoritarian school governance. In order to separate themselves from the inspectoral and autocratic supervision of the past, they knew they must radically alter the conception of "modern" supervisory practice. Supervisors, in this effort, promoted democracy and cooperation in their relationships with teachers. Figure 4 depicts, in cartoon form, the shift away from "fault-finding" supervision to a more modern view of supervisory practice.[37] Note the remnants of inspectoral supervision and "superior/inferior" ideology present in supervisory practice even during this time when "democratic" supervision was endorsed. Vestiges of bureaucratic governance were difficult to overcome.

In an article published in *The Journal of Educational Method*, R. K. Keyes maintained that "the new conception of supervision" was based on "not merely a stereotyped looking-on or even looking-over the things within its immediate scope, but a clear, open-eyed vision from the higher places." Keyes stated that supervision was "not merely planning plus criticism, pruning here, cutting there to bring the supervised into harmony with the supervisor's preconceived notion, but great-minded breadth and depth of observation which sees in order to inspire. . . . Supervision's main purpose is to improve instruction, . . . be cooperative rather than critical, . . . provides professional growth, . . . must be constructive."[39] In an impassioned address before the Department of Rural Education, William T. Melchior urged his audience, comprised mainly of supervisors, "May your purpose in 1924 and every year thereafter be to be not inspectors, but supervisors, 'technically trained, ennobled by character, sanctified by faith. . . .' Supervision leads; inspection drives. . . . Supervision says, 'Come on, let's go; inspection says, 'Go on.'" M. W. Sloyer, a supervisor from Pennsylvania, considered the work of supervision under three main categories, favoring category number three:

Figure 4
SPEARS' CARTOON

Modus Operandi
1. The swivel-chair artist
2. The inspectional type
3. The sympathetic helper

Modus Juricandi
1. The destructive, cynical type
2. The optimistic, impressionist
3. The constructive, cooperative type

Modus Discendi
1. The disciplinary method
2. The socialized method
3. The proposing method[41]

The democratic drive in public school supervision was reflective of the general tone of American society in the twenties and thirties. President Woodrow Wilson, speaking before Congress in April 1917, asked for a declaration of war on Germany. Wilson incarnated the progressive idealism of the twenties, which embraced the idea that America's goal should be to "make the world safe for democracy." National democratic idealism influenced the urgent call for greater democracy in the nation's public schools. Speaking before the NEA in 1917, Mary D. Bradford, a superintendent from Kenosha, Wisconsin, reaffirmed America's faith in democracy domestically and in foreign affairs. According to Bradford, "The evils of the world" were being "cured by more democracy. . . . That cure, more democracy," was being "applied to the internal affairs of the nation's schools. . . . The democratic trend in school administration seems to parallel this general trend in civic affairs." In her closing remarks, Bradford said that "the apparent trend of the day is moving away from autocratic and centralized management of the schools towards cooperative and democratic principles."[42]

The most profound and comprehensive treatment of democracy in education can be found in the work of Dewey. Writing in 1903, Dewey explained that "modern life means democracy, . . . how does the school stand with reference to this matter? Does the school as an accredited representative exhibit this trait of democracy as a spiritual force?"[43] Dewey lamented the fact that schools, "as currently constructed," do not foster democracy. Hosic, affected in large part by the work of Dewey, wrote an article appearing in *School and Society* entitled, "The Democratization of Supervision." Hosic cautioned the supervisor to eschew his "autocratic past." "The fact that he is invested for the time being with a good deal of delegated authority does not justify him in playing the autocrat.... To do so is neither humane, wise, nor expedient." Continuing to build a philosophic rationale for the supervisor's involvement in "democratic pursuits," Hosic explained that it is no longer viable to apply techniques of the past. Hosic believed, as did Dewey, that it was possible to reshape a school system originated on the idea of bureaucratic maintenance to comply with the principles of democracy.[44]

Hosic, in his now classic article, analyzed "the factors involved in democratic supervision." They are: (1) a clear delimitation of the supervisory function; (2) genuine, constructive leadership, (3) adequate professional preparation of the supervisor; (4) scientific and impersonal standards by which to determine results; and (5) recognition of the human element. In explaining the first two factors of democratic supervision, Hosic discussed supervision as a specific function "not identical with administration," employing effective and cooperative methods best exemplified by enthusiasm, encouragement, and leadership on the part of the supervisor. In his third category, Hosic emphasized the fact that the supervisor would no longer be "chosen from the ranks merely because he was a good teacher." Professional preparation, wide experience, said Hosic, and "sound knowledge of educational method," would characterize the supervisor. Regarding the fourth point, Hosic admonished against scientific management without concern for the human element because without this element supervision becomes undemocratic, unscientific, and autocratic. Hosic insisted that the Prussian system, based on dictatorial principles, was not applicable to a country like the United States where the democratic attitude was the "key to the future." However, Hosic believed, as did many supervisors of the time, that discipline and authority were important, but that they should "progressively be supplanted by cooperation."[45]

Some seventeen years after the publication of Hosic's article, William H. Burton, a widely known professor of education, declared that democratic supervision was a reality. "Supervision is an expert technical service primarily concerned with bettering the conditions which surround learning. . . . It is sincerely hoped that the new definition [of supervision] will aid in eliminating from our thinking the implications of inspection, imposed improvement, and of the superiority-inferiority of the older relationship between supervisors and supervised." According to

Burton, "democracy" had indeed suppressed "monarchical rule."[46] The message was plain and clear: snoopervision and whoopervision were vestiges of past supervisory practice; today's supervision is unquestionably democratic, or so they hoped.

The Problems of Efficiency, Democracy, and Science

The endorsement of democracy as the impetus for supervisory practice did not occur in isolation of other advocated themes. "Science" and "efficiency" had their share of popularity among supervisors of the 1920s and 1930s. Supervisors apparently were not concerned about any possible conflicts resulting between science and democracy; to the contrary, the two were seen as complementary. David Snedden, a well-known proponent of science in education, formulated a theory in which all three elements were harmoniously joined. Snedden acknowledged that democracy in education had a long history dating back to the days of decentralization. Snedden contended that democratic principles could be fostered within a centralized school system as long as equal emphasis is given to efficiency and science. Although, maintained Snedden, efficiency is not a natural outgrowth of democracy, the two can function quite effectively. In fact, charged Snedden, democracy is vital for the continued progress of an efficient and scientifically minded educational system.

> In the administration of public education a large and ultimately indispensable elements of efficiency is popular interest and cooperation. . . . It should be well within the province and possibilities of a constructive statesmanship to formulate principles and devise methods of administration which should combine, . . . the merits of democratic and popular participation in school administration with the efficiency that results from the development of large school units, the presence of the expert, and centralized supervision."[47]

Others agreed that democracy and efficiency could be effectively combined. In 1934, William A. Smith, in an article entitled "Dictatorship and Democracy in Education from Teacher's Viewpoint," asked: "Will the schools prepare for the efficiency of an autocrat in government or will they prepare for the less efficient, more complicated, and idealistic democracy?" His answer was obvious. "Efficiency and democracy should not be viewed as competing ideas, but rather as one entity." Schools, thought Smith, can be efficient democracies utilizing scientific technology.[48] Perhaps the most widely read book that outlined in very precise terms the notion that science and democracy can be partners in the "educational enterprise," was the Third Yearbook of the Department of Supervisors and the Directors of Instruction, published in 1930, entitled *Current Problems of Supervisors: An Analysis of the Status of Supervision in American Public Schools.*

1. Supervision is cooperative.
Supervision works with teachers toward the solution of mutual problems. This involves the creation of situations in which teachers become aware of their problems and seek assistance in their solution. It eliminates every vestige of dictation or inspection. The question of superiority or inferiority of position does not enter. The teacher turns to the supervisor because the latter has proved his or her capacity to be useful—the divine right of leadership.
2. Supervision is scientific.
Supervision applies the scientific method to its study of the teaching process. It stimulates constructive, critical thinking. It sees in the classrooms of today the beginning of a processes that will lead to the gradual and constant improvement of generations of men to come. . . . Supervision seeks to . . . measure . . . evaluate objectively. . . . It seeks constantly objective evidence as to the results of the experimentation.[49]

This, indeed, was the supervisory dream! To equip the progressive supervisor with efficient, cooperative, and scientific methods to improve instruction in the nation's schools. While this certainly was the advocated theme, the "dream" was never fully realized. One of the reasons for the failure to reconcile efficiency with democracy was that much confusion ensued regarding their implementation in schools. How in fact was it possible to combine both "ideals" in a supervisory program? Jesse H. Newlon, for one, realized the dilemma at hand. Newlon, a professor of education at Teachers College, Columbia University, and a former school superintendent, claimed that a reconciliation "between cooperation and dictatorship" was impossible. He argued that it was not feasible to require "obedience to constituted authority," and at the same time, encourage "teacher participation and freedom." Newlon explained:

Almost all writers on the subject emphasize the importance of the authority of the principal. The advantages of a co-operative type of supervisory relationship are stressed by most of the writers, but the practice which they advocate often seems inconsistent with these doctrines. Burton, for example, says: "Democracy has implicitly in it the idea of delegated authority and of obedience to properly constituted expert leadership." Burton has really stated the crux of the whole problem, but he does not make clear how obedience to expert authority is to be reconciled with genuine teacher participation in the formulation of policies and freedom to exercise professional judgment in carrying out these policies.[50]

The "authority" and "freedom" debate of the late nineteenth century, although never really disappeared, gained greater attention in the twenties and thirties. Was it possible to maintain an efficient and bureaucratic school system and, at the same time, promote democracy? The problem has not changed. A school system that is fundamentally based on authoritarian and hierarchical rule cannot, by its very definition, accept participatory democracy. S. A. Courtis realized the inherent dilemma. "Can you supervise me scientifically and respect my personality? I'm afraid not."[51] Supervisors during this time did not or could not understand that, at their core, efficiency and democracy were conflicting, competing ideologies. A reconciliation between the two was tenuous, to say the least. To the supervisor in the 1920s and 1930s, "hope" obscured "reality."

The Status of School Supervision

Supervisors, between 1920 and 1940, strove to attain recognition for their work in schools. They sought to gain control over their activities by establishing new methods and standards for performance. To eschew autocracy and inspectoral supervision and accentuate cooperation and democracy were the primary objectives of the public school supervisor. However, there is little evidence to suggest that these ideals gained much popularity in the schools. The persistence of teacher criticism, the lack of specialized training in graduate schools, the problems encountered with scientific method, and the continued clamoring for professional status by writers of supervision, were indicative of the difficulty supervisors had in maintaining a professional outlook.

Supervisors, in their attempt to attain professional recogni-

tion, encountered problems that severely restricted their ability to accomplish their goals. First, while the organization they formed, in its early years, received notoriety, with a respectable membership of nearly 1,600, by the mid-thirties the National Conference was losing members (almost a 50 percent decline) and did not attract a large audience as it once did.[52] Partly for this reason the supervisory organization wished to merge with the Society for Curriculum Workers, as will be discussed in the next chapter. Second, supervisors experienced difficulties due to their interpretation of scientific method. Supervisors looked toward science for ready-made, immediate, utilitarian purposes. They sought to translate tentative and theoretical scientific notions into prescriptive and practical applications in schools. Their overconfidence and narrow empiricism associated with rating schemes proved to be a troubling issue in their quest for professionalism.

A third problem that supervisors confronted concerns the nebulous distinction between supervision and administration. Supervisors had a difficult time removing the stigma associated with school administration. Administration's legacy is steeped in authoritarian school governance. Supervisors after 1900 tried to disassociate themselves from administrative practices of the past but had much difficulty in doing so. To many, supervision was a natural outgrowth of school administration. The difference between the two, it was thought, was only a matter of definition of function and that both desired to accomplish similar goals. Alvin S. Barr, echoing this sentiment, stated that the distinction between supervision and administration was a "purely academic one." "The two can be separated only arbitrarily for the sake of analysis, a separation in function is impossible."[53] Indicative of the failure of educators to separate the two functions, is the fact that supervision of instruction and administration is carried out in schools by one functionary. In many businesses and corporations there is a clear differentiation made between the two. There is usually one person in charge with supervisory responsibilities and another concerned with administrative matters. If the same were to hold true in schools, then you would find one individual concerned only with the supervision and improvement of teaching, with no unnecessary involvement in administrative matters. A second person would then be hired to assume control over all the administrative affairs in operating a school. Many principals and subject supervisors often complain how much of their time is preoccupied with nonteaching responsibilities, leaving little, if any, time for the improvement of instruction. The primary reason for this rests with the inability of educators in the early twentieth century to clearly and definitely demarcate the boundaries of each function. Hence, a clear distinction between supervision and administration was never realized.[54]

Fourth, the supervisor's attempt to remove vestiges of authoritarian supervision and replace it with democratic supervision never came to fruition. Teachers and other educators continued to criticize supervisors and their antidemocratic methods. The ideals of democracy were difficult to fulfill in a system of school organization that relied on authoritarian and hierarchical governance. In surveying the situation in 1928, F. C. Ayer and A. S. Barr observed that the public school system maintained a rigid "line and staff type organization" flowing from the superintendent to the principal to school supervisors and then to teachers.[55] The issue of finding a balance between bureaucracy and democracy was an intractable problem for public school supervision. The challenge remains with us to this very day.

Finally, supervisors had a formidable task in seeking professionalism because of their vulnerable status in the school hierarchy. As middle-management personnel, supervisors were often torn between their administrative obligations to the principal and superintendent and, on the other hand, to teachers. The supervisor was made responsible for handling both administrative as well as curricular matters, for supervising and evaluating teachers, and for establishing school-community relations. The burden of these duties was so great that no time remained to offer assistance and guidance to teachers on a daily basis. Furthermore, the supervisor had to depend upon the superintendent and principal for authority to act, and at the same time, upon the teaching staff to cooperate regarding instructional and curricular matters. As a result, the primary role of a supervisor became that of a bureaucratic functionary, overseeing the day-to-day management of the school and acting as "foreman" of teachers.[56] Therefore, supervisors found it difficult to become professionals when the demands of the school bureaucracy were so overpowering.

With the supervisory "dream" shattered, supervisors redirected their energies in the late thirties and forties in another effort to attain professional recognition. An alliance with curriculum workers, they thought, would be advantageous and could elevate their status in the public schools. Professionalism assumed considerable importance in years to come.

4

The Alliance between Supervisors and Curriculum Workers: The Quest for Professionalism Revisited

Supervisors, toward the midthirties, began to sense the problem of being members at lower ends of the educational hierarchy. They realized that their recognition as a profession was hampered by their vulnerable position in the school organization. The supervisor had to rely on the cooperation of teachers, while at the same time remaining subservient to the pressures of school administrators. Supervisors sought to strengthen their position in schools through organizational means; an alliance with another group, they thought, would increase their political strength to attain professional recognition. This chapter begins by offering three possible explanations for the supervisors' inability to achieve control over their work. A discussion then follows exploring their revitalized efforts toward professional status.

The Supervisory Dream Shattered: Three Possible Explanations

Supervisors had difficulty achieving professional status for three reasons. The first centers on their interpretation of scientific method. The second concerns their historic commitment to bureaucracy. The third explanation focuses on the emergence of a new area of specialization, curriculum development.

Supervisors looked toward science as a way of legitimating their work in schools. Supervisors believed the use of scientific principles in their work with teachers would enable them to gain acceptance as professionals. Unfortunately, their scientific notions were highly speculative and visionary, and as such did not gain acceptance in the public schools. This was due in large measure to their lack of attention to, and understanding of, the ideas of a man whose views of science in education were profound. The work of John Dewey, particularly his work about the "science of education," did not gain enough notoriety among educators in general, and supervisors, in particular. Dewey believed that the future of civilization depended "upon the widening spread and deepening hold of the scientific habit of mind; and that the problem of problems in our education is therefore to discover how to mature and make effective this scientific habit." Dewey held that

> science must have something to say about what we do, and not merely about how we may do it most easily and economically. . . . When our schools truly become laboratories of knowledge-making, not mills fitted out with information-hoppers, there will no longer be need to discuss the place of science in education. . . . The problem of educational use of science is to create an intelligence pregnant with belief in the possibility of the direction of human affairs by itself. . . . The method of science engrained through education in habit means emancipation from rule of thumb.

Dewey asserted that science, to have any lasting effect in schools, must be grounded in the "lived experience" of the members of each school.

> Science is experience becoming rational. The effect of science is thus to change men's idea of the nature and inherent possibilities of experience. By the same token it changes the idea and the operation of reason. Instead of being something beyond experience, remote, aloof, concerned with a sublime region that has nothing to do with the experienced facts of life, it is found indigenous in experience: the factor by which past experiences are purified and rendered into tools for discovery and advance.

Dewey, in sum, believed that scientific theory was related to practice "as the agency of its expansion and its direction to new possibilities."[2]

Dewey's most scathing critique of existing scientific practices in the schools, as well as the most lucid exposition of his ideas on scientific inquiry, was set forth in his widely read, if not understood, book, *The Sources of a Science of Education*. In response to the question: "Is there a science of education? . . . Can there be a science of education?" Dewey replied that while scientific and systematic investigation sheds light on a range of facts by enabling "us to understand them better and to control them more intelligently, less haphazardly and with less routine," our current utilization of science in schools is inadequate and misdirected. Dewey denounced the current practice of science in education. There is "a strong tendency to identify teaching ability with use of procedures that yield immediately successful results, success being measured by such things as order in the classroom, correct recitations by pupils in assigned lessons, passing of examinations, promotion of pupils to a higher grade, etc." Supervisors, charged Dewey, "want recipes for classroom success." This view of "science is antagonistic to education as an art," declared Dewey. Dewey claimed the use of rating schemes was not an "enhancement of science in education" but a detraction from the true aims of science. "Such attempts, even when made unconsciously and with laudable intent to tender education more scientific, defeat their own purpose and create reactions against the very concept of educational science." Dewey concluded his little book with a recapitulation and final admonition. The only way, said Dewey, to create a science of education is to involve oneself in the "educational act itself." The intense interaction between practitioner and pupil will in and of itself yield "scientific formulations." "Education is by its nature an endless circle or spiral, . . . in its very process it sets more problems to be further studied, which then react into the educative process to change it still further, and thus demand more thought, more science, and so on, in everlasting sequence." Dewey warned that to ignore the value of "experimentation and discovery" will lead to a mistaken conception of the "true meaning of scientific inquiry." Science based on experimentation, said Dewey, is emancipatory and purposeful.[3]

Dewey's ideas of science as applied to educational practice did not receive much attention. Supervisors, in particular, did not adopt Dewey's model of scientific inquiry. Much of his writing, especially about the science of education, was technical and enigmatic in its presentation. As a result, confusion and misinterpretation of Dewey's views prevailed. Given the fact that there was much misunderstanding it was not surprising that supervisors did not adopt Dewey's ideas. In addition, supervisors eschewed his ideas about science because they were more interested in definite, ready-made prescriptions. Dewey's admonition to avoid definitive scientific formulations in favor of gradual experimentation of ideas in the classroom did not find favor among supervisors. Supervisors desperately wanted instant solutions to the problems they faced in schools. Rating schemes, for example, were appealing to supervisors because they could, it was thought, accurately assess the performance of teachers' work. In doing so, supervisors hoped to gain respect and stature. Unfortunately, their ideas backfired; rating provoked a reaction among teachers that supervisors were not expecting. This marked opposition prompted supervisors to reconsider their notions of science in education.

The second major reason for the supervisor's unsuccessful attempt to achieve professional status, although not recognized as such by supervisors at the time, rests on the inherent conflicts between middle- and low-level school personnel and bureaucracy. Supervisors encountered serious problems, as middle-management personnel, in their pursuit of professional autonomy. Supervisors did not, as middle-management personnel, achieve dominance over their work because of organizational constraints imposed by bureaucracy. Public school supervisors, unlike doctors, for example, did not achieve autonomy because they were required to carry out bureaucratically prescribed evaluative procedures. Doctors, on the other hand, who often work within a bureaucratic structure, have much greater authority to determine and shape bureaucratic regulations. They are not passive acceptors of bureaucratic governance. Supervisors never achieved professional dominance, but were in fact dominated by district superintendents, central board officers, and bureaucratic school policy in general. Compounding these pressures from the educational hierarchy, supervisors never received adequate recognition for their work. Teachers severely criticized supervisors as bureaucratic functionaries whose sole purpose was evaluation, not the improvement of teaching. Teachers did not perceive supervisors as partners in the educational enterprise but as intrusive bureaucrats whose interests were inimical to theirs. Hence, supervisors lacked both dominance over their work and recognition from those they supervised.

Supervisors, like other school personnel, must, by the nature of their work, labor in large organizations. Supervisors, however, fully accepted bureaucracy and worked within and used its hierarchical structure to further their own ends. Ironically, as middle-management personnel, bureaucracy worked, sometimes latently and at times in manifest ways, to counteract the attempts of supervisors to attain professionalism. Supervisors did not fully realize the consequences of working within a school bureaucracy until the late thirties and forties. At no time, however, did supervisors attempt to alter the bureaucratic phenomenon. To the contrary, they saw bureaucracy as a necessary ingredient in their pursuit of professional status. Supervisors, in sum, failed to realize that bureaucratic interests might be inimical to professional behavior in the schools.

A third reason why the supervisory dream of attaining professional status was shattered was due to certain important events occurring in curriculum development during the thirties and forties. These events would change the course of supervision over the next ten to fifteen years. There were two main groups of individuals who were responsible for instruction besides the classroom teacher; namely, the supervisor and the curriculum worker. The interests of both these groups remained, however, remarkably aloof. Problems concerning courses of study and curriculum seemed to have been thoroughly neglected by the supervisor. On the other side, administrative and supervisory aspects, which facilitate the implementation of curriculum theory, also received inadequate study by curriculum workers. In other words, curriculum specialists and supervisors usually went about their work in schools without considering the necessary interrelationships between the two.

Courses of study, selection of textbooks, and other matters related to the instructional aspects of schooling were controlled in the early part of the nineteenth century by laymen, school boards, and in the latter part of that century by the school superintendent. Curriculum development was minimal and episodic. The duty of the supervisor was to carry out the rigid and fixed courses of study determined by the superintendent. Curriculum was construed as that aspect of instruction controlled by the administrative members of the organization. In other words, both curriculum and supervision were under administrative control. This, of course, does not imply that schoolpeople were not concerned about curriculum. On the contrary, the evidence suggests that curricular matters were important concerns.[4] Systematic attention to curriculum became a national concern in the late nineteenth century. Curriculum thinking was influenced by men such as Francis Wayland Parker and William Torrey Harris as well as by Herbartian philosophy. Curriculum issues were given voice at various important national and local meetings. However, despite some attention to curriculum, it remains undeniable that schoolmen were chiefly interested in structural, administrative reform to achieve their goals of standardization and uniformity of urban education and that the superintendent took major responsibility for determining the course of study.

By the third decade of this century, however, it was quite evident that there was growing attention given to curriculum. This was evidenced in a number of ways: (1) the widely disseminated work of Thorndike, Strayer, and Terman in scientific methods of education; (2) Franklin Bobbitt's work in Los Angeles, as well as his important book, *The Curriculum;* (3) curriculum revisions in city systems, such as Denver and Detroit; (4) the formation of curriculum bureaus; and (5) the important role played by national committees and commissions, as well as by the growing state curriculum projects.[5] Clearly, the watchword of the day was *curriculum.* In place of Payne, Harris, McMurray, and Butler, were men such as Kilpatrick, Cocking, Charters, Harap, Dale, and Lindquist, who were now concerned with curriculum development in schools. The administrative structure of schooling was secure; emphasis was now placed on more instructional and curricular issues.

While interest in curriculum increased nationwide, there was no central clearinghouse or organization to meet the needs of curriculum workers. W. W. Charters stated in his significant book entitled *Curriculum Construction,* published in 1923, that there was an insufficient number of studies in various curriculum areas. Charters said, "But with no central magazine existing devoted to curriculum construction, or other central agency, it is impossible to be certain that all significant studies have been secured."[6] Charters felt that some sort of agency of curriculum was needed. Similarly, Henry Harap, a professor at the Cleveland School of Education, in a book published in 1928, entitled *The Technique of Curriculum Making,* stated at the very outset that "there is a great need for continued study in the field of curriculum making." Harap emphasized that "we have not yet entirely cleared the woods"; much remains to be done. Harap considered work in curriculum to be a "pioneer" venture. His own book was not a "theoretical treatise" but rather a "workbook." The chief aim of the volume was "to help students to make a new course of study, to revise a course of study, to evaluate a course of study and to interpret intelligently the extensive revision of curricula which is now in progress."[7] Harap, like Charters, inexorably tried to establish some sort of curriculum agency.

The publication of two volumes by the National Society for the Study of Education in 1926, proved to be a contributing factor to the increased interest in curriculum across the country. Harold Rugg and George Counts, in a discussion of the current methods of curriculum-making, stated that "a nation-wide movement is under way, . . . whatever the causes, the movement for curricu-

lum-revision is here." Still, Rugg and Counts were highly critical of the current methods of curriculum-making. They said, "partial, superficial, and timorous 'revision' rather than general, fundamental, and courageous reconstruction characterizes curriculum-making in the public school."[8] The authors criticized the methods used across the country as being of the "scissors and paste" type. Still, the tone and character of the yearbook was unequivocally devoted to the advocacy of a trained, competent, professional curriculum specialist.

A fundamental reason why supervisors during this period had a difficult time in securing professional status commensurate to that, for example, of the school superintendency is based on the fact that curriculum, not supervision, was the primary concern among educators. Supervision had its problems in the early twentieth-century. For example, supervisors, as was noted, had a difficult time finding legitimacy for their work in schools. At the same time, curriculum planning and development grew steadily and achieved wide popularity and, most important, was perceived as a useful function in reconstructing the courses of study. Special training in curriculum was viewed as a desirable and sought after skill. Importantly, curriculum specialists were not perceived, for the most part, by teachers as intrusive, but were viewed as integral partners in the educational process. Attention in educational circles, therefore, focused on curriculum development. Supervisors realized that in order to attain their goal of professionalism they had to accommodate to curriculum issues. Before long, curriculum theory was being advanced as the new supervision. The supervisor, now equipped with new knowledge of curriculum, would be recognized as a complete professional. It was not that supervisors felt threatened; rather, they saw an excellent opportunity to heighten their professional status by involving themselves in curriculum development.[9] Supervisors, at this time, had no alternative. The choice was rather simple: Get with it or quickly sink into oblivion.

Curriculum as the New Supervision

By the 1930s it was apparent to many that a unified effort on the part of supervisors and curriculum workers was necessary. Supervisors could no longer involve themselves in instructional matters without attention to, and knowledge about, curriculum. Curriculum workers also realized that an affiliation with supervision would be necessary to effectively carry out curriculum revisions in the schools. As a result, coordinated efforts between supervisors and curriculum experts were under way in different parts of the country. One of the early efforts at combining supervisory methods with curriculum revision was undertaken in the Detroit public schools. Stuart A. Courtis, an educational consultant for the Detroit school system, reported that the Detroit schools were unique in that supervisors were busily engaged in assisting curriculum specialists in various revisions of the courses of study. Courtis asserted that these efforts were "indicative of the prevalent trend at coordinating supervision and curriculum."[10]

Perhaps the most widely publicized attempt at coordinating activities of supervision and curriculum took place in Denver under the leadership of Jesse H. Newlon, a superintendent of schools, and A. L. Threlkeld, a deputy superintendent in charge of supervision. Newlon stressed that these coordinated efforts found acceptance in his school system because the schools were democratically administered. As such, efforts to combine the talents of supervisors and curriculum workers were welcomed. A conducive environment was present, said, Newlon, that encouraged "curriculum experimentation, continuous curriculum revision, and teacher participation." Newlon and Threlkeld believed that supervision had a vital role to play in curriculum implementation.[11] Newlon believed that these coordinated efforts would prove to be especially beneficial for supervisors. According to Newlon, curriculum involvement by supervisors gave them opportunities to work with teachers in a "joint, cooperative effort." This, Newlon felt, would enhance the perception of supervision among teachers. Writing in 1923, in an article entitled "Reorganizing City School Supervision," Newlon asked: "How can the ends of supervision best be achieved?" He maintained that the school organization must be set up to "invite the participation of the teacher in the development of courses." The ends of supervision can be realized when teacher and supervisor work in a coordinated fashion. Newlon developed the idea of setting up "supervisory councils" to offer "genuine assistance" to teachers. In this way, he continued, "The teacher will be regarded as a fellow-worker rather than a mere cog in a big machine."[12]

The idea that curriculum development is an important part of the work of a supervisor quickly spread across the country. Many school systems encouraged supervisors to engage in curriculum work. An increasing number of educators also realized that the image of the supervisor would dramatically improve by working cooperatively with teachers and with other school personnel. Threlkeld contended that autocratic supervision is no longer viable, nor desirable in a school system. Today's schools, said Threlkeld, "are committed to a democratic philosophy in its curriculum construction." Supervisors, said Threlkeld, likewise committed to democratic ideals. He explained: "Curriculum revision emphasizes the idea of constant change and improvement rather than the idea of maintaining the status quo. This constant search for a better way tends to cause supervision to depart from methods that are primarily inspectional. Curriculum construction promotes the spirit of research; . . . a research attitude is developed which should be welcomed by any constructive supervisor."[13]

A review of the literature of the period suggests a clear change in conception of public school supervision. Not only were supervisors calling for more democracy, but much emphasis was placed on greater cooperation with teachers and curriculum workers in an effort to improve curriculum-making throughout the schools. An editorial appearing in *The Journal of Educational Method* in April 1929 stated that "the supervisor should be, first of all, a curriculum expert. . . . The supervisor should be able to take the lead in some part of the educational work of the system."[14] In an address delivered before the Northern California Conference of Supervisors and Directors of Instruction in 1933, A. H. Horall, an assistant superintendent of schools in San Jose, discussed in great detail the various duties of the supervisor in curriculum revision. These duties were noted as follows:

1. Choosing the course to be revised.
2. Determining who shall do the revising.
3. Helping to revise the course.
4. Following up the tentative course.
5. Revising the tentative course after an adequate trial.
6. Submitting the final revised draft to the superintendent.
7. Directing the printing of the new course in loose-leaf form.
8. Assisting the teacher in properly using the printed course.

Horall explained that the supervisor need not feel inadequate "in the particular subject to be revised because his expertise is more concerned with supervising the program to ensure its completion. The supervisor should act to organize committees, provide stimulus, chair committees, and see that the course of study is completed satisfactorily."[15]

A prominent professor of education, Gordon N. Mackenzie, analyzed this changing conception in supervision. He argued that although "much supervision retains the autocratic characteristics reminiscent of an earlier period," supervision appears to be taking a whole new direction. MacKenzie explained this new direction in terms of an alliance with the "modern curriculum" in which supervisors seek to promote its "development and improvement." This amalgamation of supervision and curriculum was seen by MacKenzie as an important step in the professional development of supervision. When supervisors participate in democratic relationships in schools, maintained MacKenzie, "supervision is bound to realize its full potential. . . . Supervisory leadership should be democratic in a society which has a school curriculum aimed to attain democratic ideals." MacKenzie asserted that "democratic leadership does not proceed on the basis of authority. It suggests, guides, and gives opportunity for experimental learning. It is cooperative and it encourages individual initiative." MacKenzie concluded his article by saying that

> the fact that the new curriculum presents a challenge to supervision is clear. . . . Supervision must meet this challenge. . . . Supervision faces a two-fold task, one, to provide leadership in adapting the curriculum to the needs of this society, and two, to adjust and adapt its own philosophy and methods so that they will harmonize with this developing curriculum and improve its vitality and functioning quality.[16]

Two of the most prominent educators of the time concurred that the conception of supervision was radically altered. Helen Heffernan of the California State Department of Education, and William H. Burton of the University of Southern California, who were both very active in the Department of Supervisors and Directors of Instruction, clearly stated that "the supervisor is increasingly the person responsible for the development of curriculum materials and experience. In fact the heart of modern supervision is in the curriculum program."[17] Henry Harap, one of the foremost scholars in curriculum development stated that "it is being recognized that the study of the curriculum offers an opportunity to combine disjointed professional activities and courses around the learning activities of children." He continued, "Administrative and supervisory agencies are realizing that the study of the curriculum, more than any other phase of education, emphasizes learning as opposd to instruction; and cooperative professional growth as opposed to critical supervision."[18] Writing two years later, Dorothy Heubauer, a curriculum director in Illinois, stated that "we cannot define supervision nor indicate its function apart from our educational philosophy and our conception of the curriculum."[19]

More and more schoolpeople were realizing the significant interrelationships between curriculum and supervision. Hollis L. Caswell of Teachers College, Columbia University, said that "the public school curriculum has developed under the influence of specialization." Improvements in curriculum will occur, said Caswell, only when there is a mutual support on the part of both supervisors and curriculum workers.[20] Three years later Caswell expanded on this theme by stating that

> a good educational program cannot be developed when curriculum work and supervision are considered as separate. Supervision is a means of developing the curriculum and should take its setting in a total curriculum program.... Curriculum development must involve supervision if changes actually are to be accomplished. It is necessary, therefore, if good supervision is to be provided, that the activities of supervisors be related to fundamental educational issues and problems such as are involved in a curriculum program.... Such a relationship gives added significance to supervisory activities and makes curriculum programs actually effective in modifying instruction.[21]

Curriculum development, thus, became an essential activity of the public school supervisor. As a result of a number of successful coordinated efforts between supervisors and curriculum workers all across the nation, supervisors and curriculum workers began to urge for greater organizational unity between the two groups. Supervisors understood that association with the curriculum specialist could possibly upgrade their image and remove the stigma related to their authoritarian legacy. Supervisors viewed an alliance with the curriculum worker as an important and necessary step closer to professionalism. The curriculum worker also viewed involvement with supervision as crucial to their enhanced status in the school system. As middle-management personnel, curriculum workers experienced similar problems such as lack of authority and acceptance among teachers, although not to the same degree as did supervisors. Curriculum developers also realized that successful implementation of curriculum revision was dependent on being attentive to administrative and supervisory matters. They therefore welcomed an alliance with supervisors. Hence, the quest for professionalism was revitalized by the end of the third decade of the twentieth century.

The Society for Curriculum Study and the Joint Committee

In 1929, a group of college professors, under the leadership of Henry Harap, then of Western Reserve University, banded together to form the National Society of Curriculum Workers. Three years later, after a merger with a public school curriculum group, chaired by Walter Cocking, then a professor of education at George Peabody College, the new association was called the Society for Curriculum Study. The final agreement was stated as follows:

1. The new executive committee shall consist of the combined executive committees of the public school group and the college group.
2. That the combined executive committee be progressively reduced to seven by decreasing the number of replacements by half each year.
3. That the officers of the current year shall be Henry Harap, Chairman, Prudence Cutright, Vice-Chairman.
4. That the chairman continue the duties that he performed in the past and that he keep the vice-chairman informed of all important action taken.
5. That the present programs and activities of the two groups be immediately consolidated.
6. That the name of the society shall be THE SOCIETY FOR CURRICULUM STUDY.[22]

"The purpose of the Society," according to a *News Bulletin* published in 1935, "is to enable those interested in curriculum making to be of mutual help to each other, and to advance the movement of thorough and progressive curriculum revision." The society was made up of the following types of people: "curriculum directors, administrative officers in charge of curriculum making, supervisory officers in charge of curriculum making, special or general consultants in curriculum revision, authors or investigators in curriculum making, and instructors in curriculum making."²³ It was not until a year later that the society included teachers in their organization, which was composed of a rather small and selected membership. The dues per year, by the way, were one dollar. At the time that the *Curriculum Journal* began publication in 1935, the society's membership was 682. The highest membership the society reached was 807 in 1939. The leaders of the society were described by Saylor as "liberal in point of view on educational matters and probably to a considerable extent in political, economic, and social issues. . . . They were dynamic persons, many of whom were actively engaged in curriculum planning."²⁴

Unlike the Department of Supervisors and Directors of Instruction, the Society for Curriculum Study did not publish yearbooks. They did publish mimeographed news bulletins from 1931 to 1935. The bulletin consisted of brief descriptions of the curricular activities of people like Cocking, Dale, Harap, and Courtis. The bulletin functioned to coordinate the curricular interests of a wide variety of people by reporting on conferences, outstanding courses of study, curriculum projects. "I have just received the *News Bulletin* and once again let me say how important I think this publication is," stated Paul Hanna. "There must be a tremendous lot of curriculum work going on in the country and it ought to be reported in our *News Bulletin*."²⁵ They also published a number of books on curriculum issues, the first appearing in 1935, entitled *The Workbook*. This was followed by *A Challenge to Secondary Education*, 1935; *Integration: Its Meaning and Application*, 1937; *The Changing Curriculum*, 1937; *Family Living in Our Schools*, 1941; *Consumer Education*, 1942; and *An Evaluation of Modern Education*, 1942.²⁶

The Department of Supervisors and Directors of Instruction and the Society for Curriculum Study operated as two separate organizations with very little interaction. Educators for a long time considered curriculum and supervision as two unrelated and distinct functions. Each would engage in their own activities without considering the significant interrelationships involved in the planning of curriculum and the supervision of instruction. Yet, by the midthirties these apparently disjointed and unrelated groups formed an alliance based on a common effort "to establish a strong, viable, dynamic organization."²⁷ A committee was formed, for the first time, in 1936 to discuss many common issues that affected both supervisors and curriculum workers. There are number of reasons why the two organizations decided to undertake this joint effort. First, there was an awareness that a unified and powerful organization was needed to serve the best interests of curriculum making in the nation's schools. As separate groups, they realized their political clout would be minimal. A coalition would command more prestige and recognition. Second, both organizations had overlapping memberships, especially toward the end of the thirties. For example, Rudolph Lindquist of California was both president of the Department of Supervisors and Directors of Instruction and also an active member in the Society for Curriculum Study. Hollis Caswell was also chairman of the executive committee of the Society for Curriculum Study in 1936–37, and earlier served as the first vice president of the supervisory group as well as a member of the Board of Directors from 1935 to the merger. A third reason for the collaborative effort between the two associations was that these people really believed that in order to successfully carry out the instructional aspects of schooling a unified effort between supervisors and curriculum workers was needed. It became evident that to talk about curricular change without considering matters involving school governance, administrative programming, and other institutional variables that supervision attended to would be senseless and educationally unsound. Fourth, both groups had rather obvious limitations. One group had a small and limited membership, although at first the society wanted a select membership. The supervisory group had a considerable membership, but was unable to realize its professional objectives.

Specifically, the joint effort was begun early in 1936. Paul Rankin, of the Department the Supervisors and Directors of Instruction, and C. L. Cushman, of the Society for Curriculum Study, met in February of that year to discuss plans to work on a joint yearbook to summarize and update work done in curriculum construction. Final arrangements were made and a group of ten people formed the Joint Committee. Of the members, two were assistant superintendents, six were professors of education, one was a supervisory director of curriculum research, and one member was a dean. The chairman, Henry Harap, stated that "all the conferences were held in an atmosphere of comfort, friendliness, and geniality, but pleasantness did not dull the edge of criticism."[28] A reading of the volume that resulted in this joint effort indicates that in fact there was little disagreement about the methods of curriculum development.

The book was divided into two parts: the first presented a

theoretical base for the curriculum and the second an appraisal of current curriculum projects across the country. "In a very real sense the committee wishes this volume to be regarded as a report of progress," said Harap. As a whole, the volume demonstrated the "current social orientation toward curriculum." The committee felt that the central problem in education was the "achievement of a good society." School life, it was postulated, should be "social-centered rather than child-centered."[29] Some of the other themes were that (1) the teacher must participate in a cooperative manner with other school people to work on curriculum construction, (2) evaluation was an important aspect of curriculum building, (3) the learner should play an active role in the instructional process, and (4) curriculum was a paramount issue in education.

In a review of the book, J. Paul Leonard of Stanford University, in December 1937, stated that "certain chapters are far superior to others, not only in their style of writing but also in the clearness with which they present their thinking." He continued, "There is a need for more definitive language in the treatment of modern curriculum theories and practice." Leonard continued further: "One also feels that the yearbook missed an opportunity to be more critical in its evaluation of present theories and practices. The volume appears to be more of an explanation and a defense rather than an appreciative but critical study of the present curriculum movement." Despite these criticisms, Leonard stated that *The Changing Curriculum* was a significant contribution to curriculum thought.[30]

Following this joint effort, a merger seemed inevitable. Despite voiced opposition to a merger there is every indication that this criticism was limited and quickly overlooked. Helen Heffernan of the California State Department of Education and a very active member of the Department of Supervisors and Directors of Instruction, voiced her opposition by stating that the supervisory organization was the stronger of the two, due to a more substantial membership, and merger would not aid their efforts toward professionalism. In addition, Heffernan stated that "curriculum development and supervision seemed to be related but not identical functions. Both required a distinctive type of expertness. . . . I have never been enthusiastic about the 'big umbrella.' "[31] Of equal interest, Dr. Alice Miel, Professor Emeritus at Teachers College, Columbia University, a prolific writer of both supervisory and curricular matters, and later a president of the newly formed organization Association for Supervision and Curriculum Development (ASCD), in a interview in 1976, maintained that an important reason for the conflict about merger centered on male-female relationships. The supervisory group, comprised of many special supervisors, feared that merger with the curriculum group, mostly male, would eventuate in a male-dominated organization.[32] Regardless of these criticisms, merger was inevitable. For the most part, most supervisors and curriculum workers welcomed the merger. Many realized that the goal of professionalism which both groups hoped for could now be attained as a result of the merger. In May 1943, an editorial in the *Curriculum Journal* stated: "The editor feels somewhat like the parent who is about to give away a favorite child in marriage. He approves his going, but parts with him reluctantly.[33] Thus, the merger took place. The new organization was called the Department of Supervision and Curriculum Development. Three years later, the name was changed to the Association for Supervision and Curriculum Development.

The End of an Era

It was during this period that supervision, faced with a deluge of demands and a dearth of creative solutions, realized, to some extent, the problem or dilemma of seeking professional status within a demanding, imposing bureaucratic organization. The supervisor's rather inauspicious birth during the early twentieth century marked the beginning of what proved to be a tide of circumstances that led supervisors to become aware of their vulnerable status and position in the school organization. Supervisors pursued a professional orientation while at the same time accepting the bureaucratic framework, with the belief that once they attained the status of a profession these problems would be resolved. The supervisor, however, met several obstacles in his drive for professionalism. The doctrines of science, democracy, and cooperative leadership were unable, by themselves, to elevate supervision to its ambitious goal of professional autonomy. Confronted with the possibility of obscurity and an indeterminate future, supervision renewed its striving for professional status through an alliance with the curriculum worker. These two groups of people realized that by themselves they would be unable to affect change or wield power to strengthen and buttress their efforts to be recognized as professional people. A merger, they thought, would enable them to establish a strong professional organization in order to effectuate the changes they desired.

Public school supervision passed through three major periods in the United States. First, the late nineteenth century was characterized as a period in which bureaucracy flourished. Second, the period between approximately 1900 and 1920 was depicted as a time during which the supervisor realized his bureaucratic legacy and decided to make a conscious effort to counteract bureaucratization. Third, the post-1920 period was a time during which supervisors sought to professionalize. Thus, bureaucracy and professionalism were important processes affecting the nature, conception, and direction of public school supervision.

The drive to improve instruction and to help teachers, while at the same time maintaining bureaucratic role relationships in schools, were antagonistic objectives. This strain between bureaucracy and professionalism was a serious problem for the public school supervisor. Supervisors grew cognizant of the fact that their organizational membership restricted certain professional needs. The supervisor's remedy for this condition was to strengthen his position in the bureaucracy by attempting to manipulate rather than transform the structural aspects of the organization. In other words, professionalism was conceived by supervisors as a means to gain legitimacy within the bureaucracy. Supervisors never wished to alter fundamental bureaucratic role relationships in schools. Therefore, supervisors sought bureaucratic means to counteract bureaucratic tendencies—a dubious panacea.

Within the context of this analysis, it appears that the "why" is as intriguing as the "what." Why did supervisors adopt these bureaucratic means? Why did supervisors seek professional status within a bureaucracy which, by its very nature, was programmed to neutralize the autonomy, individuality, and professional behavior of its participants? Indeed, why the persistence of bureaucracy, which permeates almost every aspect of schooling? While these crucial questions are addressed, to some extent, in an interpretive way, the thrust of this study has been to examine the professionalization of supervision and how it was shaped by bureaucratic organization. We have found that the events and practices in this early history of supervision were influenced by the degree to which they served the goals of professionalism. The professionalization of supervision was not driven by a desire to improve education and improve the plight of teachers. Rather, a desire to serve professional interests was more the point. I see no reason, in this study, to defend or attack supervisors for what they did. My intention, as historian, has been to explain the rise and evolution of an occupational group and its efforts to professionalize.

Epilogue
Bureaucracy and Professionalism Revisited

I have described the bureaucratic-professional dilemma that has troubled public school supervision in the United States from the late nineteenth century through the thirties of the twentieth century.[1] In certain ways, William H. Payne, William H. Maxwell, and William T. Harris would have applauded the persistence of bureaucratically controlled schools. On the other hand, these nineteenth-century supervisors would be surprised that standardization of urban education has come to mean extreme subordination of the individual, usurpation of power by certain people with vested interests, red tape, waste, and inefficiency. These reformers would be aghast that the very conditions they sought to abolish in the late nineteenth century have continued to the present. Hence, we see one of the fundamental paradoxes of bureaucracy. On the one hand, bureaucracy is considered the quintessence of rationality and efficiency. On the other hand, bureaucracy, with its demand for uniformity, is incongruent with individual initiative and responsibility. However, reformers in the late nineteenth century like Harris, progressives like Dewey in the early twentieth century, and supervisors through the forties believed that it was possible to attain professionalism within a bureaucratic organization. This belief was epitomized when the supervisory and curriculum groups met to work on a yearbook in 1937. Supervisors believed that through a merger with the curriculum group, professional status was within reach.

Was it possible for supervisors to become professionals within a bureaucratically controlled organization? Alice Miel, Professor Emeritus of Education at Teachers College, Columbia University, felt that some supervisors were able to maintain professionalism and to work with teachers in a democratic environment.[2] That is, in some instances professionalism did succeed. Supervision, in certain school settings, became a constructive and cooperative function. The term *supervisor* was, in these situations, not invoked and supervisors became partners with teachers in the effort to promote learning. Professional diaries of teachers, supervisors, and principals, indicate that cooperation, thoughtfulness, good judgment, and a democratic philosophical outlook were repeatedly cited as characteristics of professional supervisors.[3] These isolated instances indicate that different degrees of bureaucratization and professionalism existed within the school system.[4] Indeed, more studies exploring the circumstances that allowed for a greater degree of professional autonomy are needed. However, on the basis of examining supervision from a broad perspective, it is clear that most supervisors were unable, for a variety of reasons, to circumvent the demands of the bureaucratic organization. Supervisors, by and large, were not perceived as helpful partners, but as imposing bureaucrats. Examination of the same professional diaries just noted, indicates a persistent and perplexing dilemma for the supervisor; that is, the search for a balance between authority and freedom. Apparently, many supervisors were unable to discover a workable balance between the two. Many supervisors were characterized by teachers as "authoritarian, dictatorial, and unprofessional."[5]

As a result of this historical investigation of public school supervision, it is clear that supervisors were not able to achieve a high degree of professionalism within the school bureaucracy. It is important to note, that even if professionalism did fully materialize for supervisors, the problem of being professionals at low levels of the bureaucracy was never recognized nor rectified. Decker Walker recognized this problem when he discussed the problem of curriculum workers and supervisors in schools. He stated:

> The primary professional was placed within the regular school district administrative hierarchy—above the teachers and below the superintendent—and was made responsible for organizing committees to handle curriculum revision for all the schools in the district and for all subjects, for supervising the operations of these committees, and for disseminating the results through the staff. The burden of these duties was so great that no time remained for research or scholarship, . . . the curriculum worker had to depend upon the superintendent for authority to act, and upon the teaching staff to conduct the bulk of the curriculum development without power. . . . As a result, the primary professional role became that of a bureaucratic functionary, overseeing periodic revisions of courses of study. . . . At best the local curriculum specialist was a gate-keeper operating within the bureaucracy.

Walker concluded his discussion of the professional curriculum specialist working within the confines of a bureaucracy by stating that they were "condemned to inefficiency by the location of their influence, in the limbo of middle management."[6] It seems clear that supervisors experienced similar problems.

The query: Were supervisors able to become professionals within a bureaucratically controlled organization, is fundamental. The problem was concisely posed by Stephen T. Kerr. "How should specialized professional services be provided in an educational system that is bureaucratically organized, but that also takes as fundamental the principle of client involvement."[7] Examination of the post-1937 period indicates the persistence of this bureaucratic-professional dilemma for public school supervision. Supervisors, since 1937, have been faced with a plethora of problems created by a compelling bureaucracy. In a sense, the problems encountered by supervisors before 1937, not only persisted but, in many instances, grew worse. One is reminded of something William Faulkner once said. "The past is never dead; it is not even past." As a theoretical and normative concept, supervision remains inconsistent with the ideals and objectives of participatory democracy. Supervision necessarily implies, among other things, evaluation from the top, hierarchical relationships, autocratic practices, and conformity to the welter of bureaucratic regulations. Seen in this light, supervision appears most compatible with the values and assumptions upon which bureaucracy is based. Supervisors want to help teachers and improve instruction in schools. However, they are ideologically committed to a mode of practice that is fundamentally grounded in bureaucratic governance. In essence, while several factors were brought into play after 1937, the bureaucratic-professional tension has remained a vital concern for supervisors, teachers, administrators, curriculum workers, children, and parents in our schools to this very day.

SUPERVISION AND CURRICULUM DEVELOPMENT: THE NEW RHETORIC

The same type of problems confronting supervisors in the early period have continued to frustrate efforts at professionalization since 1937. One of the main reasons why supervisors experienced difficulty at professionalization can be traced to the merger between the Department of Supervisors and Directors of Instruction and the Society for Curriculum Study to form the Department of Supervision and Curriculum Development. Between October 1942 and March 1943, members of both the curriculum and supervisory organizations formed committees to complete arrangements for merger.[8] Ruth Cunningham, later to be named executive secretary of the new department, announced in April 1943 that the merger was complete.[9] In May 1943, both journals, the *Curriculum Journal* and *Educational Method,* in their last issues published the "Program of the Department of Supervision and Curriculum Development." The authors of this statement contended that "in the life of every organization there come times when its members should pause and state their beliefs."[10] The authors reaffirmed their commitment to democratic ideals, patriotism, schooling in America, training of teachers, and improvement of student learning. Unquestionably, the formation of the new department excited supervisors and curriculum workers. H. Ruth Henderson, a supervisor in Richmond, Virginia, and the president of the new department, exclaimed that "dynamic leadership is essential. . . . Let us go ahead with vigor and courage to meet the challenge of providing experiences for children, youth, and adults appropriate for the demands of our time."[11] The organization changed its name officially on February 1, 1946, to the Association for Supervision and Curriculum Development. Interestingly, as part of the NEA, this new organization preferred to be called an "association" rather than a "department." Galen Saylor explained that "the change in name would more clearly state the nature and status of the organization."[12]

More important than these organizational matters involved in the forming of the new association was a profound shift in emphasis in the conception of supervision. Supervision, after 1937, was no longer considered a function to be performed by only one individual in a school system. The proliferation of titles for supervisors became evident. For example, special supervisors, consultants, principals, department chairmen, coordinators, deans, directors, and many others performed supervisory functions. The January 1945 issue of *Educational Leadership* carried an article entitled "Who Is Supervisor?" in which the author contended that "everyone who is helping teachers do a better and more satisfying job" is called a supervisor.[13] The emphasis was not on supervisor, but on the functions of supervision. G. Franklin Stover, acting as a consultant-supervisor in the Pennsylvania Department of Public Instruction, described his position in the school system. "They call me a consultant, a resource person available at the request of the teacher, . . . a supervisor, etc."[14] Mildred E. Swearingen, a specialist in elementary education in Florida, explained that "supervision is varied in nature, calling for the work of persons serving in different capacities. Not all supervision is carried on by people whose titles include such a word as supervisor, director, or consultant."[15] Gordon N. Mackenzie also explained that the word "'supervisor' is used here as a generic term to include all whose unique or primary concern is instructional leadership. . . . Supervisors may be called helping teachers, curriculum consultants, curriculum directors or assistant superintendents in charge of instruction. The word 'role' is used to indicate what the holder of a position does."[16]

Herein lies one of the important problems supervisors faced after 1937. The emphasis shifted to the activities that are essential in the performance of supervision, rather than focusing on the person carrying out the function. The theory behind this idea was that this would attract much less negative reaction. A major problem with this change in conception of supervision is that much confusion resulted in the notion that anyone can perform supervision. Supervision was suffering, so to speak, from an identity crisis. Under the circumstances, it is highly unlikely that supervisors would ever achieve the dominance and recognition they sorely craved. J. Harlan Shores, the president of the ASCD, explained the problem, in 1967, as follows: "Everybody knows what a teacher's and superintendent's roles and duties are—not so with supervision and curriculum work."[17] Indicative of the confusion is the fact that among writers of supervision there was no agreement on who the supervisor was and what he did. Supervision during this time not only severely lacked a theoretical basis, but was lacking in definition. "Teachers have become confused about the meaning of supervision, because they encounter many methods in the supervisors they know."[18]

Although lacking theoretical clarity, supervision did find some degree of focus principally through its involvement in curriculum revision, which was widespread throughout the nation. Supervisors joined with curriculum people in a cooperative venture to make and revise curriculum. This connection to, and involvement with, curriculum development gained favor. During this time, supervisors were urging for greater cooperative and democratic methods. Supervisors, more so than any time in the past, advocated democratic supervision in much stronger language and in more definite ways. "The supervision of curriculum development, . . . is fundamentally a democratic service rather than an administrative function."[19] Glenys G. Unruh, the president of the ASCD in 1975, stated that "supervision at its best is an art that can release teachers initiative, responsibility, creativity, internal commitment and motivation."[20] It is undeniable that a great many supervisors and curriculum workers advocated supervision as a function that is "cooperative, democratic, and helpful."[21] Supervisors once again thought that waving the banner of democracy would advance their professional objectives. Democracy and unified efforts between supervisors and curriculum workers were the latest rhetorical tools by which supervisors would achieve legitmacy as a profession.

An influential pamphlet that called for the dismissal of traditional supervision to democratic supervision was prepared by the Commission on Teacher Evaluation of the ASCD. Published in 1950 it was entitled, *Better than Rating: New Approaches to Appraisal of Teaching Services,* which unequivocally stated that the improvement of instruction cannot be fostered through rating. The commission of five members appointed by the Executive Committee in March 1948 stated that "this bulletin opposes administrative or supervisory rating of teachers as undemocratic, as actually harmful in many instances, and as generally unproductive of wholesome change, growth and development on the part of individuals who may be affected by such practices."[22] Interestingly, even Alvin S. Barr, a staunch advocate of rating, stated that "teacher rating, albeit still an issue, is no longer viable." Barr realized that strong democratic leadership must replace the traditional view of "supervisor as rater."[23] Even though supervision was being advocated as a democratic and leadership function, vestiges of traditional supervisory practices remained. One such vestige was classroom visitation. H. R. Douglass, R. K. Bent, and C. W. Boardman, in a popular college text published in 1961, stated that "classroom visitation is a procedure by which the educational leader who possesses wisdom and vision can be of great assistance in aiding the teacher to improve both his instructional techniques and the learning of the students."[24] Classroom visitation was considered by these and other writers as a democratic activity unlike an inspectoral function of the past. The difference between visitation and inspection was never fully made clear.

Compounding these problems, the merger between supervisors and curriculum workers in 1943 had another serious consequence for school supervision. Simply stated, supervision became indistinguishable from curriculum development. It became difficult, if not impossible, to talk about supervision without attending to curriculum development. As one noted author put it, "Supervision *is* Curriculum Development."[25] The inattention to supervision as a field to be studied in its own right is undeniable. Arthur J. Lewis and Alice Miel, in a book published in 1972 titled *Supervision for Improved Instructions: New Challenges, New Responses,* lamented the lack of attention to supervision and expressed the view that "hindsight suggests that the profession went too far in its efforts to turn supervision into a helping function, a teaching function, a curricular function—anything, . . . but the function it literally names, overseeing with a view to improving the quality of an operation."[26] An examination of supervision as a field of study and practice since 1937 reveals the lack of attention paid to school supervision apart from curriculum development.[27] In the February 1976 issue of *Educational Leadership,* Robert J. Krajewski, a professor of education at Texas Tech University, urged that if supervisory leadership was to be restored, then greater emphasis must be placed on supervision as a field of study. The author of this article, entitled "Putting the 'S' Back in ASCD," observed that "curriculum has taken priority over supervision consistently." The tone of the article was doleful, to say the least. The article indicated dissatisfaction with ASCD as a professional organization supposedly formed to meet the needs of both curriculum specialists and supervisors. Indeed, in October 1947, when the organization changed its name from a department to an association, the object of the association was clearly stated. "The object of the Association shall be the general improvement of instruction and supervision." The object of the association, according to Krajewski, was not carried out. "There is no time to falter now," insisted Krajewski. "Present indicators look promising for putting the 'S' back into ASCD."[28] Once again, under these circumstances, it is little wonder why supervisors had difficulty achieving dominance and professional recognition for their work.

This complaint about inattention to supervision at the expense of curriculum development is curious considering the views of many who advocated the importance of equal attention to both curriculum and supervision. "Supervision and curriculum development have always been central concerns of the Association for Supervision and Curriculum Development."[29] Galen Saylor, the president of the ASCD in 1966, stated that "*the* national professional organization for supervisors" is ASCD.[30] Similarly, J. Harlan Shores, the president of the ASCD in 1967, stated that "the Board of Directors and Executive Committee are quite conscious of the 'S' in ASCD. There are times when it seems that supervision is neglected with the increased attention being given to curriculum development. . . . Supervision and curriculum development are as intimately related as we thought they should be."[31] However, supervisors and curriculum workers never fully defined their own parameters and areas of specialization; confusion was inevitable. Supervisors were unclear as to their responsibilities in schools and as a result were perceived as anything but professional.

The amalgamation of supervision and curriculum, as a result of the merger, presented a host of problems for supervisors. Supervisors, after 1937, sought to define and clarify their role in the schools and to achieve greater professional recognition. Supervision, however, was unable to break away from its history as an autocratic function. With little or no conceptual foundation, deficiency of theoretical constructs, and lack of definition and direction, the supervisor's quest for professional recognition remained illusory.

THE SUPERVISOR: BUREAUCRAT OR PROFESSIONAL?

The persistence of bureaucratic modes of operations has been perplexing yet characteristic of America's public schools. The bureaucratization of schooling grew in response to the unique and arduous demands placed on it. Depersonalization in the schools was a major consequence of the systematization of the educational system, but that seemed not to disturb many reformers who supported bureaucracy. After all, their goal of establishing an organizational structure had been accomplished. The newly developed system applied collective decision-making, employed supervision, inspection, punishments and rewards to encourage uniformity, enforced an administrative hierarchy for teachers, and a curriculum hierarchy for students. Still, bureaucracy has met with much criticism.

William Van Til, a professor of education at New York University, stated in 1965, that "bureaucracy has made its influence felt in education, too; the probability is that still stronger influence is in the offing. . . . Bureaucracy is reflected in the lives of both faculty members and students in large schools and in the daily experiences of staff members in large educational organizations."[32] Recently, David S. Seeley, a professor of education and program director of educational supervision and administration at the

College of Staten Island, charged that "the present educational bureaucracy is antilearning; it must be turned upside down."³³ Bureaucracy, it has been argued, is ill-suited to the interests and well-being of children, teachers, and supervisors. James B. Macdonald, in an article entitled "Helping Teachers Change," stated that "most teachers are in fact caught up in the 'organization,' the educational bureaucracy. . . . It is little wonder that few of our teachers can overcome the burden of the 'system' and become self-educating."³⁴ Thomas A. Shaheen, an educational consultant in San Francisco, wrote that "I have seen very competent, well-intentioned staff members and many of my colleagues trapped and overwhelmed by the bureaucracy. I have seen the stifling impact of bureaucracy on curriculum and instruction." Shaheen held that "the bureaucracy was a system well suited to yesteryear's industrial society." Shaheen concluded by declaring that if the school was to survive as a democratic institution then "the bureaucracy must not only be 'damned,' it must go!"³⁵ Michael B. Katz stated quite emphatically in *Class, Bureaucracy, and Schools: The Illusion of Educational Change in America,* that "one of the greatest weaknesses of education has been its bureaucratic form of organization."³⁶ Max G. Abbott concurred that "we must be willing to admit that we do not necessarily live in the best of all possible organizational worlds."³⁷ Similarly, Warren G. Bennis stated that "bureaucracy was a monumental discovery for harnessing the muscle power of the industrial revolution. In today's world, it is a lifeless crutch that is no longer useful."³⁸ Recently the point was clearly made by John E. Chubb, in a *New York Times* article, entitled "To Revive Schools, Dump Bureaucracies." "If New York and other cities are to save their staggering public schools, they must first kill off their central educational bureaucracies." Chubb makes the point that research on effective schools indicate "that better schools are much less likely to have organizational structures imposed on them by external authorities." Teachers, continues Chubb, are more likely to perform better if "given the freedom to organize themselves without the imposition of bureaucratic regulations." Private schooling, explains Chubb, provide "an important lesson for the improvement of public schools." Private schools succeed because they are decentralized, competitive, and seek to meet the satisfaction of parents. "If private schools were to tie the hands of teachers and principals, and vest vital decision-making power in a central bureaucracy beyond the reach of parents, they would quickly find themselves out of business, as frustrated parents, exercising their freedom of choice, took their business elsewhere." Public schools, concludes Chubb, must be given greater autonomy "to reorganize . . . along lines that rely less on the top-down controls of bureaucracy."[39]

Bureaucracy in school supervision received no less criticism. Arthur J. Lewis and Alice Miel, in *Supervision for Improved Instruction,* expressed the view that supervision must be carried out with respect for individual and group concerns and that "the bureaucratic organization is not compatible with this style of leadership nor is it conducive to a school's ability to adapt." Lewis and Miel continued to offer an alternative to bureaucratic organization. They advocated a synergetic organization in which "the centralized decision-making characteristic of a bureaucratic organization is replaced by shared control and responsibility based on mutual confidence and trust stemming from common commitment to organizational goals." The authors contended that "a change from bureaucratic organization in the schools will be evolutionary rather than revolutionary.[40] The urging for alternatives to bureaucratic organization received some voice. William H. Whyte, writing in *Educational Leadership* in October 1956, exclaimed that "organizations have been made by men; they can be changed by men and with intelligence we may be able to make them as compatible with individual expression as institutions in the past."[41] Few practical proposals were developed to replace bureaucracy. Throughout the twentieth century, bureaucratic school organization enjoyed unprecedented vitality. Supervision, as a function, simply reflected this bureaucratic tendency.

Supervisors accepted bureaucracy as the dominant form of school organization not only because it was perceived as the most effective and stable form of management, but it served, they thought, their professional self-interests. The hierarchical structure of bureaucracy afforded supervisors a position of authority which, they thought, would be advantageous in securing a professional footing. They did not realize that their position as middle-management within the school bureaucracy would be the very reason they had so much difficulty achieving professional recognition. While supervisors acknowledged that bureaucracy was not necessarily the best of all organizational worlds, they reacted rather harshly to suggestions at dismantling it. It seems clear that supervisors, although not fully understanding the nature of bureaucracy and its effects on the educational process, nevertheless shared an ideology and vested interest in maintaining the school hierarchy. They were not very sensitive to how stifled teachers, for instance, felt under the scrutiny of the autocratic supervisor. They also did not acknowledge the detrimental effects of bureaucratic supervision on parents and students. They believed in bureaucracy, as did reformers in the late nineteenth-century. Supervisors, admitting to the negative effects of bureaucracy, insisted that any detrimental effect caused by bureaucracy could be mitigated.[42] They thought it was possible to find a balance between freedom and authority, democracy and autocracy, and professionalism and bureaucracy. Earl S. Johnson, in an article entitled "The Human Dimensions of Supervision," restated a recurrent theme throughout the history of supervision by quoting Martin Buber. Buber, said Johnson, described the 'authority/freedom' debate as a "strange paradox." Johnson believed that the democratic "thinking and loving" orientation could be fostered through "the human dimensions of supervision."[43] In other words, "professionalism" can counteract the ill-effects of "bureaucracy." However, few, if any, practical proposals were offered to demonstrate exactly how this balance between freedom and authority would take place.

According to some observers, supervisors were unable or unwilling to remove the yoke of bureaucracy. Paul R. Klohr, in an article entitled "Looking Ahead in a Climate of Change," stated that "never before has such potential power been available. Yet, there is a pervasive tendency for many supervisors and curriculum workers to feel alienated from the educational scene. . . . They frequently act in ways that almost deny their sense of being—personal and professional."[44] Similarly, Arthur Blumberg in a study completed in 1974, found that teachers saw supervisors "having, in a sense, forsaken professionalism for a role in the bureaucracy with the major function of protecting and maintaining organization norms and values." According to Blumberg, teachers perceived themselves as professionals and supervisors as bureaucrats, while supervisors perceived both teachers and themselves as professionals.[45]

It is the thesis of this book that supervisors as an occupational group were constrained by conflicting bureaucratic and professional pressures. This inherent conflict between bureaucracy and professionalism persisted after 1937. Supervisors, in most cases, wanted to professionalize, improve instruction, and provide leadership, but were hindered by bureaucratic red tape and other organizational demands. One of the effects of the struggle to attain professionalism while maintaining membership in bureaucracy has been the insecurity, uncertainty, and anxiety associated with the supervisor's status. Shirley Markowitz, an instructor of elementary and special education at Cleveland State University, writing in the February 1976 issue of *Educational Leadership,* discussed the bureaucratic-professional interface of authority in supervisory behavior. The confusion of the supervisory role was, to a large extent, she contended, reflective of the authority structure of American schools. "The supervisor in the educational system is plagued by ambiguities. His or her position in the authority structure is ill-defined and quite often vulnerable," said Markowitz. "There is a lack of clarity in the definition of his or her role and a lack of agreement on the functions associated with supervision."[46] Robert J. Alfonso, Gerald R. Firth, and Richard F. Neville described this role ambiguity in terms of a "power limbo." That is, supervisors are "neither line nor staff, neither administration nor faculty, but somewhere in between."[47] Fred T. Wilhelms concurred that supervision had witnessed tremendous change. "Roles are changing; staff organization is swirling; titles and functions are shifting, . . . But whether his title is 'principal,' 'supervisor,' 'curriculum coordinator,' or what not, the person in a position of supervisory leadership is caught in the middle."[48] Supervisors were indeed in a dilemma, wrote Markowitz in an article entitled "The Dilemma of Authority in Supervisory Behavior." On the one hand, their duty was to carry out the mandates of the bureaucratic organization. On the other hand, supervisors, as middle management, wished to secure a professional basis for their work and to maintain "authentic human concerns."[49]

Put concisely, the problems supervisors face today and have faced throughout this century originate in the late nineteenth century when supervision was cast within a bureaucratic mold. Bureaucratic supervision was desirable because it promoted efficiency, organizational stability, and predictability. According to Herbert A. Shepard, "Bureaucratic structures are designed to do programmable things in a stable, predictable environment."[50] Supervision, as a policing function, is important for ensuring predictability and stability. Supervisors did not create bureaucracy, but certainly played a role in perpetuating bureaucratic policy. In other words, the school bureaucracy developed rules and regulations in order to control behavior among individuals. The few available studies buttress the contention that supervision in schools serves a maintenance rather than an innovative function.[51]

In terms of the history of public school supervision in this country, the bureaucratic phenomenon emphasized three basic elements: (1) centralized control through supervision, (2) hierarchy of authority, and (3) impersonality of rules. Once initiated in the late nineteenth century, these three basic elements of bureaucracy were not only sustained but gained momentum as the school organization increased in complexity in the twentieth century. For example, when a neophyte teacher enters a school he quickly realizes that there are prescribed rules for behavior. The teacher soon is introduced to the grade supervisor who, among other things, makes sure the teacher understands and follows school regulations. Furthermore, there are different rules governing supervisors, teachers, and children. In other words, the school system stratifies its members into various groups, appearing even castelike at times.[52]

The public school system, reflecting the organizational structure of society, perpetuates bureaucratic rules needed to maintain itself. Bureaucracy thrives on these rules and formalized behavior. Rewards and punishments are distributed by bureaucratic functionaries (administrators) whose main concern is to see that the organization is running efficiently. Underlying these sanctions and rules are, of course, values and beliefs of the members of the organization. Bureaucracy developed in response to a particular set of beliefs held by the members of the system. The school organization has persisted because individuals valued the assumptions underlying bureaucracy. In essence, as it relates to this study, there exists three basic groups or functionaries in schools: (1) the top group (administrators), (2) the middle group (supervisors), and (3) the lower group (teachers). Frequently, the group at the lower end of the hierarchy advocates change and criticizes bureaucratic practices of those above them. At the other end of the hierarchy, the top group tends to be rather complacent and secure in knowing its members have the authority to govern the organization. It is the middle group of supervisors that is of concern in this study. The middle group is in a precarious, and at the same time, pivotal position in the schools. The supervisors are close enough to the top so that all hope is not lost of achieving greater legitimized authority. At the same time, acting as middle management, they are vulnerable to attack from both ends—the teachers and administrators.

The important point to be made is that analysis of the history of supervision since the late nineteenth century, reveals that supervisors sought to become professionals within this bureaucratic framework. However, professionalism represented an attempt to attain higher status within the bureaucracy. In other words, supervisors did not envision professional interests as inimical to bureaucratic operations, although they often were. Nor did they question the viability of bureaucracy. Supervisors wanted to serve a useful and helping function. They wanted higher status. They believed in bureaucracy. Supervisors believed that professionalism could mitigate harmful bureaucratic effects. Supervisors, through their organization, the ASCD, wanted to gain legitimacy for their work; that is, they sought to make supervision a professional activity. This meant seeking higher status. However, professionalism, sought by supervisors, can be viewed as an expedient, political, and conservative ideology of a group of educators seeking a certain vested interest—the maintenance of bureaucracy. The fact remains that supervision, in 1990, is still a nebulous function. Given the exigencies of the organizational framework of schooling, it is dubious that supervisors ever had a chance to attain their professional goals.

Notes

Introduction

1. See, for example, Arno A. Bellack, "History of Curriculum Thought and Practice," *Review of Educational Research* 39 (June 1969), pp. 283–92; Barry M. Franklin, "The Curriculum Field and the Problem of Social Control, 1918–1938: A Study in Critical Theory" (Ph.D. dissertation, University of Wisconsin, 1974); Herbert M. Kliebard, "Persistent Curriculum Issues in Historical Perspective," *Educational Comment* (1970), pp. 31–41; Mary L. Seguel, *The Curriculum Field: Its Formative Years* (New York: Teachers College Press, 1966); and, more recently, Herbert M. Kliebard, *The Struggle for the American Curriculum, 1893–1958* (Boston: Routledge and Kegan Paul, 1986).

2. According to the authors of a publication sponsored by the ASCD, "a definitive history of educational supervision has not been published." *Curriculum Leaders: Improving Their Influence* (Washington, D.C.: ASCD, 1976), p. 13. In 1977 I argued that "supervision as a field of study has little by way of history." Jeffrey Glanz, "Ahistoricism and School Supervision: Notes Toward a History," *Educational Leadership* 35 (November 1977), p. 154.

There have been two noteworthy doctoral dissertations dealing with educational supervision. The first was a history of supervision completed in 1961 by Henry Warren Button, under the sponsorship of Raymond Callahan at Washington University. For a discussion of this work see the Bibliographical Essay at the end of the book. Button, "A History of Supervision in the Public Schools, 1870–1950" (Ph.D. dissertation, Washington University, 1961). The second dissertation was completed by this author in 1977. Although by no means a comprehensive treatment on the subject, it does analyze and interpret certain developments crucial in the history of supervision. See Glanz, "Bureaucracy and Professionalism: An Historical Interpretation of Public School Supervision in the United States, 1875–1937" (Ed.D. dissertation, Teachers College, Columbia University, 1977).

Besides these studies, there has been a paucity of published work on school supervision. See, for example, Clarence Karier, "Supervision in Historic Perspective," in Thomas J. Sergiovanni, ed., *Supervision of Teaching*, 1982 Yearbook of the ASCD (Washington, D.C.: ASCD, 1982); Arthur Blumberg, "Where We Came from: Notes on Supervision in the 1840s," *Journal of Curriculum and Supervision* 1 (Fall 1985), pp. 56–65; and Daniel Tanner and Laurel N. Tanner, *Supervision in Education: Problems and Practices* (New York: Macmillan, 1987), pp. 3–26. Also see my recently published article titled "Beyond Bureaucracy: Notes on the Professionalization of Public School Supervision in the Early Twentieth Century," *Journal of Curriculum and Supervision* 5 (Winter 1990), pp. 150–70.

3. David B. Tyack, *The One Best System: A History of American Urban Education* (Cambridge: Harvard University Press, 1974).

4. See, for example, Diane Ravitch, *The Great School Wars: New York City, 1805–1973* (New York: Basic, 1974); William A. Bullough, *Cities and Schools in the Gilded Age* (Port Washington, N.Y.: Kennikat Press, 1974); and Joseph M. Cronin, *The Control of Urban Schools: Perspective on the Power of Educational Reformers* (New York: Free Press, 1973).

5. P. M. Blau and W. R. Scott, "The Nature and Types of Formal Organizations," in F. D. Carver and T. J. Sergiovanni, eds., *Organizations and Human Behavior* (New York: McGraw-Hill, 1969), p. 9.

6. Tyack, *One Best System*. My discussion of bureaucracy and supervision in this book covers developments that occurred throughout many cities in the late nineteenth century. Certainly, the emergence of bureaucracy as the main source of school governance was not a unitary phenomenon that took hold at "one fell swoop" across the nation. Bureaucratization of schooling and of supervision in particular was a piecemeal and complicated process. For more specific explorations into the emergence of bureaucracy and the importance of supervision see, for example, Michael B. Katz, *Recontructing American Education* (Cambridge: Harvard Univerity Press, 1988), chapter 3, "How Urban School Systems Became Bureaucracies: The Boston Case, 1850–1884."

7. This idea was first developed in a paper presentation in 1978. See Glanz, "Controlling the Schools: An Essay on the Bureaucratization of School Supervision in the Late Nineteenth Century," Paper presented at the Annual Meeting of the American Educational Research Association, Toronto, March 20, 1978. For a general treatment of control in schooling see, for example, Gerald A. Ponder, "Schooling and Control: Some Interpretations of the Changing Social Function of Curriculum," in O. L. Davis, Jr., ed., *Perspectives on Curriculum Development, 1776–1976*, 1976 Yearbook of th ASCD (Washington, D.C.: ASCD, 1976).

8. See Glanz, "From Bureaucracy to Professionalism: An Essay on the Democratization of School Supervision in the Early Twentieth Century," Paper presented at the Annual Meeting of the American Educational Studies Association, Washington, D.C., November 1978).

9. K. C. Mayhew and A. C. Edwards, *The Dewey School: The Laboratory School of the University of Chicago 1896–1903* (New York: Atherton Press, 1965), p. 465.

10. Ivan Illich, *Deschooling Society* (New York: Harper, 1970), p. 108; Samuel Bowles and Herbert Gintis, *Schooling in Capitalist America* (New York: Basic, 1976), p. 246.

11. Tanner and Tanner, *Supervision in Education*, p. 103.

12. Evelyn F. Carlson, Introduction, *Role of Supervisor and Curriculum Director in a Climate of Change*, 1965 Yearbook of the ASCD (Washington, D.C.: ASCD, 1965), p. 2.

13. William H. Payne, *Chapters on School Supervision: A Practical Treatise on Superintendence; Grading; Arranging Courses of Study; The Preparation and Use of Blanks, Records, and Reports; Examinations for Promotion, etc.* (New York: Wilson, Hinkle and Company, 1875), p. 13.

14. Josiah L. Pickard, *School Supervision* (New York: Appleton, 1890), p. 1.

15. Willard S. Elsbree, *The American Teacher* (New York: American Book, 1939), p. 71.

16. See, for example, Button, "History of Supervision in the Public Schools," pp. 3–4.

17. Ellwood P. Cubberley, "Organization of Public Education," *NEA Addresses and Proceedings*, 53rd Annual Meeting, Oakland, 1915, pp. 91–97.

18. Payne, *Chapters on School Supervision*. Also, see Theodore L. Reller,

The Development of the City Superintendency of Schools in the United States (Philadelphia: The Author, 1935).

19. U.S. Bureau of the Census, *Historical Statistics of the United States, Colonial Times to 1957* (Washington, D.C.: U.S. Government Printing Office, 1960), pp. 207–10, 214.

20. Willard S. Elsbree and E. Edmund Reutter, Jr., *Staff Personnel in the Public Schools* (Englewood Cliffs, N.J.: Prentice-Hall, 1954), p. 231.

21. Ibid., p. 231.

22. The title "general supervisor" later changed to "assistant principal," which more precisely defined his relationship to the building principal in the school hierarchy. A similar relationship existed between the assistant superintendent and the superintendent. The title "assistant principal," however, did not gain wide usage until the late thirties and early forties.

23. Medicine, law, architecture, and accounting were in fact bureaucratic from their origins. The growth of professionalization of these groups was enhanced by bureaucratization. As Andrew Abbott recently explains, "Bureaucratic organization among professions enabled them to meet the challenges of the modern world and transformed the nature and location of interprofessional competition." Abbott, *The System of Professions: An Essay on the Division of Expert Labor* (Chicago: University of Chicago Press, 1988), p. 155.

24. Ibid., pp. 150, 155.

25. See, for example, H. J. Friesdam, "Bureaucrats as Heroes," *Social Forces* (March 1954), pp. 269–74.

26. Bel Kaufman, *Up the Down Staircase* (New York: Avon, 1989).

27. Robert K. Merton, "Bureaucratic Structure and Personality," *Social Forces* 18 (May 1940), pp. 561–68.

28. The following discussion is from chapter 4, "Rationalism Rediscovered: Bureaucracy and the Study of Administration," in Roald F. Campbell; Thomas Fleming; L. Jackson Newell; and John W. Bennion, eds., *A History of Thought and Practice in Educational Administration* (New York: Teachers College Press, 1987).

29. Ibid., p. 196.

30. While there is no need to recite the history of sociological ideas from Weber through Merton, Parsons, and Blau, it should be pointed out that Webers' theory, while contributing much to our understanding of the character of bureaucratic systems, did encounter criticism for its incompleteness and narrowness. See, for example, Talcott Parsons, *Structure and Process in Modern Societies* (New York: Free Press, 1960); Amitai Etzioni, *Modern Organizations* (Englewood Cliffs, N.J.: Prentice-Hall, 1964); Peter Blau, *The Dynamics of Bureaucracy* (Chicago: University of Chicago Press, 1955; Merton, *Social Theory and Social Structure* (Glencoe, Ill.: Free Press, 1959); and Alvin Gouldner, *Patterns of Industrial Bureaucracy* (Glencoe, Ill.: Free Press, 1954).

31. See Walter Doyle, "Education for All: The Triumph of Professionalism," in O. L. Davis, Jr., ed., *Perspectives on Curriculum Development, 1776–1976* (Washington, D.C.: ASCD, 1976), p. 27.

32. See, for example, Ronald G. Corwin, *Sociology of Education* (New York: Appleton, 1965; Kenneth R. Howey and William E. Gardner, *The Education of Teachers* (New York: Longman, 1983); and Robert B. Howsam et al., *Educating a Profession* (Washington, D.C.: American Association of Colleges for Teacher Education, 1976).

33. See, for example, Myron Lieberman, *Education as a Profession* (En-

glewood Cliffs, N.J.: Prentice-Hall, 1956); and Morris L. Cogan, "Toward a Definition of Profession," *Harvard Educational Review* 23 (Winter 1953), pp. 33–50.

34. Eliot Freidson, *Profession of Medicine: A Study in the Sociology of Applied Knowledge* (New York: Harper, 1970), pp. xvii, 5, 71–84.

35. Corwin, *Militant Professionalism: A Study of Organizational Conflict in High Schools* (New York: Appleton, 1970), p. 43.

36. Stephen T. Kerr, "Teacher Specialization and the Growth of a Bureaucratic Profession," *Teachers College Record* (Spring 1983), p. 634.

37. Corwin, *Militant Professionalism,* p. 12.

38. Ibid., p. 19.

39. Corwin, "Professional Persons in Public Organizations," in F. D. Carver and T. J. Sergiovanni, eds., *Organizations and Human Behavior* (New York: McGraw-Hill, 1969), p. 222.

Chapter 1. Bureaucracy and School Supervision

1. U.S. Bureau of the Census, *U.S. Census of 1890* (Washington, D.C.: U.S. Government Printing Office, 1895), Introduction.

2. Andrew Carnegie, *Triumphant Democracy or Fifty Years' March of the Republic* (New York: Scribner, 1886), p. 1.

3. U.S. Bureau of the Census, *Historical Statistics of the United States, Colonial Times to 1957* (Washington, D.C.: U.S. Government Printing Office, 1960), p. 207.

4. F. Louis Soldan, "The Progress in Public Education," *NEA Proceedings,* 1899, p. 177.

5. William A. Mowry, *Recollections of a New England Educator, 1838–1908* (New York: Silver, Burdett, 1908), p. 279.

6. The struggles that ensued in the late nineteenth century between superintendents and ward boards to control policy in public schools has been extensively treated. See, for example, Raymond E. Callahan, *The Superintendent of Schools: An Historical Analysis* (Bethesda, Md.: ERIC Document Reproduction Service, 1967); and Joseph M. Cronin, *The Control of Urban Schools: Perspective on the Power of Educational Reformers* (New York: Free Press, 1973).

7. Robert H. Wiebe, *The Search for Order, 1877–1920* (New York: Hill and Wang, 1967), p. 145.

8. For perhaps the best treatment of this period see David B. Tyack, *The One Best System: A History of American Urban Education* (Cambridge: Harvard University Press, 1974).

9. Joseph M. Rice, *The Public-School System of the United States* (New York: Century Company, 1893), pp. 1–2. For biographical information on Rice, see the *National Cyclopedia of American Biography* 12 (New York, 1904): pp. 203–4.

10. Rice's proclamations regarding the American school system received much stricture, particularly among the cities that were characterized by Rice as "deplorable." The journal *Education,* between May 1894 and February 1895, ran a series of articles attacking Rice's extensive study. However, much of this criticism focused on personal offensives against Rice rather than actually denying the conditions that Rice found as inaccurate and misleading.

11. William A. Mowry, "Powers and Duties of School Superintendents," *Educational Review* 9 (January 1895), p. 41.

12. William G. Bruce, "The Politician in the Schools," *American School Board Journal* 10 (January 1895), p. 8.

13. Lewis H. Jones, "The Politician and the Public School: Indianapolis and Cleveland," *Atlantic Monthly* 77 (March 1896), pp. 810, 815.

14. "Confessions of Public School Teachers," *Atlantic Monthly* 28 (July 1896), pp. 97–110.

15. "Confessions of Three School Superintendents," *Atlantic Monthly* (November 1898), pp. 650, 652–53.

16. Rice, *Public School-System*, p. 11. As to instilling more "humane" education, I do not believe that was the intent of reformers. Certainly, they earnestly wanted to change American education for the better. However, more "autocratic" means would be applied to achieve their stated objective.

17. Ibid., pp. 14–17, 96–98.

18. Ibid., p. 230.

19. John D. Philbrick, *City School Systems in the United States* (U.S. Bureau of Education, Circular of Information No. 1, Washington, D.C.: U.S. Government Printing Office, 1885), pp. 6, 14–15. For biographical information on Philbrick see the *National Cyclopedia of American Biography*, p. 242.

20. Ibid., p. 58.

21. B. A. Hinsdale, "Business Side of City School Systems," *NEA Proceedings*, 1888, p. 317.

22. Aaron E. Gove, "The Rise of the Superintendent," *Education* 19 (May 1899), p. 520.

23. See the discussion following B. A. Hinsdale, "Supplementary Report of the Committee on School Systems," *NEA Proceedings*, 1890, pp. 358–61; Emerson E. White, Discussion, *Committee of Fifteen Report* (New York: American Book, 1895), p. 362.

24. White; Discussion, *Committee of Fifteen*, p. 224.

25. Andrew S. Draper, "Plans of Organization for School Purposes in Large Cities," *NEA Proceedings*, 1894, pp. 307–8.

26. See the discussion following W. H. Maxwell, "City School Systems," *NEA Proceedings*, 1890, pp. 447–60; Draper, "Plans of Organization," p. 467.

27. Israel H. Peres, "What Constitutes an Efficient Superintendent?" *NEA Proceedings*, 1901, pp. 826–28.

28. A. E. Winship, "What the Superintendent Is Not," *NEA Proceedings*, 1899, p. 309.

29. Editorial, *Education* 7 (September 1886), p. 61.

30. Seventh Annual Report of the City Superintendent of Schools in New York, 1905, p. 42.

31. See the discussion following H. F. Harrington, "The Extent, Methods and Values of Supervision in a System of Schools," *NEA Proceedings*, 1872, pp. 245–57, J. P. Wickersham, p. 257.

32. White, *Committee of Fifteen* (New York: American Book, 1895), pp. 115–26.

33. John T. Prince, *School Administration* (New York: C. W. Bardeen, 1906), p. 150.

34. F. Louis Soldan, *Report of the Superintendent of Instruction* (December 1, 1903, Board of Education of the City of St. Louis, Missouri, 1904), p. 235.

35. Draper, *The Supervision of Country Schools* (New York: C. W. Bardeen, 1904), p. 39.
36. James M. Greenwood, "Discussion of Gove's Paper," *NEA Proceedings,* 1891, p. 227.
37. Andrew W. Edson, "School Supervision," *Education* 13 (March 1893), pp. 394, 396.
38. Edson, "Leadership in the Superintendent," *Education* 24 (October 1903), pp. 70–71.
39. Thomas M. Balliet, "What Can Be Done to Increase the Efficiency of Teachers in Actual Service?" *NEA Proceedings,* 1894, p. 377.
40. Balliet, "Discussion of Anderson's Paper," *NEA Proceedings,* 1891, pp. 437–38.
41. Frank A. Fitzpatrick, "How to Improve the Work of Inefficient Teachers," *NEA Proceedings,* 1893, p. 76.
42. E. E. Cates, "The Trained Teacher," *The School Review* 7 (1899), p. 24.
43. William T. Harris, "City School Supervision," *Educational Review* 3 (1892) pp. 171–72.
44. James M. Greenwood, "Efficient School Supervision," *NEA Proceedings,* 1888, pp. 519–21.
45. Greenwood, "Discussion of Gove's Paper," p. 227.
46. Aaron Gove, "How to Test the Quality of a Teacher's Work" *NEA Proceedings,* 1891, p. 224.
47. Ibid., Discussion, p. 226.
48. Greenwood, "Efficient School Supervision," p. 227.
49. Burke, p. 227.
50. William T. Harris, "The Present Status of Education in the United States," *NEA Proceedings,* 1891, p. 136.
51. Harris and Duane Doty, *A Statement of the Theory of Education in the United States as Approved by Many Leading Educators* (Washington, D.C.: U.S. Government Printing Office, 1874), p. 15.
52. Gove, "The Trail of the City Superintendent," *NEA Proceedings,* 1900, p. 219.
53. Samuel T. Dutton, *School Management: Practical Suggestions Concerning the Conduct and Life of the School* (New York: Scribner, 1904); Emerson E. White, *School Management: A Practical Treatise for Teachers and All Other Persons Interested in the Right Training of the Young* (New York: American Book, 1894).
54. John Kennedy, "The Philosophy of School Discipline," 1879, p. 18, reproduced in pamphlet form in *School Room Classics,* Columbia University. Also, see A. D. Mayo, "The Spirit of School Discipline," *The National Teacher* 1 (1871), pp. 39–48.
55. James L. Hughes, "Harmony between Control and Spontaneity," *NEA Proceedings,* 1892, p. 187.
56. William T. Harris, "The Relation of School Discipline to Moral Education," in Charles A. McMurray, ed., *National Herbart Society for the Scientific Study of Teaching, Third Yearbook* (Chicago: University of Chicago Press, 1897), p. 72.
57. John Trainer, *How to Grade and Teach a Country School* (Decatur, Ill.: Burgess, Trainer and Company, 1885), pp. 20–21.
58. For a more complete discussion of the system see, for example, Carl F.

Kaestle, "The Origins of an Urban School System: New York City, 1750–1850" (Ph.D. dissertation, Harvard University, 1970, pp. 366–67.

59. David MacRae, *The Americans at Home* (New York: Dutton, 1952 [originally published in 1875), pp. 601–3.

60. Barbara Joan Finkelstein, "Governing the Young: Teacher Behavior in American Primary Schools, 1820–1880; A Documentary History" (Ed.d dissertation, Teachers College, Columbia University, 1970), p. 378 and quoted by David Tyack, *The One Best System: A History of American Urban Education* (Cambridge: Harvard University Press, 1974), p. 51.

61. Trainer, *How to Grade and Teach a Country School*, p. 22.

62. Lotus D. Coffman, "The Control of Educational Progress Thru School Supervision," *NEA Proceedings*, 1917, p. 194. Also, see L. H. Marvel, "The Province of Supervision," *American Institute of Instruction*, 1885; *Journal of Proceedings of the American Institute of Instruction* (Portsmouth: American Institute of Instruction, 1869); William E. Chancellor, *Our Schools Their Administration and Supervision* (Boston: Heath, 1904).

63. Larkin Dutton, "School Discipline," *Education* 12 (February 1892), p. 325.

64. See the discussion following C. B. Gilbert, "The Ethics of School Management," *NEA Proceedings*, 1888, pp. 528–42, Greenwood, "Efficient School Supervision," p. 543.

65. Homer Seeley, "City Supervision," *Education* 15 (May 1895), p. 519.

66. C. L. Biedenbach, "High School Discipline," *The School Review* 4 (1896), p. 230.

67. William Harold Payne, *Chapters on School Supervision: A Practical Treatise on Superintendence; Grading; Arranging Courses of Study; the Preparation and Use of Blanks, Records, and Reports; Examinations for Promotion, etc.* (New York: Wilson, Hinkle and Company, 1875).

68. George Cleveland Poret, *The Contributions of William Harold Payne to Public Education* (Peabody Contributions to Education, no. 81, Nashville, 1930), p. 43. For biographical information on Payne, see the *Dictionary of American Biography* 14 (New York, 1934), pp. 331–32; and *National Cyclopedia of American Biography* (New York, 1900), pp. 134–35. According to William A. Mowry, Payne "was one of our foremost educators, having had long experience in responsible positions in the state of Michigan. He was a prolific writer and translator." Mowry, *Recollections of a New England Educator, 1838–1908* (New York: Silver, Burdett, 1908), p. 255.

69. Payne, *Contributions to the Science of Education* (New York: Harper, 1887), pp. viii, 3. 331.

70. Payne, *Chapters on School Supervision*, pp. 13–14.

71. Ibid., p. 17

72. Josiah Little Pickard, *School Supervision* (New York: Appleton, 1890), p. 2.

73. J. W. Errant, "Reform in School Administration," *NEA Proceedings*, 1897, p. 967. Also, see Anna Burstall, *Impressions of American Education in 1908* (London, n.p., 1909).

74. Albert P. Marble, *The Powers and Duties of School Officers and Teachers* (New York: C. W. Bardeen, 1887), pp. 3, 4, 7.

75. Norman A. Calkins, "School Supervision," *Education* 2 (May 1882), pp. 497, 500.

76. Payne, *Chapters on School Supervision,* pp. 13–14.
77. Ibid., p. 73.
78. Chancellor, *Our Schools,* p. 417.
79. William T. Harris, *Seventeenth Annual Report of the Board of Directors of the St. Louis Public Schools,* 1871, p. 31. For biographical information on Harris, see the *Dictionary of American Biography* 8 (New York, 1932), pp. 328–30; and *National Cyclopedia of American Biography* 6 (New York, 1896), p. 344. According to Mowry, Harris "is one of the most learned and most noted educators in the world." Mowry, *Recollections of a New England Educator,* p. 247.
80. Payne, *Chapters on School Supervision,* p. 53.
81. William T. Harris, "City School Supervision," *Educational Review* 3 (1892), p. 168.
82. Ibid., pp. 171–72.
83. Ibid., p. 172.
84. Chancellor, *Our Schools,* p. 106.
85. Payne, *Chapters on School Supervision,* p. 49.
86. Chancellor, *Our School,* p. 210. Note that Chancellor allowed women to assume supervisory positions. He was referring to subject supervisors in schools, such as music supervisors. These supervisors, as shall be explained later, did not have any independent authority and were subject to the "supervision" of the principal and superintendent. Also, see H. L. Getz, "Hints on School Administration," *NEA Proceedings,* 1897. "Married women should not be employed in our public schools as teachers, except in emergencies." (pp. 964–65); and *Committee of Fifteen Report,* Appendix." [the superintendent] should be a well man with a good physique and a strong personality, capable of easily influencing women and children" (Earl Barnes, p. 201).
87. Payne, *Chapters on School Supervision,* pp. 13–14.
88. E. C. Warriner, "Unity Gained from School Supervision," *NEA Proceedings,* 1911, pp. 312, 314.
89. William H. Maxwell, "Supervision of City Schools," *NEA Proceedings,* 1894, p. 315. For a biography on Maxwell see Samuel P. Abelow, *Dr. William H. Maxwell, The First Superintendent of Schools of the City of New York* (Brooklyn: Scheba, 1934); and Selma C. Berrol, "William Henry Maxwell and a New Educational New York," *History of Education Quarterly* 8 (1968).
90. Albert B. Hart, "The Teacher as a Professional Expert," *The School Review* 1 (1893), p. 14.
91. Josiah L. Pickard, "The Extent, Methods and Values of Supervision in a System of Schools," *NEA Proceedings,* 1872, p. 259.
92. Louis J. Block, "School Supervision," *Education* 12 (May 1892), pp. 558, 561.
93. Emerson Elbridge White, "Ohio Superintendent's Association, Proceedings of the Annual Meeting held at Sandusky City, July 4, 1871," *The National Teacher* 1 (1871), p. 515.
94. White, "Several Problems in Graded-School Management," *The National Teacher* 4 (September 1874), p. 411.
95. Burke Aaron Hinsdale, *Common School Education* (Cleveland, Ohio: Robison, Savage & Co., 1877), pp. 21, 24.
96. Franklin Bobbitt, "Some General Principles of Management Applied to the Problems of City-School Systems," *Twelfth Yearbook of the National Society*

for the Study of Education, part 1 (Chicago: University of Chicago Press, 1913), p. 89.

97. Sallie Hill, "Defects of Supervision and Construction Suggestions Thereon," *NEA Proceedings,* 1919, p. 506.

98. Francis E. Harden, "A Plea for Greater Democracy on Our Public Schools," *NEA Proceedings,* 1919, p. 391.

99. Aaron Estellus Gove, "The Rise of the Superintendent," *Education* 19 (May 1899), p. 520; Gove, "Limitations of Superintendents' Authority and of the Teacher's Independence," *NEA Proceedings,* 1904, p. 155.

100. Margaret A. Haley, "Why Teachers Should Organize?" *NEA Proceedings,* 1904, pp. 147–48. Also, see Sarah L. Brooks, "Supervision as Viewed by the Supervised," *NEA Proceedings,* 1897, pp. 225–32.

101. Michael Katz, among other historians, maintains that we need to analyze the value system of those persons whom we are studying in order to fully understand their viewpoints. See, for example, Katz, *Class, Bureaucracy, & Schools: The Illusion of Educational Change in America* (New York: Praeger, 1973).

102. Oscar T. Corson, "The Superintendents' Authority and the Teacher's Freedom," *NEA Proceedings,* 1906, pp. 80–81.

103. Jesse H. Newlon, "Attitude of the Teacher Toward Supervision," *NEA Proceedings,* 1923, p. 548.

104. Henry Sabin, "The Kind of Supervision Most Needed," *NEA Proceedings,* 1897, p. 127, Sabin, "Suggestions for the Improvement of a System of City Schools," *Education* 10 (September 1898), p. 3.

105. Sarah L. Arnold, "The Duties and Privileges of the Supervisor," *NEA Proceedings,* 1898, pp. 228, 236.

106. See the discussion following Sabin, "Organization and System vs. Originality and Individuality on the Part of Teacher and Pupil," *NEA Proceedings,* 1890, pp. 228–34; Bardeen, p. 234.

107. Bardeen, pp. 234–35.

108. Ibid., p. 235.

109. Anderson, p. 241.

110. Consult U. S. Bureau of the Census, *Historical Statistics,* 14, 139, 427; and Kenneth T. Jackson and Stanley K. Schultz, eds., *Cities in American History* (New York: Knopf, 1972).

111. Albert P. Marble, "City School Administration," *Educational Review,* 1894, p. 166.

112. Henry Warren Button, "A History of Supervision in the Public Schools, 1870–1950" (Ph.D. dissertation, Washington University, 1961), p. 81.

113. Michael B. Katz, *Class, Bureaucracy, & Schools: The Illusion of Educational Change in America* (New York: Praeger, 1973), p. 144.

114. P. M. Blau and R. W. Scott, "The Nature and Types of Formal Organizations," in F. D. Carver and T. J. Sergiovanni, *Organizations and Human Behavior,* eds. (New York: McGraw-Hill, 1969), p. 9.

115. Talcott Parsons, *Max Weber: The Theory of Social and Economic Organization* (New York: Free Press, 1947), p. 53.

116. David S. Seeley, *Education Through Partnership* (Washington, D.C.: American Enterprise Institute for Public Research, 1985), p. 21.

117. Ibid., pp. 41–49.

118. John Dewey, *Democracy and Education* (New York: Macmillan, 1916);

James F. Hosic, "The Democratization of Supervision," *School and Society* 11 (March 20, 1920), pp. 331–36.

119. Samuel T. Dutton, *School Management: Practical Suggestions Concerning the Conduct and Life of the School* (New York: Scribner, 1904), p. 75.

Chapter 2. From Cautious Optimism to Confirmed Despair: The Supervisor's Newly Found Status within the School Organization

1. Lawrence A. Cremin, *The Transformation of the School: Progressivism in American Education, 1876–1957* (New York: Knopf, 1961), p. 88. Also, see Cremin, *American Education: The Metropolitan Experience, 1876–1980* (New York, Harper, 1988), part 2.

2. John Dewey, "Democracy in Education," *The Elementary School Teacher* 4 (December 1903), p. 196.

3. Lawrence A. Cremin, "John Dewey and the Progressive Education Movement," *The School Review* 7 (1959), p. 160.

4. Dewey, "My Pedagogic Creed," in Martin S. Dworkin, etc., *Dewey on Education* (New York: Teachers College, Columbia University, 1959), p. 30.

5. Charles E. Merriam, *Civic Education in the United States* (New York: Scribner, 1934), pp. 67–68.

6. Diane Ravitch felt that Nicholas Murray Butler did not envision a bureaucracy in the 1890s. She said, "Nicholas Murray Butler, for example, imagined that centralization would remove capriciousness and error; he expected his reforms to empower visionary experts, not bureaucratic functionaries." See Ravitch, The Great School Wars: New York, City, 1805–1973 (New York: Basic, 1974), p. 400.

7. Annual Report of the United States Commissioner of Education, 2 (1888–89), p. 772; 2 (1895–96), pp. 1488–89.

8. For example, in 1875 a school board described the duties of supervisors as follows: "1. to visit and examine the schools in detail twice each year. 2. to visit all the schools . . . inquire into the character of the discipline, . . . 3. to collate and combine their reports" etc. "Report of the Committee Appointed to Represent the School Committee before the Legislature," Annual Report of the School Committee, 1875, Boston.

9. Ibid. (1900–1901), p. 1527; 1 1905), p. XXIX; 1 (1911), p. 121.

10. William E. Chancellor, *Our Schools: Their Administration and Supervision* (Boston: Heath, 1904), p. 210.

11. Frank E. Spaulding, *School Superintendent in Action in Five Cities* (Ringe, N.H., Richard R. Smith Publisher, 1955), p. 130.

12. U.S. Bureau of the Census, *Historical Statistics of the United States, Colonial Times to 1957* (Washington, D.C.: Bureau of Census), p. 214.

13. See Linda Murgatroyd, "Gender and Occupational Stratification," *Sociological Review* 30 (November 1982); Barry H. Bergen, "Only a Schoolmaster: Gender, Class, and the Effort to Professionalize Elementary Teaching in England, 1870–1910," *History of Education Quarterly* 22 (Spring 1982); Myra Strober, "Segregation by Gender in Public School Teaching: Toward a General Theory of Occupational Segregation in the Labor Market," Stanford University, 1982; Marta Danylewycz and Alison Prentice, "Teachers, Gender, and Bureaucratizing School Systems in Nineteenth Century Montreal and Toronto,"

History of Education Quarterly 24 (Spring 1984); Sheila Rothman, *Women's Proper Place* (New York: Basic, 1978); Michael W. Apple, *Teachers and Texts: A Political Economy of Class and Gender Relations in Education* (New York: Routledge, 1986); Polly Welts Kaufman, *Women Teachers on the Frontier* (New Haven, Conn.: Yale University Press, 1984); John Richardson and Brenda Wooden Hatcher, "The Feminization of Public School Teaching: 1870–1920," *Work and Occupations* 10 (February 1983); Myra Strober and David Tyack, "Why Do Women Teach and Manage?: A Report on Research on Schools," *Signs* 5 (Spring 1980); and Carl A. Grant and Christine E. Sleeter, "Race, Class, and Gender and Abandoned Dreams," *Teachers College Record* 90 (Fall 1988).

14. Payne, *Chapters on School Supervision*, p. 49.

15. Strober and Tyack, "Why Do Women Teach and Men Manage?" p. 500.

16. The "principal" in charge of a school prior to about 1900 was a teacher selected on presumed excellence in teaching, although more probably because he knew the right politician; he was known as the "principal" teacher.

17. M. W. Sloyer, "Subject Supervision," *Education* 48 (April 1928), p. 479. Also, see James R. McGaughy, "Tendencies in Supervision," *Teachers College Record,* 29 (April 1928), pp. 579–86; Thomas W. Gosling, "The Adjustment of the Duties of the Supervisor to those of the Principal," *The Elementary School Journal* 26 (Summer 1925), pp. 18–21; and M. Madden, "The Right Relationship of Cooperation between the Principal and Supervisors: The Chicago Plan," *NEA Proceedings,* (1924), pp. 548–51.

18. Alice E. Reynolds, "The Assistant to the Superintendent—His Functions and Methods of Work," *NEA Proceedings* (1904), pp.2 64–71.

19. Editorial, *The Journal of Educational Method* 7 (May 1928), p. 343. Several studies confirm the confusion that existed regarding supervising in the early twentieth century. See, for example, Ernest O. Melby, *A Critical Study of the Existing Organization and Administration of Supervision: A Study of Current Practice* (Bloomington, Ill.: Public School Publishing Company, 1929); B. F. Moore, "Supervision of Instruction in Cities from 15,000 to 50,000 Population" (Master's thesis, Columbia University, 1913); Charles H. Elliott, "Types of Supervision in American Cities," (Master's thesis, Columbia University, 1926); M. B. Fry, "Supervision" (Master's thesis, Columbia University, 1931); T. M. Risk, "Supervisory Organization and Procedure in Public Schools" (Master's Thesis, University of Wisconsin, 1925); and L. J. Neidert, "The Administrative Aspects of Supervisory Organization in 44 American Cities" (Master's thesis, University of Washington, 1926).

20. William H. Lucio and John D. McNeil, *Supervision: A Synthesis of Thought and Action* (New York: McGraw-Hill, 1962), p. 11. Indeed, administration was the prime concern. See W. E. Chancellor, *Our City Schools: Their Direction and Management* (Boston: Heath, 1908); Hollis Caswell, *City School Survey* (Contributions to Education, no. 358, New York: Bureau of Publications, Teachers College, Columbia University, 1929); Ellwood P. Cubberley, *School Funds and Their Apportionment* (Contributions to Education, no. 2, New York: Teachers College, Columbia University, 1906); Paul H. Hanus, *School Administration and School Reports* (New York: Houghton, 1920); George D. Strayer, *City School Expenditures* (Contributions to Education, no. 5, New York: Teachers College, Columbia University, 1905); and George D. Strayer and Edward L. Thorndike, *Educational Administration: Quantitative Studies* (New York: Macmillan, 1913). Later, we will indicate that supervisors tried to alter their relative obscurity in the schools. However, in addition to being overshadowed by

the administrator, the supervisor found his problems compounded by the fact that curriculum, in the post-1920 era, dominated the educational scene. Their attempts to gain professional autonomy will be discussed later.

21. See C. S. Hobson, "Franklin Bobbitt: Pioneer in Curriculum-Making," *Curriculum Journal* 14 (1943), pp. 14–17.

22. It is a curious irony that supervisors were confused and ill-at-ease regarding their role and function in the school. It would seem logical that since schools were cast as bureaucratic organizations, supervisors would find definite and clear job specifications. Bureaucracies, by their very definition, are characterized by precision and clarity of function. Apparently, however, "bureaucracy" in education was far from Weber's "ideal type." The reason for this is because, in my opinion, bureaucracy is ill-suited as a form of organization for schools. Bureaucracy is perhaps more appropriate for factories, for example. However, schools that are chiefly responsible for fostering the intellectual and social development of young people are more concerned with democratic, "humane" relationships. Bureaucracy is antithetical to the pursuits of schooling.

23. For an extensive treatment of the "efficiency movement" in education, see Raymond E. Callahan, *Education and the Cult of Efficiency* (Chicago: University of Chicago Press, 1962).

24. Frederick Winslow Taylor, *The Principles of Scientific Management* (New York: Harper, 1911).

25. Franklin Bobbitt, "Some General Principles of Management Applied to the Problems of City-School Systems," *Twelfth Yearbook of the National Society for the Study of Education,* part 1 (Chicago: University of Chicago Press, 1913), p. 7.

26. Ibid., pp. 8–12, 70.

27. Ibid., pp. 12–12, 15.

28. Ibid., pp. 27, 30.

29. Ibid., pp. 51, 53, 57.

30. Ibid., pp. 66–70.

31. Ibid., pp. 89–94.

32. Bobbitt's views ultimately failed not because the opponents to "scientific supervision" gained support for their views, but rather due to the fact that his plan was simply too costly. Curiously, although the public was strongly in favor of "efficiency," they were more concerned with cost. This was a point made and clarified by Raymond E. Callahan, "The Superintendent of Schools: An Historical Analysis" (Bethesda, Md.: ERIC Document Reproduction Service, 1967), p. 205.

33. James F. Hosic, "The Concept of the Principalship—II," *The Journal of Educational Method* 3 (March 1924), p. 283.

34. William McAndrew, "The Schoolman's Loins," *Educational Review* (September 1922), p. 114.

35. Alvin S. Barr and William H. Burton, *The Supervision of Instruction: A General Volume* (New York: Appleton, 1926), p. 75.

36. Bobbitt, "Principles of Management," p. 95.

37. Ibid., p. 12.

38. Bobbitt, "Mistakes Often Made by Principals—Part I," *The Elementary School Journal* 20 (January 1920), pp. 338–39.

39. Ibid., p. 338

40. Ibid., p. 434.

41. Joseph S. Taylor, "Measurement of Educational Efficiency," *Educational Review* 44 (November 1912), pp. 350–51, 359.

42. Clyde C. Green, "The Promotion of Teachers on the Basis of Merit and Efficiency," *NEA Proceedings*, 1915, p. 474.

43. William M. Davidson, "How to Measure the Efficiency of Teachers," *NEA Proceedings*, 1913, pp. 286–87.

44. Charles J. Dalthorp, "Shall We Rate Teachers?" *Educational Method* 12 (November 1932), p. 19.

45. Henry D. Hervey, "The Rating of Teachers," *NEA Proceedings*, 1921, p. 825. Also, see N. Skala, "Superfishin' or Supervision," *The Nebraska Educational Journal* 10 (October 1930), pp. 437–38; and A. Shiels, "The Rating of Teachers in New York City Public Schools," *School and Society* 2 (November 20, 1915), pp. 752–54.

46. For a survey of a number of rating scales used in schools in the early 1900s see J. H. Johnston, "Scientific Supervision of Teaching," *School and Society* 5 (February 17, 1917), pp. 181–88. Also, see F. B. Knight and R. H. Franzen, "Pitfalls in Rating Schemes," *The Journal of Educational Psychology* 11 (April 1922), pp. 145–55.

47. Edward C. Elliott, "How Shall the Efficiency of Teachers Be Tested and Recorded?" *NEA Proceedings*, 1915, pp. 472–73. Also, see Edward C. Elliott, *Tentative Scheme for the Measurement of Teaching Efficiency* (Madison, n.p., 1910).

48. Arthur Clifton Boyce, "Methods for Measuring Teachers Efficiency," *Fourteenth Yearbook of the National Society for the Study of Education*, part 2 (Chicago: University of Chicago Press, 1915), pp. 14–15, 77.

49. H. O. Rugg, "Self-Improvement of Teachers through Self-Rating: A New Scale for Rating Teachers," *The Elementary School Journal* 20 (May 1920), pp. 674, 676.

50. Ibid., pp. 670, 675, 684.

51. A Study by a Committee of Southern Educators, "The Rating of Teachers," *American School Board Journal* 63 (November 1921), p. 45.

52. Franklin W. Johnson, "The Supervision of Instruction," *The School Review* 30 (December 1922), p. 745.

53. Leroy A. King, "The Present Status of Teacher Rating," *American School Board Journal* 70 (February 1920), pp. 44–46.

54. *National Conference on Educational Method*, "Educational Supervision: A Report of Current Views, Investigations, and Practices," First Yearbook (New York: Teachers College, Columbia University, 1928), pp. 176–77.

55. Willard S. Elsbree, *Teachers' Salaries* (New York: Bureau of Publications, Teachers College, Columbia University, 1931), p. 84.

56. J. W. Crabtree, "Rating of Teachers," *NEA Proceedings*, 1915, pp. 1165, 1167.

57. Ava L. Parrott, "Abolishing the Rating of Teachers," *NEA Proceedings* 1915, pp. 1168, 1170–73. Also see H. W. Nutt, "The Attitude of Teachers Toward Supervision," *Ohio State University Research Bulletin*, no. 3, (February 6, 1924), pp. 59–64; A. Temple, "Value of Supervision from the Standpoint of the Teacher," *Childhood Education* 12 (March 1928), pp. 315–17; Editorial, *Industrial Arts Magazine* 13 (February 1926), p. 60; and E. Wilson, "Can the 'Shun' be Taken Out of Supervision?" *Journal of Educational Method* 4 (May 1926), pp. 379–83.

58. Jesse H. Newlon, "Attitude of the Teacher toward Supervision," *NEA Proceedings,* 1923, p. 548. Also, see Charles H. Judd, "The Principal as a Supervisor of Classroom Teaching," *NEA Proceedings,* 1926.

59. H. C. Storm, "Three Elements of Effective Supervision," *American School Board Journal* 66 (May 1923), p. 58.

60. Angelo Patri, *A Schoolmaster of the Great City* (New York: Macmillan, 1921), pp. 29–30.

61. Editorial, *The American Teacher* (April 1912), p. 45.

62. *Fiftieth Annual Report,* Brooklyn Teachers Association, New York City Archives, Teachers College, Columbia University (September 1924), p. 105. Wayne Urban, a noted historian, posited that teachers, generally, opposed educational reform (centralization and increased supervision by "professionals") because "it threatened their economic well being and job security." Urban, "Organized Teachers and Educational Reform During the Progressive Era: 1890–1920," *History of Education Quarterly* 16 (Spring 1976), p. 50.

63. "Master and Servant," *The American Teacher* 2 (January 1913), p. 11.

64. Franklin J. Keller, "The Graces of Supervision," *American Teacher* 4 (May 1915), p. 78.

65. Abraham Lefkowitz, "The Product of Autocracy," *The American Teacher* 9 (September 1920), p. 135.

66. Sallie Hill, "Defects of Supervision and Constructive Suggestions Thereon," *National Educational Association Proceedings* 1918, p. 506. Also, see C. B. Stillman, "Democracy in Management of the Schools," *NEA Proceedings,* 1917; Fannie B. Hayes, "Supervision from the Point of View of the Teacher," *The School Review* 33 (March 1925), pp. 220–26; N. Rodriguez, "Attitudes of Teachers toward Supervision and a Constructive Program of Supervision" (Master's Thesis, Teachers College, Columbia University, 1928); and Carrie Koons, "Supervision of Teaching: Viewpoint of the Teacher," *Pennsylvania School Journal* (April 1920).

67. W. C. Bagley, "The Status of the Classroom Teacher," *NEA Proceedings,* 1918, p. 384. Also, see John Dewey, "Professional Spirit among Teachers," *The American Teacher* 4 (1915), pp. 115–16.

68. Many surveys indicate that supervisors wanted to improve instruction. See, for example, Melvin C. Hart, "Supervision from the Standpoint of the Supervised," *Education* 50 (February 1930), pp. 364–68.

69. J. S. Kinder, "A Rating Scale for Practice Teachers," *Education* 46 (October 1925), p. 108.

70. Frank McMurray, *Elementary School Standards* (Yonkers-on-Hudson, New York World Book Company, 1917), p. 131.

71. Orville Brim, "Reconstructing Our Concept of Scientific Supervision," *Education* 53 (June 1933), p. 586.

72. Romiett Stevens, "Stenographic Reports of High School Lessons," *Teachers College Record* 11 (September 1910), entire issue; Stevens, *The Question as a Measure of Efficiency in Classroom Practice* (New York: Contributions to Education, no. 48, Teachers College, Columbia University, 1912).

73. W. J. Hoetker and W. P. Ahlbrand, "The Persistence of the Recitation," *American Educational Research Journal* 6 (March 1969), p. 150.

74. See, for example, J. D. Brooks, "Learning to Quiz by Quizing," *Journal of Education* 115 (November 1932), pp. 630–32; N. E. Crout, "Art Lesson: A Stenographic Report of a Lesson," *Platoon School* 5 (December 1931), pp. 38–41; H. Halter, "Stenographic Report of a Junior High School Social Science Class," *Clearing House* 6 (December 1931), pp. 240–44; W. L. Matthews, "Super-

vising the Recitation by Lesson Analysis" (Master's thesis, George Peabody College, 1930; and M. N. Woodring, "The Use of Stenographic Records in Improving Instruction," *Teachers College Record,* 37 (March 1936), pp. 504–17.

75. John D. Rossman, "Economy in Supervision," *American School Board Journal* 68 (February 1924), pp. 39–40.

76. Walter D. Cocking, "The Stenographic Report as a Supervisory Instrument," *Peabody Journal of Education* 8 (November 1930), p. 139.

77. Stevens, "High School Lessons," p. 56.

78. Rossman, "Economy in Supervision," p. 40.

79. Interview with Professor Emeritus Florence H. Stratemeyer, Department of Education, Teachers College, Columbia University, December 1, 1976.

80. Many of these ideas regarding the distinctions between rating and stenographic reports were affirmed by Professor Stratemeyer in my interview with her in 1976.

Chapter 3. The Fall of Autocracy and the Emergence of Efficient, Cooperative, Democratic Methods and Scientific Supervision: The Supervisor's Dream

1. Ross L. Neagley and N. Dean Evans, *Handbook for Effective Supervision of Instruction* (Englewood Cliffs: N.J.: Prentice-Hall, 1980), p. 99.

2. Arthur Costa and Charles Guditus, "Do Districtwide Supervisors Make a Difference?" *Educational Leadership* (February 1984), p. 84.

3. Anonymous, "The Snoopervisor, the Whoopervisor and the Supervisor," *Playground and Recreation* 23 (December 1929), p. 558.

4. I am not equating professionalism with democracy. Indeed, physicians are anything but democratic in their deliberations with clients and subordinate medical workers. If I were to use the trait model of professionalism I might have missed the importance that democratic supervision played in the advancement of supervision as a profession. Analyzing supervision as an occupational group struggling to gain acceptance within the school bureaucracy indicates that supervisors, wanting to raise their status and gain recognition in schools, sought to align themselves with democratic principles of school management. In this sense, professionalism and democracy can be equated, at least, in discussing the history of supervision during the post-1920 era.

5. "The Opening Meeting of the National Conference," *The Journal of Educational Method* 1 (September 1921), pp. 38–39.

6. Editorial, "Supervision as a Profession," *The Journal of Educational Method* 1 (May 1922), p. 34.

7. "Opening Meeting of the National Conference," p. 38.

8. Editorial, "What's in a Name?" *The Journal of Educational Method* 1 (November 1921), p. 85.

9. Editorial, "Supervision as a Profession," p. 347.

10. W. G. Coburn, "Preparation of Supervisory and Administrative Officers," *NEA Proceedings,* 1919, p. 251.

11. J. M. Gwynn, "The Selection and Tenure of Office of Assistant Superintendents and Supervisors," *NEA Proceedings,* 1913, p. 303.

12. George C. Kyte, *Problems in School Supervision* (Boston: Houghton, 1931). The subjective approach to supervisory training is discussed in William

Penn Dyer, *Activities of the Elementary School Principal for the Improvement of Instruction: The Kind of Supervisory Program which a City Superintendent Should Set Up for His Elementary School Principals* (New York: Contributions to Education, no. 274, Teachers College, Columbia University, 1927); A. M. Clem and S. J. McLaughlin, "A Study of the Professionalization of the High School Principalship in Maine," *Educational Administration and Supervision* 13 (January 1927), pp. 1–12; and U.S. Office of Education, Bulletin, no. 18, "Preparation of Supervisors" (Washington, D.C.: U.S. Government Printing Office, 1937), pp. 44–45.

13. Ethel I. Salisbury, "Supervision," *American School Board Journal* 57 (October 1918), p. 22.

14. F. E. Bamberger, "Supervision: A Look Forward," *School and Society* 24 (December 18, 1926), p. 752.

15. Richard D. Allen, "Three Types of School Supervision," *Educational Method* 20 (May 1930), p. 479.

16. Fannie W. Dunn, "What Is Instructional Supervision?" *NEA Proceedings,* 1923, p. 764.

17. James Hosic, "The Democratization of Supervision," *School and Society* 11 (March 20, 1920), pp. 331, 333.

18. Orville G. Brim, "Changing and Conflicting Conceptions in Supervision," *Educational Method* 10 (December 1930), p. 132.

19. "Opening Meeting of the National Conference," p. 39.

20. C. W. Stone, "A School Report by a Modern Supervisor," *Educational Administration and Supervision* 2 (June 1916), p. 387.

21. W. E. Wiley, "Objective Methods in School Supervision," *American School Board Journal* 71 (October 1925), pp. 55–56. Also, see F. W. Ballou, "Progress in the Science of Education in the Last Twenty-Five Years," *NEA Proceedings,* p. 1925.

22. E. E. Oberholtzer, "The Next Step in School Supervision," *NEA Proceedings,* 1922, p. 1443.

23. Alvin S. Barr, *An Introduction to the Scientific Study of Classroom Supervision* (New York: Appleton, 1931), pp. x–xi. Also, see Barr, "Scientific Analyses of Teaching Procedures," *The Journal of Educational Method* 4 (May 1925), p. 361; Barr, "Science and Philosophy in Supervision," *Education* 53 (June 1933).

24. Ibid., pp. 1–26.

25. Barr, "Scientific Analyses of Teaching Procedures," pp. 360, 363. Also, see Barr, *Characteristic Differences in the Teaching Performance of Good and Poor Teachers of the Social Studies* (n.p., 1929); Barr and M. Rudisill, *An Annotated Bibliography on the Methodology of Scientific Research as Applied to Education* (Bureau of Educational Research, The University of Wisconsin, Bulletin, no. 13, 1931); W. H. Lancelot and Barr, *The Measurement of Teaching Efficiency* (New York: Macmillan, 1935); and Stephen M. Corey, "The Present State of Ignorance About Factors Effecting Teacher's Success," *Educational Administration and Supervision* 18 (October 1932), pp. 481–90.

26. Charles H. Judd, "The High School Manager," *National Association of Secondary School Principals,* 1920, pp. 30–31. Also, see D. E. Scates, "Judd and the Scientific Study of Education," *The School Review* 75 (Spring 1967), pp. 2–28.

27. E. E. Lewis, "Scientific School Supervision," *American School Board Journal* 16 (February 1923), pp. 43, 146.

28. William H. Burton, "Probable Next Steps in the Progress of Supervision," *Educational Method* 9 (April 1930), p. 404.

29. Florence E. Bamberger, "Supervision: Shared Responsibility," *The Elementary School Journal* 27 (October 1926), p. 115.

30. John T. Prince, *School Administration* (New York: C. W. Bardeen Publishers, 1906), p. 264.

31. Margaret Madden, "Some Problems of Method in Supervision," *The Journal of Educational Method* 1 (October 1921), p. 10.

32. Charles A. Wagner, "Supervision of Instruction: Why?" *American School Board Journal* 66 (February 1923), p. 35.

33. John M. Foote, "A State Program of Instructional Supervision," *NEA Proceedings,* 1922, p. 1150. Also, see B. E. Holmes, "The Supervision of Instruction," *Education* 47 (May 1927), pp. 556–68; and George A. Mirick, "Administration and Supervision," *The Elementary School Journal* 19 (December 1918).

34. NEA, Department of Superintendence, "The Superintendent Survey's Supervision," *Eighth Yearbook* (Washington, D.C.: NEA, 1930), pp. 14–15. Also, see Barr, *An Analysis of the Duties and Functions of Instructional Supervisors: A Study of the Detroit Supervisory Organization* (Bureau of Educational Research, no. 7, 1926).

35. See, for example, Fannie W. Dunn, "The Distinction between Administration and Supervision," *Educational Administration and Supervision* 6 (March 1920); and S. Stacks, "Supervisors Discuss Supervision in Its Distinction from Administration and Inspection," *School Life* 11 (January 1926), p. 94.

36. E. O. Melby, "Can We Be Creative in Supervision?" *Educational Method* (December 1932), p. 130.

37. Harold Spears, *Secondary Education in American Life* (New York: American Book, 1941), p. 320.

38. R. K. Keyes, "Vision and Supervision," *The Journal of Educational Method* 1 (November 1921), p. 348. Also, see W. L. Ettinger, "The American School Program from the Standpoint of the City," *School and Society* (August 4, 1923). "Supervision too long has meant narrow-visioned dictation and strait jacketed response, . . . supervision must be based on inspiring leadership," p. 139, and W. McClure, "Co-operative Effort in Supervision," *The Elementary School Journal* (December 1926), pp. 256–64.

39. H. D. Fillers, "Supervision," *American School Board Journal* 74 (February 1927), p. 44.

40. William T. Melchior, "Supervision versus Inspection," *Journal of Rural Education* 4 (May-June 1925), pp. 456, 458.

41. M. W. Sloyer, "Subject Supervision," *Education* 48 (April 1928), p. 478.

42. Mary D. Bradford, "The Democratic Trend in School Administration," *NEA Proceedings,* 1917, pp. 234–35. Also, see S. B. Vincent, "Democracy in Supervision," *Chicago Schools Journal* 1 (February 1919), pp. 3–6; G. L. Potter, "Democracy in Supervision," *California Journal of Elementary Education* 9 (May 1941), pp. 201–7; N. C. Kearney, "What Do You Mean—Democratic Administration?" *Secondary Education* 7 (November 1938, pp. 172–76; and O. H. Bimson, "Democracy in Administration," *Curriculum Journal* 12 (November 1940), pp. 321–23.

43. John Dewey, "Democracy in Education," *The Elementary School Teacher* 4 (December 1903), p. 193.

44. James F. Hosic, "The Democratization of Supervision," *School and Society* 11 (March 20, 1920), pp. 331, 333.

45. Ibid., pp. 333–36.

46. William H. Burton, "A New Definition of the Function of Supervision," *California Journal of Elementary Education* 6 (November 1937), pp. 84, 86.

47. David Snedden, "Combining Efficiency and Democracy in Educational Administration," *American School Board Journal* 42 (January 1911), pp. 3–4. Also, see Snedden, "Centralized vs. Localized Administration of Public Education," *Education* 30 (May 1910, pp. 536–49; and W. H. Allen, *Efficient Democracy* (New York: Dodd, 1907).

48. William A. Smith, "Dictatorship and Democracy in Education from Teacher's Viewpoint," *School and Society* 39 (May 12, 1934), p. 614. Also, see R. Bruce Raup, "Dictatorship or Cooperation," *NEA*, 1938, pp. 581–86.

49. National Conference of Supervisors and Directors of Instruction, "Current Problems of Supervisors: An Analysis of the Status of Supervision in American Public Schools," *Third Yearbook* (New York: Teachers College, Columbia University, 1930).

50. Jesse H. Newlon, *Educational Administration as Social Policy* (New York: 1934), pp. 188, 196.

51. S. A. Courtis, "Ideals in Supervision," *The Journal of Educational Method* 7 (May 1928), p. 339.

52. See Galen Saylor, "The Founding of the Association for Supervision and Curriculum Development" [1976] mimeographed, pp. 10–22.

53. Alvin S. Barr, William H. Burton, and L. J. Brueckner, *Supervision: Democratic Leadership in the Improvement of Learning* (New York: Appleton, 1938), p. 27.

54. Interestingly, there are recent proposals to effect precisely this dichotomy of functions in the role of school principal. For example, Sharon F. Rallis and Martha C. Highsmith argue that there are clearly two different tasks required of school principals. The first concerns school management, in which the principal is directly responsible for administrative concerns. The second task of a principal is to provide instructional and educational leadership. Rallis and Highsmith question the ability of any person to successfully perform both tasks. "We suspect that only someone with a split personality and the time of two people can perform both functions well. We suggest that the first realistic step in school improvement is to recognize that school management and instructional leadership are two separate tasks and cannot be performed by the same individual." See Rallis and Highsmith, "The Myth of the 'Great Principal': Questions of School Management and Instructional Leadership," *Phi Delta Kappan* (1986), p. 161.

55. F. C. Ayer and A. S. Barr, *Organization of Supervision* (New York: Appleton, 1928).

56. Similar problems were experienced by curriculum workers. See Decker F. Walker, "Straining to Lift Ourselves: A Critique of the Foundations of the Curriculum Field," *Curriculum Theory Network* 5 (1975), pp. 16–18.

Chapter 4. The Alliance between Supervisors and Curriculum Workers: The Quest for Professionalism Revisited

1. John Dewey, "Science as Subject-Matter and as Method," *Science* 31 (January 28, 1910), pp. 126–27.

2. Dewey, *Democracy and Education* (New York: Macmillan, 1916), pp. 223, 225, 228.

3. Dewey, *The Sources of a Science of Education* (New York: Liveright, 1929), pp. 7–10, 14–16, 42.

4. See Herbert M. Kliebard, *The Struggle for the American Curriculum: 1893–1958* (New York: Routledge & Kegan Paul, 1987).

5. See Mary L. Seguel, *The Curriculum Field: Its Formative Years* (New York: Teachers College Press, 1966); Daniel Tanner and Laurel Tanner, *Curriculum Development* (New York: Macmillan, 1975); Decker Walker, "The Curriculum Field in Formation: A Review of the 26th Yearbook of NSSE," *Curriculum Theory Network* 4 (1975), pp. 3–25; and Hollis L. Caswell, "Emergence of the Curriculum as a Field of Professional Work and Study," in H. F. Robison, ed., *Precedents and Promise in the Curriculum Field* (New York: Teachers College Press, 1966), pp. 1–21.

6. W. W. Charters, *Curriculum Construction* (New York: Macmillan, 1923), p. 169.

7. Henry Harap, *The Technique of Curriculum Making* (New York: Macmillan, 1928), pp. v, vi, 3.

8. "Curriculum Making: Past and Present," *Twenty-Sixth Yearbook of the National Society for the Study of Education,* part 1 (Bloomington, Ill.: Public School Publishing Company, 1926), pp. 425–27.

9. Both Seguel and Krug state that supervisors were threatened by the emergence of the curriculum worker. There is little evidence that I find to support this bold assertion. Rather, supervisors realized that by making curriculum an important concern, the possibilities for professional development would be strengthened. Supervisors did not feel threatened. While the emergence of the curriculum specialty did create some confusion and uneasiness, the supervisor did accommodate himself rather well to this new function. See Seguel, *The Curriculum Field,* pp. 159–60; and Edward A. Krug, *The Shaping of the American High School, Volume 2, 1920–1941* (Madison: University of Wisconsin Press, 1972), p. 163.

10. Stuart A. Courtis, "Curriculum Construction at Detroit," *Twenty-Sixth Yearbook of the National Society for the Study of Education,* part 1 (1933), pp. 189, 194, 203.

11. Jesse H. Newlon and A. L. Threlkeld, "The Denver Curriculum-Revision Program," *Twenty-Sixth Yearbook of the National Society for the Study of Education,* part 1 (1933), pp. 229, 240. Also, see Newlon, "Outcomes of the Curriculum Program," *NEA Proceedings,* 1925.

12. Newlon, "Reorganizing City School Supervision," *The Journal of Educational Method* 2 (June 1923), pp. 406, 410–11. Also, see Newlon, "The Administration of the Curriculum," *Educational Method* 12 (May 1933), pp. 474–80; and Gary L. Peltier, "Teacher Participation in Curriculum Revision: An Historical Case Study," *History of Education Quarterly* 8 (Summary 1967), pp. 209–19.

13. Threlkeld, "The Place of Curriculum Construction in the Supervisory Program," National Conference on Educational Method, "Educational Supervision," *First Yearbook* (New York: Teachers College, Columbia University, 1928), pp. 216–18. Also, see Threlkeld, "Curriculum Revision: How a Particular City May Attack the Problem," *The Elementary School Journal* 25 (April 1925).

14. Editorial, "Full Sail Ahead," *The Journal of Educational Method* 8 (April 1929), p. 372.

15. A. H. Horrall, "The Supervisor's Function in Relation to Curriculum Making," *California Journal of Elementary Education* 2 (August 1933), pp. 150–53.

16. Gordon N. MacKenzie, "Supervision Confronts a Changing Curriculum," *California Journal of Elementary Education* 5 (February 1937), pp. 136, 142–43. Also, see J. A. Clement, "Supervision of Instruction and Curriculum Making in Secondary Schools as Complementary Processes," *Educational Administration and Supervision* 13 (March 1927), pp. 170–77.

17. Helen Heffernan and William H. Burton, "Adjusting Theory and Practice in Supervision," *Educational Method* 18 (April 1939), p. 328.

18. Henry Harap, "Annual Report of the Executive Secretary," *Curriculum Journal* (February 1937), p. 70.

19. Dorothy Heubauer, "The Curriculum Approach to Supervision," *Curriculum Journal* 10 (March 1939), p. 132.

20. Hollis L. Caswell, "The Function of the Curriculum Director," *Curriculum Journal* 9 (October 1938), p. 246. Also, see A. A. Douglas, "The Teacher, The Expert and Curriculum Improvement," *Curriculum Journal* 8 (November 1937), pp. 305–9.

21. Caswell, "How Shall Supervision Be Advanced?" *Educational Method* 21 (October 1941), pp. 7–8.

22. Society for Curriculum Study, "News Bulletin" 3 (March 25, 1932), p. 1.

23. Ibid., 6 (1935).

24. Ibid., 5 (January 12, 1934), p. 16.

25. Ibid.

26. Galen Saylor, "The Founding of the Association for Supervision and Curriculum Development" [1976], mimeographed, p. 10.

27. Ibid., p. 13.

28. Joint Committee on Curriculum of the Department of Supervisors and Directors of Instruction and the Society for Curriculum Study, *The Changing Curriculum* (New York, 1937), p. v.

29. Ibid., pp. vii, 54, 331.

30. J. Paul Leonard, Reviews, The Joint Committee on Curriculum, *Curriculum Journal* 8 (December 1937), pp. 373–74.

31. Saylor, "The Founding of the Association for Supervision and Curriculum Development," pp. 21–22, from a personal letter to Saylor dated March 3, 1967.

32. Interview with Alice Miel, Professor Emeritus of Education, Teachers College, Columbia University, November 18, 1976.

33. Editorial, "Hail and Farewell," *Curriculum Journal* 14 (May 1943), p 193. Also, see "Program of the Department of Supervision and Curriculum Development," *Educational Method* 22 (May 1943), pp. 344–53.

Epilogue

1. For discussions of bureaucracy and professionalism in general see, for example, Myron Lieberman, *Education as a Profession* (Englewood Cliffs, N.J.: Prentice-Hall, 1956); Morris L. Cogan, "Toward a Definition of Profession," *Harvard Educational Review* 23 (Winter 1953), pp. 33–50; Corrine Lathrop Gilb, *Hidden Hierarchies: The Professions and Government* (New York: Harper, 1966); Gerald E. Markowitz and David Karl Rosner, "Doctors in Crisis: A Study of

the Use of Medical Education Reform to Establish Modern Professional Elitism in Medicine," *American Quarterly* 25 (March 1973), pp. 83–107; Daniel H. Calhoun, *Professional Lives in America* (Cambridge: Harvard University Press, 1965); and Walter Doyle, "Education for All: The Triumph of Professionalism," in O. L. Davis, Jr., ed., *Perspectives on Curriculum Development, 1776–1976* (1976 Yearbook of the ASCD (Washington, D.C.: ASCD, 1976).

2. Interview with Alice Miel, Professor Emeritus of Education, Teachers College, Columbia University, New York, November 18, 1976.

3. Joyce Cooper and Miel, eds., "Personal Experiences with Supervision: Excerpts From Professional Diaries," n.p., Spring 1948, (mimeographed).

4. For a discussion of this idea as it relates to supervision see, for example, Gerald R. Firth and Keith P. Eiken, "Impact of the Schools' Bureaucratic Structure on Supervision," in Thomas J. Sergiovanni, ed., *Supervision of Teaching* (1982 Yearbook of the ASCD, 1982). Also, see K. F. Punch, "Interschool Variation in Bureaucratization," *The Journal of Educational Administration* 7 (October 1970), pp. 124–34.

5. Ibid.

6. Decker Walker, "Straining to Lift Ourselves," *Curriculum Theory Network* 5 (1975), p. 17.

7. Stephen T. Kerr, "Teacher Specialization and the Growth of a Bureaucratic Profession," Teachers College Report (Spring 1983), p. 645.

8. See "Announcement of Merger," *Curriculum Journal* 12 (December 1942), p. 337.

9. Ruth Cunningham, "Merger Now Complete," *Educational Method* 22 (April 1943), p. 336.

10. "Program of the Department of Supervision and Curriculum Development," *Curriculum Journal* 13 (May 1943), p. 197; *Educational Method* 12 (May 1943), pp. 344–53.

11. H. Ruth Henderson, "A Message from the President," *Educational Leadership* 1 (October 1943), p. 39.

12. Galen Saylor, "The Founding of the Association for Supervision and Curriculum Development" (mimeographed) (1976), p. 27.

13. Virgil M. Rogers, "Who Is Supervisor?" *Educational Leadership* 2 (January 1945), p. 152.

14. G. Franklin Sloyer, "Trouble-Shooter and Eye-Opener," *Educational Leadership* 2 (January 1945), p. 158.

15. Mildred E. Swearingen, "Looking at Supervision," *Educational Leadership* 3 (January 1946), p. 150.

16. Gordon N. Mackenzie, "Role of the Supervisor," *Educational Leadership* 19 (November 1961), p. 86. Also, see W. H. Lucio and J. D. McNeil, *Supervision: A Synthesis of Thought and Action* (New York: McGraw-Hill, 1962), and Ronald C. Doll, *Curriculum Development: Decision-Making and Process* (Boston: Allyn, 1964).

17. J. Harlan Shores, Foreword, in R. P. Wahle, ed., *Toward Professional Maturity of Supervisors and Curriculum Workers* (Washington, D.C.: ASCD, 1967), p. v. For studies in role confusion see N. J. Vigilante, "A Role Perception Study of Elementary Principals and Elementary Supervisors in the State of Ohio" (Ph.D dissertation, Columbus, Ohio State University, 1964); and Richard F. Neville, "The Supervisory Function of the Elementary School Principal as Perceived by Teachers" (Ph.D. dissertation, University of Connecticut, 1963).

18. Wiles, *Supervision for Better Schools,* pp. 4–5. Confusion continues to

this very day. Educators are presently seeking to arrive at a precise definition of supervision. See, for example, Francis S. Bolin, "On Defining Supervision," *Journal of Curriculum and Supervision* 2 (1987), pp. 368–80.

19. Chester Babcock, "The Emerging Role of the Curriculum Leader," in Robert R. Leeper, ed., *Role of Supervisor and Curriculum Director in a Climate of Change* (Washington, D.C.: ASCD, 1975), p. vii.

20. Glenys G. Unruh, Foreword, in Thomas J. Sergiovanni, ed., *Professional Supervision for Professional Teachers,* (Washington, D.C.: ASCD, 1975), p. vii.

21. See William H. Burton and Leo J. Brueckner, *Supervision: A Social Process* (New York: Appleton, 1955); H. R. Douglass, R. K. Bent, and C. W. Boardman, *Democratic Supervision in Secondary Schools* (Boston: Houghton, 1961); Hilda Taba, *Curriculum Development: Theory and Practice* (New York: Harcourt, 1962); and Margaret Williamson, *Supervision: Principles and Methods* (New York: Woman's Press, 1950).

22. ASCD, *Better than Rating: New Approaches to Appraisal of Teaching Services* (a pamphlet prepared by the Commission of Teacher Evaluation of the ASCD, NEA, 1950), p. 8.

23. Alvin S. Barr, "Teaching Efficiency," *Encyclopedia of Educational Research* (1941), pp. 1280–81.

24. Douglass, Bent, and Boardman, *Democratic Supervision in Secondary Schools,* p. 80.

25. Wiles, *Supervision for Better Schools,* chapter 12.

26. Arthur J. Lewis and Alice Miel, *Supervision for Improved Instruction: New Challenges, New Responses* (Belmont, Calif.: Wadsworth Publishing Company, 1972), p. 43.

27. For example, a perusal of the *Education Index* evidences the lack of research dealing with school supervision. Sources on supervision were frequently listed under curriculum headings.

28. Robert J. Krajewski, "Putting the 'S' Back in ASCD," *Educational Leadership* 33 (February 1976), p. 376.

29. Harold D. Drummond, Foreword, in Leeper, *Role of Supervisor and Curriculum,* Louise M. Berman and Mary Lou Usery, eds., *Personalized Supervision: Sources as Insights* (Washington, D.C.: ASCD, 1966), p. v.

30. Galen Saylor, Foreword, in Louise M. Berman and Mary Lou Usery, eds., *Personalized Supervision: Sources and Insights* (Washington, D.C.: ASCD, 1966), p. v.

31. J. Harlan Shores, Foreword, in *Supervision: Perspectives and Propositions,* p. v.

32. William Van Til, "In a Climate of Change, in Leeper, *Role of Supervisor and Curriculum Director,* p. 16.

33. David S. Seeley, *Education through Partnership* (Washington, D.C.: American Enterprise Institute for Public Policy Research, 1985), p. 211.

34. James B. Macdonald, "Helping Teachers Change," in James Raths and Leeper, eds., *The Supervisor: Agent for Change in Teaching* (Washington, D.C.: ASCD, 1966), p. 2.

35. Thomas A. Shaheen, "A Choice: Bureaucracy or Curriculum Renaissance?" *Educational Leadership* 31 (March 1974), pp. 494–95.

36. Michael B. Katz, *Class, Bureaucracy, and Schools: The Illusion of Educational Change in America* (New York: Praeger, 1971), p. 135.

37. Max G. Abbott, "Hierarchical Impediments to Innovation in Educational

Organizations," in Fred C. Carver and Thomas J. Sergiovanni, eds. *Organizations and Human Behavior*, (New York: Mcgraw-Hill, 1969), p. 49.

38. Warren G. Bennis, "Changing Organizations," in Warren G. Bennis, Kenneth D. Benne, and Robert Chin, eds., *The Planning of Change* (New York: Holt, 1969), p. 579.

39. John E. Chubb, "To Revive Schools, Dump Bureaucracies," *New York Times*, (December 9, 1988), p. A35.

40. Lewis and Miel, *Supervision for Improved Instruction*, p. 68.

41. William H. Whyte, "Creativity vs. Organizational Life," *Educational Leadership* 13 (October 1956), p. 15.

42. See, for example, Lucio and McNeil, *Supervision*.

43. Earl S. Johnson, "The Human Dimensions of Supervision," in Robert R. Leeper, ed., *Supervision: An Emerging Profession*, (Washington, D.C.: ASCO, 1969) p. 8.

44. Klohr, "Looking Ahead in a Climate of Change," in Leeper, *Role of Supervisor and Curriculum Director*, p. 144.

45. Arthur Blumberg, *Supervisors and Teachers: A Private Cold War* (Berkeley, Calif.: McCutchan Publishing Company, 1974), p. 35.

46. Shirley Markowitz, "The Dilemma of Authority in Supervisory Behavior," *Educational Leadership* 33 (February 1976), p. 367.

47. Robert J. Alfonso, Gerald R. Firth, and Richard F. Neville, *Instructional Supervision* (Boston: Allyn and Bacon, 1975), p. 342.

48. Fred T. Wilhelms, Introduction, in *Supervision: Emerging Profession*, p. x.

49. Markowitz, "Dilemma of Authority in Supervisory Behavior," p. 372.

50. Herbert A. Shepard, "Changing Relationships in Organizations," in James G. March, ed., *Handbook of Organizations* (Chicago: Rand McNally, 1965), pp. 1141–42.

51. Blumberg, *Supervisors and Teachers*.

52. Ray C. Rist, in an observational study, has described the relationships between the "caste system" of the classroom and the "caste system" of society. See Rist, "Student Social Class and Teacher Expectations: The Self-Fulfilling Prophesy in Ghetto Education," *Harvard Educational Review* 50 (August 1970), pp. 411–51. Also, see Philip Jackson, *Life in Classrooms* (New York: Holt, 1968).

Bibliographical Essay

According to *Curriculum Leaders: Improving Their Influence* (Washington, D.C.: ASCD, 1976, p. 13), "A definitive history of educational supervision has not been published." To be sure, there is ample published documentary material relating to many aspects of public school supervision in the United States. Unfortunately, one must concur with the statement just quoted, which indicates the lack of historical inquiry into "educational supervision." Perusal of any text on supervision and some curriculum books should give the researcher a broad overview of the history of public school supervision. However, much of this history is sketchy, general, and, at times, inaccurate. The best general study on supervision was undertaken in 1961 by Henry W. Button, under the sponsorship of Raymond Callahan at Washington University. Button, "A History of Supervision in the Public Schools, 1870–1950" (Ph.D. dissertation, Washington University, 1961).

Button's study suffers from two basic flaws. The first deals with the treatment of the history of supervision in terms of periods. The writing of public school supervision cannot be undertaken by merely describing its development through periodization; that is, specific periods tied within specific time frames. The historical trends occurring in supervision are frequently contradictory and confusing. It is not possible, for example, to state that scientific supervision began during such and such a time and was immediately followed by democratic supervision. Rather, to obtain a more realistic view, these events must be viewed as trends occurring concurrently. Therefore, the notions of scientific, philosophical, cooperative, democratic, creative, authoritarian, and effective supervision, as a totality, expressed the trend in school supervision across the country during, at least, the twenties and thirties. A second major flaw of the Button study centers on the author's neglect of curriculum as a valuable source into supervisory procedures in the early twentieth century. Button stated that "the functions of supervision and of developing curriculum seem to have followed separate paths, so disparate as to make the consideration of both in a single study exceedingly cumbersome. . . . For present purposes the individual in the school system is not engaged in supervision when he is considering the curriculum" (p. 3). The fact of the matter is that individuals in school systems, called supervisors, were engaged in curriculum matters. To overlook this fact is to negate a valuable source into supervisory practice. The researcher can glean important information on supervisory practice by examining cities such as Denver, where curriculum revision was occurring.

Some other notable works, which only tangentially study school supervision, are Raymond Callahan, *Education and the Cult of Efficiency* (Chicago: University of Chicago Press, 1962); David Tyack and Elisabeth Hansot, *Managers of Virtue: Public School Leadership in America, 1820–1980* (New York: Basic, 1982); and Roald F. Campbell; Thomas Fleming, L. Jackson Newell; and John W. Bennion, *A History of Thought and Practice in Educational Administration*

(New York: Teachers College Press, 1987). Few historians have addressed supervision apart from administration.

Other historians have attempted to analyze supervision historically. However, these studies do not serve to further our knowledge of supervision to a higher level of sophistication. Rather, certain studies, such as A. Arrington, "An Historical Analysis of the Development of Supervision in the Public Schools in the United States from 1870 to 1970" (Ph.D. dissertation, George Washington University, 1972), were repetitive and in some instances identical to the Button study.

To reiterate, due to the lack of historical inquiry into supervision, studies that have been done, including my own, out of necessity tend to be general treatments. A number of studies are sorely needed on a wide range of topics dealing with public school supervision in the United States.

This book is essentially based on a dissertation entitled "Bureaucracy and Professionalism: An Historical Interpretation of Public School Supervision in the United States, 1875–1937" (Ed.D. dissertation, Teachers College, Columbia University, 1977). It is by no means a comprehensive treatment of the subject. Rather, the writer envisions the attempt as one effort to raise our historical awareness to certain critical issues in the field. It is also hoped that the interested reader will join in the provocative venture of exploring, historically, school supervision in the United States. See Jeffrey Glanz, "Ahistoricism and School Supervision," *Educational Leadership* 2 (November 1977), 149–54, where I urge historians to investigate supervision more closely.

The purpose of the remainder of this bibliographical note is to highlight the relevant sources used in this study, to briefly indicate further gaps in our knowledge of public school supervision, and to provide additional information and bibliographical material.

I

This study would not be possible if not for the numerous journals, manuscripts, proceedings, and other recorded sources. The following periodicals and journals were most helpful in the study of school supervision:

American Institute of Instruction 1831–1908
American School Board Journal 1891–1949
American Teacher 1912–49
Curriculum Journal (News Bulletins and Journal) 1931–43
Education 1880–1948
Educational Administration and Supervision 1915–60
Educational Leadership 1943–76
Educational Method 1921–43
Educational Review 1891–1928
Elementary School Journal 1900–1946
Elementary School Teacher volumes 2–14 of *ESJ* called *EST*
Journal of Education 1875–1949
National Education Association 1871–1940
National Teacher 1870–75
School Review 1893–1949

School and Society 1915–72
Teachers College Record 1900–1976

Other journals contained articles dealing with school supervision, intermittently. Some of these include:

Atlantic Monthly
California Journal of Elementary Education
Chicago School Journal
Education Research Bulletin
Forum
High School Quarterly
Industrial Arts Magazine
Journal of Educational Research
Journal of Experimental Research
Journal of Rural Education
Nation's Schools
Nebraska Education Journal
Ohio Schools
Playground and Recreation
Primary Education
School Life
Secondary Education

A variety of publications and yearbooks also provided essential information:

Department of Elementary School Principals (organized in 1922)
National Associations of Secondary School Principals (Yearbooks 1–4, 1917–20)
National Conference on Educational Method (organized in 1921, in 1928 became National Conference of Supervisors and Directors of Instruction, became NEA department in 1929, and became Department of Supervisors and Directors of Instruction)
The National Herbart Society for the Scientific Study of Teaching (1895 *First Yearbook*, in 1902 became the National Society for the Study of Education and in 1910 it dropped "Scientific" to become the NSSE)
The National Society for the Study of Education (NSSE)
Society for Curriculum Study (founded in 1929, originally called the Society for Curriculum Specialists, Four Yearbooks, 1935, 1937, 1937, and 1938, merged with the Department of Supervisors and Directors of Instruction in 1943 and became, initially, the Department of Supervision and Curriculum Development, then, the Association for Supervision and Curriculum Development)

Although not extensively cited in the study, several other sources proved useful in the study of public school supervision. Some of these sources included state and local documents; proceedings, manuals, and journals of boards of education; state education department reports; Annual Reports of the U.S. Commissioner of Education; Annual Reports of Superintendents, Assistant Superintendents, Principals, and Supervisors; U.S. Bureau of Education, Circulars of Information; and other miscellaneous public school reports across the country. Additionally, while archival and other types of correspondence need to be explored pertaining to public school supervision, the following materials may serve as a worthwhile beginning: the Nicholas Murray Butler Papers in the Manuscript Room at Butler Library, Columbia University, and the Teachers College Library Archives (New York City school system).

Specifically, the following documents proved helpful as well:

American Diaries (W. Mathews)
Bibliography of American Autobiographies (Louis Kaplan)
A Cyclopedia of Education (New York: Macmillan, 1911)
Davis, Sheldon E. *Educational Periodicals during the Nineteenth Century* (Bureau of Education, no. 28, 1919)
Dictionary of American Biography (New York 1928–43, 1944–73)
Educational Resources Information Center—*Office of Education Research Reports*
Encyclopedia of Educational Research (New York: Macmillan, 1969)
Education in the States: Historical Development and Outlook (Washington, D.C.: NEA of the United States, 1969)
Education index
Index to the Reports of the Commissioner of Education 1867–1907 (Bulletin, no. 7, 1909)
International Index to Periodicals (1907–15)
Leaders in Education (1932)
List of Publications of the U.S. Bureau of Education (Bulletin, no. 2, 1908)
Mott, F. L. *A History of American Magazines, 1885–1905* (Cambridge: Harvard University Press, 1968)
National Cyclopedia of American Biography (New York, 1982–)
Reader's Guide to Periodical Literature
U.S. Bureau of the Census, *Statistical Abstracts of the U.S.* (Washington, D.C., 1878–)
U.S. Bureau of the Census, *Historical Statistics of the U.S.: Colonial Times to 1970*, part 1, 360–88 (Washington, D.C.: U.S. Department of Commerce, 1975)
U.S. Office of Education, *Biennial Survey of Education*

II

In a strange sort of way, this study opens more questions than it answers. The gaps in our knowledge of school supervision are vast. First, we need to know more about how supervision was conducted in various cities throughout the country. For example, were there supervisors in Portland, Oregon? If so, who were these people and what duties did they perform? How was supervision, in general, conducted in the Portland school system between 1900 and 1920, for example?

Second, we need educational biographies of various personages, such as W. H. Payne, J. D. Philbrick, A. S. Draper, J. M. Rice, E. E. White, J. F. Bobbitt, A. S. Barr, W. H. Burton, and C. H. Judd.

Third, a number of organizations are in dire need of study, such as the American Federation of Teachers, the National Conference on Educational Method, the Society for Curriculum Study, and the Association for Supervision and Curriculum Development. For example, an in-depth study is sorely needed into the merger between the Department of Supervisors and Directors of Instruction, and the Society for Curriculum Study. For background information on the teacher organization known as the American Federation of Teachers, see Wayne Urban, "Organized Teachers and Educational Reform during the Progressive Era," *History of Education Quarterly* 16 (Spring 1976), pp. 35–52, "The AFT at 60: Maturity, Vitality, Vision," *The American Teacher* 61 (September 1976); Aileen W. Robinson, *A Critical Evaluation of the American Federation of Teachers* (Chicago: AFT, 1935), Commission on Educational Reconstruction, *Organizing the Teaching Profession: The Story of the AFT* (Glencoe: Free Press, 1955); William E. Eaton, *The AFT, 1916–1961: A History of the Movement* (Illinois: Southern Illinois University Press, 1974); and Wayne J. Urban, *Why Teachers Organized* (Detroit: Wayne State University Press, 1982). For background information on the National Conference on Educational Method and the Society for Curriculum Study, see Galen Saylor, "The Founding of the Association for Supervision and Curriculum Development" [1976] (mimeographed); also, see M. Mugan, "Aims and Purposes of the Department of Supervisors and Directors of Instruction," *NEA Proceedings* (1929), 805–6; J. F. Hosic, "A Balanced Program in Supervision," *NEA Proceedings* (1929), 815–19, and Mary L. Seguel, *The Curriculum Field: Its Formative Years* (New York: Teachers College Press, 1966), pp. 156–58. Also see *ASCD in Retrospect: Contributions to the History of the ASCD,* W. V. Til, Editor, ASCD, 1986.

Fourth, various aspects of school supervision warrant further investigation. Some topics include the origins and early development of public school supervision, the origins and duties of special supervisors, general supervisors, principals and assistant superintendents, scientific supervision, teachers' reactions to supervisors, rating procedures used by supervisors, supervision in the social efficiency era, and the relationship between supervision and curriculum, and supervision and administration. Additionally, we need to know more about the persistence of the bureaucratic form of school organization. Bureaucracy, in varying degrees, has characterized the American public school system from the 1840s to the present. We need to know how different generations of educators dealt with this bureaucratic phenomenon, what alternatives, if any, were available, and why certain people under different circumstances were able to circumvent the bureaucracy.

Fifth, our knowledge of supervision as a function would be greatly enhanced by examining supervision in various institutional settings, such as private schools and industrial plants.

Additionally, the number of sources into supervisory practice has not been fully tapped. We need to find relevant primary sources that might include diaries of school supervisors, oral histories, surveys, letters, and other kinds of personal correspondence and, of course, other public documents.

III

PART ONE

The period in the late nineteenth century, with which this part of the study dealt, was a time, in our history, during which a number of important societal transformations occurred. For an explanation of the influence of the frontier, see Ray A. Billington, *Westward Expansion: A History of the American Fron-*

tier (New York: Macmillan, 1967); and Fredrick Jackson Turner, *The Frontier in American History* (New York: Holt, 1920). For an explanation of urban growth, see B. McKelvey, *The Urbanization of America, 1860–1915* (New Brunswick, N.J.: Rutgers University Press, 1963). For an explanation of the growth of industry, see Samuel P. Hays, *The Response to Industrialism, 1855–1914* (Chicago: University of Chicago Press, 1957); Allan Nevins, *The Emergence of Modern America, 1865–1878* New York: Macmillan, 1927); and Ida Tarbell, *The Nationalizing of Business, 1878–1898* (New York: Macmillan, 1898). For an explanation of agriculture, see Fred A. Shannon, *The Farmer's Last Frontier: Agriculture, 1860–1897* (New York/Toronto, Farrar, and Rinehart, 1945). For the growth of cities, see W. T. Harris, "The General Government and Public Education Throughout the Country," *NEA Proceedings,* (1890), 481–99; A. F. Weber, "Growth of Cities in the Nineteenth Century," *Municipal Affairs* 3 (1899), 534–61; and A. M. Schlesinger Sr., *The Rise of the City, 1878–1898* (New York: Macmillan, 1933). For an explanation of the changes in the economic status of the country, see Robert Bremner, *From the Depths: The Discoveryn of Poverty in the United States* (New York: NYU Press, 1956; Ellwood P. Cubberley, *Public Education in the United States* (New York: Houghton, 1934); Arthur Mann, *Yankee Reformers in the Urban Age* (Cambridge: Belknap Press of Harvard University Press, 1954); and Arthur M. Schlessinger, *The Rise of the City, 1878–1898* (New York: Macmillan, 1933).

These transformations frequently were interpreted as signs of progress. The philosophical rationale for this program was expressed by one of the leading proponents of the evolutionary ideas of Charles Darwin and Herbert Spencer, John Fiske. Fiske advocated the survival of the fittest of those "pacific communities," which would inevitably rule over the inferior races of the world, thereby "rendering warfare illegal all over the globe." See Fiske, "Manifest Destiny," *Harper's New Monthly Magazine* (1885), pp. 578–90. For alternative views concerning these philosophical doctrines, see Edward Bellamy, *Looking Backward, 2000–1887* (New York: Houghton, 1926, first published 1888), Henry George, *Progress and Poverty: An Inquiry into the Cause of Industrial Depressions and of Increase of Want with Increase of Wealth . . . the Remedy* (New York: Doubleday and McClure Company, 1899), Henry Demarest Lloyd, *Wealth Against Commonwealth* (New York: Harper, 1899), and Lester Ward, *The Psychic Factors of Civilization* (New York: Johnson Reprint Corporation, 1970 [originally published in 1893]).

Undeniably, progress affected almost every aspect of American society. For an explanation of developments occurring in education and schooling, in particular, see Nicholas M. Butler, *Education in the United States* (New York: J. Blyon Company, 1900); Nicholas M. Butler, *Monographs on Education in the United States* (Washington, D.C., 1900); Lawrence A. Cremen, "The Curriculum Maker and His Critics: A Persistent American Problem," in M. D. Alcorn and J. M. Linley, eds., *Issues in Curriculum Development: A Book of Readings* (Yonkers-on-Hudson: World Book Company, 1959); Lawrence A. Cremen, *The Transformation of the School: Progressivism in American Education, 1876–1957* (New York: Knopf, 1961); Andrew S. Draper, "The General Government and Popular Education," *NEA Proceedings,* (1896), 201–8; Samuel T. Dutton and David Snedden, *The Administration of Public Education in the United States* (New York: Macmillan, 1922); Neil McCluskey, *Public Schools and Moral Education: The Influence of Horace Mann, William Torrey Harris and John Dewey* (New York: Columbia University Press, 1958); Rush Welter, *Popular Education and Democratic Thought in America* (New York: Columbia University Press, 1962); and Merle Curti, *The Social Ideas of American Educators* (New York: Scribner, 1935).

The late nineteenth century was also an era of virulent criticism. See Louis Filler, *Crusades for American Liberalism* (Yellow Springs, Ohio: Antioch Press, 1950); Frank Norris, *The Octopus* (New York: Wessels Company, 1901); C. C. Regier, *The Era of the Muckrakers* (Chapel Hill: University of North Carolina Press, 1932); Upton Sinclair, *The Jungle* (Cambridge: R. Bentley, 1971, 1946); Lincoln Steffens, *The Shame of the Cities* (New York: Hill and Wang, 1957, 1904); and Ida Tarbell, *The History of the Standard Oil Company* (New York: Macmillan, 1925, 1904).

This study described the criticism leveled by Joseph M. Rice in the 1890s. Rice's proclamations regarding the American school system received much stricture, particularly among the cities that were characterized by Rice as "deplorable." The *Education* journal ran a series of articles attacking Rice's extensive study between May 1894 and February 1895. However, much of this criticism focused on personal offensives toward Rice, rather than actually denying the conditions that Rice found as inaccurate or misleading. Rice's suggestions to put education on a scientific basis, likewise, did not find wide popularity in the nineteenth century. It is interesting, though, to compare Herbartians, such as McMurray, with Rice's views concerning scientific notions in education. Rice's pronouncements, about ten years after his extensive study was published, had little effect. He still clamored that "good schools would be found not to exceed one-third of the total number of schools." His emphasis on securing results within the school organization was soundly disregarded. See Rice, "Need for a New Basis of Supervision," *Forum* 35 (April 1904), 590–609. It should be noted that accountability, setting up standards, and securing results to augment school efficiency has been a topic of concern along a continuum from N. A. Calkins, "School Supervision," *Education* 2 (May 1882), 498–99, E. E. White, *School Management* (1894). He stated, "The most helpful supervision does not dictate or prescribe details; but it asks for *results,* and then so instructs, inspires, and guides teachers, that they freely put their best thought and effort into whatever they do. This means professional progress." p. 52), to Rice, of course, and then Bobbitt. To be sure, there were those who misunderstood Rice, for example, J. L. Pickard, "City Systems of Management of Public Schools," *NEA Proceedings* (1894), who thought that the superintendent should be "responsible only for results" (p. 78). This wholly disregarded Rice's ideas concerning method. Rice's theme, albeit lamentably misunderstood, concisely stated that the schools could be made more efficient through school supervision where the superintendent would instruct and guide the teachers in the science of education, and hold them responsible for results. Unfortunately, this was a theme that had succumbed to organizational demands.

This period, in the nineteenth century, also was important to the development of the school superintendency. In the nineteenth century, urbanization, population growths, and the general increasing complexity of the school system illustrated the need for superintendency offices. In this context, the superintendent was perceived as a vital position within the schools. For general background information into the development of the superintendency, see Thomas M. Gilland, *The Origin and Development of the Power and Duties of the City School Superintendent* (Chicago: University of Chicago Press, 1935); Theodore L. Reller, *The Development of the City Superintendency of Schools in the*

United States (Philadelphia: The Author, 1935), Daniel E. Griffiths, *The School Superintendent* (New York: Center for Applied Research in Education, 1966); Willard S. Elsbree, *The American Teacher: Evolution of a Profession in a Democracy* (New York: American Book, 1939); and David B. Tyack, "Pilgrim's Progress: Toward a Social History of the School Superintendency, 1860–1960," *History of Education Quarterly* 16 (Fall 1976), pp. 257–300. Although the superintendency arose as a functional position in the schools, the authority of the superintendent was limited and lacked clear definition. A struggle ensued between the superintendent and the school boards to control policy in public education. While this study was not directly concerned with this vital matter, it did recognize this conflict as an important factor in the development of school supervision. Supervision, during this struggle, became an important tool by which the superintendent would legitimize his existence in the school system. For an excellent account of this struggle, that eventuated in victory for the superintendent, whereby the schools were separated from partisan politics, school boards were reduced in size, and "superintendents were gradually given the power to hire teachers, and select textbooks and control the educational program generally," see Raymond E. Callahan, *The Superintendent of Schools: An Historical Analysis* (Bethesda, Md.: ERIC Document Reproduction Service, 1967). Also see, for example, Carl F. Kaestle, *Pillars of the Republic: Common Schools and American Society, 1780–1960* (New York: Hill and Wang, 1983); David Tyack, *The One Best System* (Cambridge: Harvard University Press, 1974); Selwyn Troen, *The Public and the Schools: Shaping the St. Louis System, 1838–1920* (Columbia: University of Missouri Press, 1975); and Paul E. Peterson, *The Politics of School Reform, 1870–1940* (Chicago: University of Chicago Press, 1985).

That supervision was inextricably entwined with the superintendency has been well documented, see S. T. Dutton and D. Snedden, *The Administration of Public Education in the United States* (New York: Macmillan, 1922, "The supervision of instruction is, of course, the most essential part of the work of a school superintendent." p. 300); J. L. Pickard, *School Supervision* (New York: Appleton, 1890. "Professional supervision was provided by a superintendent, devoting his entire time to the supervision of the work of his teachers." p. 18), C. A. Babcock, "What Is the True Function or Essence of Supervision?" *NEA Proceedings* (1896), 242–47, Forty-third Annual Report of the Board of Education of St. Louis, Report of the Superintendent (1898), p. 21; and J. G. Allen, "The Supervisory Work of Principals," *School Review* 1 (1893), 291–96. Historically, supervision was undertaken by the clergy through school inspections and frequent visitations. See W. S. Elsbree, *The American Teacher* (New York: American Book, 1939, pp. 71–80). Gilland stated that often when the superintendent was performing the supervisory function, "a duty which ranked high in frequency of mention was that of visiting the schools." See Gilland, *The Origin and Development of the Power and Duties of the City School Superintendent* (Chicago: University of Chicago Press, 1935, p. 267). Philbrick stated that "merely looking on and seeing teachers teach is not the supervision of instruction which is to be expected of a principal." See *Annual Report of the School Committee of Boston, Report of the Superintendent of Public Schools* (1877, p. 201). For an excellent study explicating the control function of supervision in the early days of Massachusetts, see H. Suzzalo, *The Rise of Local School Supervision in Massachusetts* (New York: Teachers College, Columbia University, 1906). On supervision to increase teacher efficiency, see John W. Cook,

"How Can the Superintendent Improve the Efficiency of the Teachers Under His Charge?" *NEA Proceedings* (1800), 276–87; R. J. Cunningham, "The Relations of a City Superintendent to His Teachers," *American School Board Journal* 42 (May 1911); J. M. Greenwood, "What Shall Be Done with Non-Progressive and Retrogressive Teachers?" *NEA Proceedings* (1894), 383–87; W. T. Harris, "How to Make Good Teachers Out of Poor Ones?" *NEA Proceedings* (1899), 310–14; and F. L. Soldan, "Efficient and Inefficient Teachers," *NEA Proceedings* (1899), 298–306.

To many, during the late nineteenth century, school supervision and the superintendency were highly professionalized. The idea was to put professional people in control over schools. See Aaron Gove, "The Trail of the Superintendent," *NEA Proceedings* (1900), 214–22; M. A. Newell, "School Superintendence as a Profession," *NEA Proceedings* (1886), 200–14; and Charles F. Thwing, "A New Profession," *Educational Review* 15 (January 1898), 65–69. According to some observers, the superintendent never reached his ideal of "educational expert," in fact, in some states he "actually retrogressed." See W. E. Chancellor, "Where Are the Leaders?" *Educational Review* 38 (November 1909), p. 410.

The shift in control of public schooling into the hands of the superintendent meant standardization, reorganization, and consolidation of power. The systematization of urban education, in the nineteenth century, resulted in a school bureaucracy. For excellent studies on early bureaucratic tendencies, see William A. Bullough, *Cities and Schools in the Gilded Age* (New York: Kennikat Press, 1974); C. F. Kaestle, *The Evolution of an Urban School System: New York City, 1750–1850* (Cambridge: Harvard University Press, 1973); M. B. Katz, "The Emergence of Bureaucracy in Urban Education: The Boston Case 1850–84," *History of Education Quarterly,* 8 (Summer 1968 and Fall 1968), 155–88, 319–57; E. M. Lazerson, *Origins of the Urban School: Public Education in Massachusetts, 1870–1915* (Cambridge: Harvard University Press, 1971); J. W. Meyer, D. Tyack; J. Nagel; and A. Gordon, "Public Education as Nation-Builders in America: Enrollments and Bureaucratization in the American States, 1870–1930," *American Journal of Sociology* 85: (1979), 591–613; and R. Wiebe, *The Search for Order 1877–1920* (New York: Hill and Wang, 1967).

Centralization of authority in the late nineteenth century enabled school people to standardize, bureaucratize, and control school operations. According to W. A. Bullough, *Cities and Schools in the Gilded Age* (New York: Kennikat Press, 1974), pp. 50–51, by the late 1890s cities, such as Baltimore, Cincinnati, Cleveland, Milwaukee, St. Louis, San Francisco, and Denver, which "became even more bureaucratic" under the direction of Aaron Gove, were centralized. New York City schools became centralized in 1896, as a result of a difficult struggle. Nicholas Murray Butler and William Henry Maxwell were prime movers of this new public school reform. See Diane Ravitch, *The Great School Wars: New York City 1805–1973* (New York: Basic, 1974); and Richard Whittemore, *Nicholas Murray Butler and Public Education, 1862–1911* (New York: Teachers College Press, 1970, chapter 6). Interestingly, in a letter written to William Torey Harris, Butler described the passage of the bill abolishing ward boards and local control in New York City as follows:

> Our New York school bill has passed after a most terrific fight with the forces of darkness. We have now removed the administrative obstacles to improvement in the schools. If improvements do not take place, we can hold the Board of Education and the Superintendent directly responsible. Heretofore, no body could be held responsible because of the complexity of the system.

See Butler to Harris, April 9, 1896, (Nicholas Murray Butler Papers, Special MS Collection, Columbia University); see also Sol Cohen, *Progressives and Urban School Reform* (New York: Teachers College Press, 1963), Joseph M. Cronin, *The Control of Urban Schools: Perspective on the Power of Educational Reformers* (New York: Free Press, 1973); Leonard Ayres, *School Organization and Administration* (Cleveland, Ohio: The Survey Committee of the Cleveland Foundation, 1916); Otis W. Caldwell and Stuart A. Courtis, *Then and Now in Education: 1845, 1923* (Yonkers-on-Hudson: World Book Company, pp. 127–33 for an example of Detroit's "strong centralized control democratically administered."), Herbert Shapiro, "Reorganizations of the New York City Public School System, 1890–1910" (Ph.D. dissertation, Yeshiva University, 1967); David C. Hammack, "The Centralization of New York Public School System, 1896: A Social Analysis of the Decision" (Master's thesis, Columbia University, 1969); A. P. Marble, "The School System of Greater New York," *American Institute of Instruction*, (1901), pp. 80–87; and D. B. Tyack, "City Schools" Centralization of Control at the Turn of the Century," pp. 57–72, in Jerry Israel, ed., *Building the Organizational Society* (New York: Free Press, 1972). Also, for a definition of centralization, see S. T. Dutton and D. Snedden, *The Administration of Public Education in the United States* (New York: Macmillan, 1922), p. 97. "Centralization in educational and other forms of administration means roughly the removal of authority and responsibility from local and popular sources to those more centralized and remote."

PART TWO

The period in the early twentieth century, with which this part of the study dealt, was a time in our history during which the country underwent significant change. For an explanation of the emergence of America as a world power, see Foster Rhea Dulles, *America's Rise to World Power, 1898–1954* (New York: Harper, 1955), Frank B. Freidel, *The Splendid Little War* (Boston: Little, Brown, 1958); John D. Hicks, *The Populist Revolt: A History of the Farmers' Alliance and the People's Party* (Minneapolis: University of Minnesota Press, 1931); Alfred Thayer Mahan, *Lessons of the War with Spain and Other Articles* (Boston: Little, Brown, 1899); and Albert K. Weinberg, *Manifest Destiny: A Study of Nationalistic Expansion in American History* (Gloucester, Mass.: Johns Hopkins University Press, 1935). For other developments occurring within this post-1900 period, see E. H. Buehrig, *Woodrow Wilson and Balance of Power* (Bloomington, Ill.: Indiana University Press, 1955, bibliographical references pp. 277–319), Josephus Daniels, *The Wilson Era: Years of Peace 1910–1917* (Chapel Hill: University of North Carolina Press, 1946); C. C. Tansill, *American Goes to War* (Boston: Little, Brown, 1938); Howard K. Beale, *Theodore Roosevelt and the Rise of America to World Power* (Baltimore, Md.: John Hopkins Press University, 1956); John D. Hicks, *Rehearsal for Disaster: The Boom and Collapse 1919–1920* (Gainsville: University of Florida Press, 1961); William E. Leuchtenburg, *The Perils of Prosperity: 1914–1932* (Chapel Hill: University of North Carolina Press, 1958); B. Mitchell, *Depression Decade: from New Era Through New Deal 1929–1941* (New York: Macmillan, 1948); H. G. Warran, *Herbert Hoover and the Great Depression* (New York: Oxford University Press, 1959); and John Steinbeck, *The Grapes of Wrath* (New York: Viking, 1939).

The history of supervision, during this period, is best understood in terms of how progressive reformers sought to deal with the problems of education and schooling, in particular. See chapter 3 in L. Cremin, *The Transformation of the School* (New York: Knopf, 1961), for a good examination of how progressives sought to solve the problems of the industrial revolution through education. For a general overview of the "progressive movement," see Daniel Aaron, *Men of Good Hope: A Story of American Progressives* (New York: Oxford University Press, 1951); Harold Underwood Faulkner, *The Quest for Social Justice 1898–1914* (New York: Macmillan, 1931); Louis Filler, *Crusaders for American Liberalism* (Yellow Springs, Ohio: Antioch Press, 1950); Samuel P. Hays, *The Response to Industrialism, 1855–1914* (Chicago: University of Chicago Press, 1957); Richard Hofstader, *The Age of Reform* (New York: Vintage Books, 1955); G. Kolko, *The Triumph of Conservatism: A Re-interpretation of American History, 1900–1916* (New York: Free Press of Glencoe, 1963); George E. Mowry, *The Era of Theodore Roosevelt, 1900–1912* (New York: Haprer, 1958); and C. C. Regier, *The Era of the Muckrakers* (Chapel Hill: University of North Carolina Press, 1932). For a detailed listing of references pertaining to progressivism in education, see L. Cremin, *The Transformation of the School* (New York: Knopf, 1961), Bibliographical Notes, pp. 355–87. For different perspectives on progressive education, see Sol Cohen, *Progressives and Urban School Reform: The Public Education Association of New York City, 1895–1954* (New York: Bureau of Publications, Teachers College, Columbia University, 1964), Patricia A. Graham, *Progressive Education: From Arcady to Academe: A History of the Progressive Education Association, 1919–1955* (New York: Teachers College Press, 1967); Colin Greer, *The Great School Legend: A Revisionist Interpretation of American Public Education* (New York: Basic, 1972); and Rush Welter, *Popular Education and Democratic Thought in America* (New York: Columbia University Press, 1962). For an insight into Theodore Roosevelt, see G. W. Chessman, *Governor Theodore Roosevelt: The Albany Apprenticeship, 1898–1900* (Cambridge: Harvard University Press, 1965); George E. Mowry, *Theodore Roosevelt and the Progressive Movements* (Madison: University of Wisconsin Press, 1947); and Henry F. Pringle, *Theodore Roosevelt: A Biography* (New York: Harcourt, 1931).

The distinction between education and schooling has been a topic of concern for educators. This distinction, however, was blurred during the early twentieth century. While Cremin's influential thesis concerning the position that education should "bear in mind the total education of the public and the many agencies that carry it on" is valid and has far-reaching implications for the history of education in the United States, it should be noted that at the turn of the century and highlighted in the years to follow, the church, the family, and other related educative institutions played a secondary role to the vast network of schools. See Cremin, *The Genius of American Education* (New York: Vintage Books, 1965), p. 14; and Cremin, *American Education: The Colonial Experience, 1607–1783* (New York: Harper, 1970); this book presented a different perspective where schooling played a rather insignificant role as compared to other "educative institutions" in Cremin's "configuration," such as the church and the printing press.

Many social ills beset early twentieth-century America. Progressive educators turned to the schools for relief. Undoubtedly, no single individual characterized the tenets of progressive education better than John Dewey. For Dewey, the schools were the primary agency to counteract the effects of industrialism. The schools, according to Dewey, would best serve the ideals of democracy. See Dewey, *Democracy and Education* (New York: Macmillan, 1916). For a discussion of the emphasis of schooling by progressive leaders, such as Jane Addams and Robert Hunder, see Allan F. Davis, *Spearheads for Reform: The Social Settlements and the Progressive Movement, 1890–1914* (New York: Oxford University Press, 1967). For a discussion of the role of the school in the twentieth century, see Sol Cohen, "The Elementary School in the Twentieth Century: A Social Context," in John I. Goodland and Harold Shane, eds., *The Seventy-Second Yearbook of the National Society for the Study of Education,* part 2 (Chicago; University of Chicago Press, 1973). While educators saw the schools as an important agency to elevate society, others envisioned the school as a means of social control; see Charles A. Ellwood, *The Psychology of Human Society* (New York: Appleton, 1925); and Charles C. Peters, *Objectives and Procedures in Civic Education* (New York: Longmans, Green, and Company, 1930).

Undoubtedly, educators, with their belief in schooling, envisioned that *progress* would be the watchword for the new century. Indeed, the schools entered the new century with the promise of unprecedented progress, best evidenced by statistical data. See *Historical Statistics of the United States: Colonial Times to 1970* (part 1, Washington, D.C.: U.S. Department of Commerce, Bureau of the Census, 1975, especially pp. 360–88); also see any statistical abstract of education from 1920 to the present and/or the U.S. Office of Education—Biennial Survey of Education and/or Annual Reports of the Commissioner of Education. On compulsory education, See David Tyack, "Ways of Seeing: An Essay of the History of Compulsory Schooling," *Harvard Educational Review* 46 (August 1976), 355–89. For a comprehensive detailed volume, combining statistics and history, on the progress of each state, see *Education in the States: Historical Development and Outlook* (Washington, D.C.: NEA of the U.S., 1969). For descriptions of the progress made in education, see N. M. Butler, ed., *Education in the United States* (New York: J. Blyon Company, 1900), Editorial, *The Journal of Educational Method* 3 (MAY 1924), 359–60; I. L. Kandel, ed., *Twenty-Five Years of American Education* (New York: Macmillan, 1929); J. H. Newlon, "The Educational Outlook at the End of the First Quarter of the Twentieth Century," *NEA Proceedings* (1925), 657–63; G. D. Strayer, "Progress in the Administration and Support of Schools During the First Quarter of the Twentieth Century," *NEA Proceedings* (1925), 17–22; and A. E. Winship, "Five Decades of Progress," *NEA Proceedings* (1920), 422–24. The reformer had much to be hopeful about. Harvard graduate and president of Western University, Charles F. Thwing, writing in 1898, was quite optimistic concerning the emergence of the "new profession," the school superintendency. The struggle between the superintendent and school boards to gain control over the schools ended on a dubious note at the turn of the century. Indeed, politics was removed from the schools, and superintendents were given the authority to hire teachers and to work out the intricacies of the course of study; however, as Callahan explained, the superintendency was still "vulnerable." Still, educators were content with the standardization of the urban schools. Hays notes that bureaucratization was a general process permeating American society during the building of the "new organization society." Progress was the vision. See Charles F. Thwing, "A New Profession," *Educational Review* 15 January (1898), 26–33; Raymonde E. Callahan, *The Superintendent of Schools: An Historical Analysis* (Bethesda, Md.: ERIC Document Reproduction Service, 1967), p. 140; and Samuel P. Hays, "The

New Organizational Society," in Jerry Israel ed., *Building the Organizational Society: Essays on Associational Activities in Modern America* (New York: Free Press, 1972), pp. 1–15.

Clearly, progress was envisioned by increasing bureaucratic control over schooling. The situation regarding the course of study at the turn of the century provides a good case in point regarding the growing bureaucratization in schools. John Dewey, in an insightful probing essay in 1901, decried the "mechanical features" of schoolwork, such as the organization of courses, arrangement of grades, the "machinery by which the course of study is made and laid out," and in general the instructional process. "Unification, organization, harmony is the demand of every aspect of life," said Dewey; it is no different in education. He believed the mandates of "school organization and administration," in effect, were at cross-purposes with the "educational side." As a result, posited Dewey, children were dealt with "*en masse*, . . . led in flocks, if not hordes, make it necessary to give the stress of attention to those studies in which some sort of definite result can be most successfully attained." Dewey attacked the way courses of study were determined. "The fact that this is fixed by the board of education, superintendent, or supervisor, by a power outside the teacher" is lamentable and all together useless. The teacher, Dewey contended, must be given a definite, authoritative position in shaping the course of study. One further example, in this context, of the standardization as exemplified by the course of study was Dewey's warning that "to enact that at a given date all the grades of a certain city shall have nature study is to invite confusion and distraction." The reader should consult this wonderful statement saturated with revealing notions of the "current" practice regarding the course of study. See Dewey, "The Situation as Regards the Course of Study" *Educational Review* 22 (June 1901), 26–49.

Educators were not able to provide viable alternatives to the bureaucratization of urban education. Dewey readily saw the problems wrought by industrialization for education. In *School and Society* he said:

> One can hardly believe there has been a revolution in all history so rapid, so extensive, so complete . . . population is hurriedly gathered into cities from the ends of the earth; habits of living are altered with startling abruptness and thoroughness; . . . Even our moral and religious ideas and interests, the most conservative because the deepest-lying things in our nature, are profoundly affected. That this revolution should not affect education in other than formal and superficial fashion is inconceivable.

While contending that the effects of industrialism had to be confronted, Dewey and his generation eschewed efforts that would have, perhaps, alleviated some of the problems. The methods and techniques used to resolve this important value-conflict between change and stability, we believe, were wholly inadequate. Even in his laboratory school at the University of Chicago, which lasted for seven years, Dewey never confronted the problems of the vast network of institutionalization and bureaucratization that were steadily obtaining hold in American society. Tyack stated that "progressives might protest against the regimentation . . . but the effects of rigid bureaucratization could not easily be erased by reading *Democracy and Education*." In chapter 1 it was explained that the conflict was between authority and freedom, and the former, of course, prevailed. In the twentieth century, supervisors were confronted by a similar dilemma, albeit in a slightly different form. The supervisor was unable or unwilling to confront the matter and, therefore, authority and bureaucracy became pervasive. Interestingly, in his last public work, Dewey alluded to this dilemma; he said that "this authoritarian principle in education . . . will never be effectively eradicated as long as the traditional notion prevails that the qualities of ideas are inherent essences." The "foundations of a democratic society" will be destroyed, concluded Dewey, if the "educational regimen" (bureaucracy) persisted. See Dewey, *The School and Society* (Chicago: University of Chicago Press, 1899), p. 22; K. C. Mayhew and A. C. Edwards, *The Dewey School* (New York: Appleton, 1936); David B. Tyack, "Bureaucracy and the Common School: The Example of Portland Oregon, 1851–1913," *American Quarterly* 19 (Fall 1967), 497–98; Dewey, "Introduction to the Use of Resources in Education by R. E. Clapp," in M. S. Dworkin, *Dewey on Education* (New York: Teachers College Press, 1959, p. 133), and Francis A. Ianni, ed., *Conflict and Change in Education* (Glenview, Ill.: Scott, Foresman, 1975), pp. 1–103.

Bureaucratic modes of operation flourished, especially in the schools, during the early twentieth century. The desire for an efficient, bureaucratic organization gained considerable attention. *Efficiency* was the key word. A perusal of any journal, for example, the NEA, will provide evidence of this fact. See Franklin Bobbitt, "The Elimination of Waste in Education," *The Elementary School Teacher* (February 1912), pp. 259–71; J. F. Hosic, "Waste in Education," *NEA Proceedings* (1916), pp. 648–52; F. E. Spaulding, "The Application of the Principles of Scientific Management," *NEA Proceedings*, (1913), p. 259; G. D. Strayer, "By What Standards and Tests Shall the Efficiency of a School or System of Schools Be Measured?" *NEA Proceedings* (1912), pp. 560–64; D. A. Anderson, "The Efficiency Expert in Education," *Educational Administration and Supervision* (October 1916), pp. 77–82; L. M. Crabbs, *Measuring Efficiency in Supervision and Teaching* (Contributions to Education, no. 175, New York: Teachers College, Columbia University, 1925); W. H. Maxwell, "How to Determine the Efficiency of a School or a School System?" *Journal of Education* 81 (January 21, 1915), p. 63; and David Snedden, "Increasing the Efficiency of Education," *Journal of Education* 88 (July 17, 1913), pp. 62–63; see Raymond E. Callahan, *Education and the Cult of Efficiency* (Chicago: University of Chicago Press, 1962). It seems to this writer that the attempt by schools, administrators, supervisors, and other educators to gain acceptance in the academic community through emulation of scientific procedures of business management was a significant weakness mirroring the immaturity of the field at the time. Indeed, other historians pointed out that administrative and supervisory actions and decisions were not made on educational basis, but as a conciliatory effort to placate critics. See Edward Krug, *The Shaping of the American High School, 1880–1920* (Madison: University of Wisconsin Press, 1964); Herbert M. Kliebard, "Bureaucracy and Curriculum Theory," in Vernon Haubrich, ed., *Freedom, Bureaucracy, and Schooling* (Washington, D.C.: ASCD, 1971); Sydney Spiegal, "The Hidden History of Educational Administration in the United States," *Changing Education* 5 (Fall 1973), pp. 6–13; and Charles R. Kelley, "Toward an Interpretation of the New Movement of 1915 in Educational Administration" (Ph.D. dissertation, Teachers College, Columbia University, 1961); curiously, Kelley maintained that Callahan's position was indefensible and polemical rather than historical. Kelley proposed that school administrators did not capitulate to the business-industrial ideologies, as Callahan said, but, rather, administrators "imposed" their ideas on the schools. Regardless of the position, the fact remained that American schoolmen became actively engrossed with efficiency engineering in industry, translated into scientific management in schools. It should be pointed out that scientific use in education, at least from within the time frame of this study, can be traced from the Herbartarians to Rice to Thorndike and Judd. See the work done by Judd and Dearborn in reading, Rice and Wallin in spelling, Stone and Courtis in arithmetic, Elliott and Cubberley in school finance, and Thorndike and Ayres in elimination of waste, and so forth. Also, see J. E. Russell, "The Scientific Movement in Education," *NEA Proceedings* (1926), pp. 719–30; E. F. Buckner, "Education as a Scientific Pursuit," *Education* 24 (November 1903), pp. 129–47; and Samuel B. Sinclair, *The Possibility of a Science in Education* (Chicago: University of Chicago Press, 1903).

Teacher efficiency was a concern for the nineteenth-century supervisor. In the twentieth century, teacher efficiency took an unprecedented vitality. The measurement of teacher efficiency was done by rating procedures. Rating was indeed widespread. See L. A. King, "The Present Status of Teacher Rating," *American School Board Journal* 70 (February 1920), pp. 44–46, 154, 157, in this study, it was reported that 76 percent of the schools in the survey had some form of plan for rating. C. W. Knudson and S. Stephens, "An Analysis of Fifty-Seven Devices of Rating Teachers," *Peabody Journal of Education* 9 (July 1931), 15–24; and A. Riddle, "Report of the Committee of One Hundred on Classroom Teachers Problems-Teacher Rating," *NEA Proceedings* (1925), pp. 200–15. Putting rating on a scientific and objective basis received wide attention. C. Alexander of George Peabody College for Teachers asked: "Haven't we reached a stage where every superintendent who claims to be efficient and up-to-date ought seriously ask himself this question: 'What use of standard tests and scales have I made in my supervision during the past year?' " See Carter Alexander, "Standard Tests as an Aid in Supervision," *American School Board Journal* 54 (January 1917), p. 69; and J. A. Nietz, "Tests and Scales as Aids to the Supervisor," *American School Board Journal* 62 (February 1921), pp. 47–48. The use of rating scales have frequently been allied with teachers' salaries. Often, these schemes had provisions allowing "for 50 percent of the teacher's rating to be determined by the teacher and the remaining half by the school authorities." See R. G. Jones, "Rating of Teachers," *American School Board Journal* 50 (January 1915), p. 17. In the Appendix, we have reproduced one such scale. Teachers protested against the use of these scales tied to salary. For teacher criticism due to salary problems, see H. W. Button, "A History of Supervision in Public Schools, 1870–1950" (Ph.D. dissertation, Washington University, 1961), pp. 188–91; W. S. Elsbree, *Teachers' Salaries* (New York: Teachers College, Columbia University, 1931), chapters 2, 5, 9); J. McKeen Cattell, "The Salaries of Teachers and the Cost of Living," *School and Society* 7 (1918); and Department of Classroom Teachers, *NEA Proceedings* (1928), p. 351.

PARTS ONE AND TWO: BUREAUCRACY AND PROFESSIONALISM

Finally, two basic concepts or processes were integral to this study: bureaucracy and professionalism. Other writers have studied these two phenomena. This study did not refer, specifically, to these studies; however, the reader may find valuable insights into bureaucracy and professionalism by consulting these sources. On bureaucracy Hans Gerth and W. W. Mills, *From Max Weber: Essays in Sociology* (New York: Oxford, V. P. Galaxy, 1958) represents an excellent overview of the work of the famous social scientist, Max Weber. Weber's classical treatment of bureaucracy served as an "ideal type" or model from which other writers could examine and test the elements of bureaucracy. Several studies of bureaucracy include Reinhard Bendix, "Bureaucracy: The Problem and Its Setting," *American Sociological Review* 12 (1947), pp. 493–503; Peter M. Blau, *The Dynamics of Bureaucracy: A Study of Interpersonal Relations in Two Government Agencies*, (Chicago: University of Chicago Press, 1969); Blau and Marshall W. Meyer, *Bureaucracy in Modern Society* (New York: Random, 1956); John W. Crider, *The Bureaucrat* (New York: Lippincott, 1944); Michel Crozier, *The Bureaucratic Phenomenon* (Chicago: University of Chicago Press, 1964); S. N. Eisenstadt, "Bureaucracy and Bureaucratization," *Current Sociology* 12 (1958), 99–163; Alvin W. Gouldner, *Patterns of Industrial Bureaucracy: A Case Study of Modern Factory Administration* (New York: Free Press, 1954); Richard H. Hall, "An Empirical Study of Bureaucratic Dimensions and Their Relations to Other Organizations Characteristics" (Ph.D. dissertation, Ohio State University, 1961); Robert K. Merton, "Bureaucratic Structure and Personality," *Social Forces* 18 (1940), pp. 560–68; Gerald H. Moeller, "The Relationship between Bureaucracy in School Systems' Organization and Teachers' Sense of Power" (Ph.D. dissertation, Washington University, 1962); Victor A. Thompson, *Bureaucracy and Innovation* (Alabama: University of Alabama Press, 1969); and Stanley H. Udy, Jr., " 'Bureaucracy' and 'Rationality' in Weber's Organizational Theory: An Empirical Study," *American Sociological Review* 24 (1959), pp. 791–95. Very much related to the study of bureaucracy is discussion of the school organization. On the study of organizations see Chris Argyris, "The Individual and Organization: Some Problems of Mutual Adjustment," *Administrative Science Quarterly* 2 (1951), pp. 1–24; Charles E. Bidwell, "The School as a Formal Organization," in James G. March, ed., *Handbook of Organizations* (Chicago: Rand McNally, 1965); Peter M. Blau and Richard W. Scott, *Formal Organizations* (San Francisco: Chandler Publishing Company, 1962); Amitai Etzioni, *Modern Organization* (Englewood Cliffs, N.J.: Prentice-Hall, 1964); Robert L. Kahn, et al., *Organizational Stress: Studies in Role Conflict and Ambiguity* (New York: Wiley, 1964); James G. March and Herbert A. Simon, *Organizations* (New York: Wiley, 1958); Nicos P. Mouzeles, *Organization and Bureaucracy: An Analysis of Modern Theories* (Chicago: Aldine, 1969); R. L. Peabody, *Organizational Authority* (New York: Atherton Press, 1964); and William H. Whyte, *The Organization Man* (New York: Simon, 1955), represent important works. James G. Anderson, *Bureaucracy in Education* (Baltimore: John Hopkins University Press, 1968), the best general analysis, demonstrates the persistence of bureaucracy as the dominant form of organization in schools. Harry L. Gracey, *Curriculum or Craftmanship: Elementary School Teachers in a Bureaucratic System* (Chicago: University of Chicago Press, 1972) represents an excellent study, from a sociological perspective, explicating the effects of bureaucracy on teachers and other school functionaries, in a specific school system. Two important studies on educational bureaucracy from an historical perspective are Michael B. Katz, *Class, Bureaucracy, and Schools: The Illusion of Educational Change in America* (New York: Praeger, 1973); and David B. Tyack, *The One Best System: A History of American Education* (Cambridge: Harvard University Press, 1974). Also, see, for example, B. Brennan, "Principals as Bureaucrats," *The Journal of Educational Administration* 11 (October 1973), pp. 171–78; M. Gosine and M. V. Keith, "Bureaucracy, Teacher Personality Needs and Teacher Satisfaction," *The Canadian Administrator* 10 (1970), pp. 1–5; E. M. Hanot, "The Modern Educational Bureaucracy and the Process of Change," *Educational Administration*

Quarterly 11 (Autumn 1975), pp. 21–36; G. B. Isherwood and W. K. Hoy, "Bureaucratic Structure Reconsidered," *The Journal of Experimental Education* 41 (May 1973), 47–50; G. B. Isherwood and W. K. Hoy, "Bureaucracy, Powerlessness, and Teacher Work Values," *The Journal of Educational Administration* 11 (May 1973), pp. 124–38; G. H. Moeller, "Bureaucracy and Teachers' Sense of Power," *School Review* 72 (Summer 1964), pp. 137–57; K. F. Punch, "Bureaucratic Structure in Schools: Toward Redefinition and Measurement," *Educational Administration Quarterly* 5 (Spring 1969), pp. 43–57; and D. A. Sousa and W. K. Hoy, "Bureaucratic Structure in Schools: A Refinement and Synthesis in Measurement," *Educational Administration Quarterly* 17 (Fall 1981), pp. 21–39.

The most useful discussions of professionalism include Morris L. Cogan, "Toward a Definition of a Profession," *Harvard Educational Review* 23 (Winter 1953), pp. 33–50; Ronald Corwin, "Professional Persons in Public Organizations," *Educational Administrative Quarterly* 1 (1965), pp. 1–22; Walter Doyle, "A Professional Model for the Authority of the Teacher in the Educational Enterprise" (Ph.D. dissertation, University of Notre Dame, 1967); Arthur W. Foshay, ed., *The Professional as Educator* (New York: Teachers College Press, 1970); Eliot Freidson, *Profession of Medicine: A Study of the Sociology of Applied Knowledge* (New York: Dodd, 1970); Corinne L. Gilb, *Hidden Hierarchies: The Professions and Government* (New York: Harper, 1966); Myron Lieberman, *Education as a Profession* (Englewood Cliffs, N.J.: Prentice-Hall, 1956); R. L. Reid, "The Professionalization of Public School Teachers: The Chicago Experience, 1895–1920" (Ph.D. dissertation, North-Western University, 1968); T. M. Stinnett, *Professional Problems of Teachers* (New York: Macmillan, 1968); and Howard M. Vollmer and Donald L. Mills, eds., *Professionalization* (Englewood Cliffs, N.J.: Prentice-Hall, 1966); M. J. Austin, *Professionals and Paraprofessionals* (New York: Human Sciences, 1978); and more recently, Andrew Abbott, *The System of Professions: An Essay on the Division of Expert Labor* (Chicago: University of Chicago Press, 1988). The following studies are representative of the attempt to explore the relationship between professionalism and bureaucracy, in other words, professional membership within a bureaucratic organization: Peter M. Blau and Richard W. Scott, *Formal Organizations: A Corporative Approach* (San Francisco: Chandler Company, 1962); Ronald G. Corwin, *A Sociology of Education: Emerging Patterns of Class, Status and Power in the Public Schools* (New York: Appleton, 1965); V. F. Dempsey, "An Assessment of Conflict Between Bureaucracy and Professionalization in a School System" (Ph.D. dissertation, New York University, 1969), Richard H. Hall, "Professionalization and Bureaucratization," *American Sociological Review* 33 (February 1968), pp. 92–104; N. Robinson, "A Study of the Professional Role Orientation of Teachers and Principals and Their Relationships to Bureaucratic Characteristics of School Organizations" (Ph.D. dissertation, University of Alberta, 1967); Richard W. Scott, "A Case Study of Professional Workers in a Bureaucratic Setting" (Ph.D. dissertation, University of Chicago, 1961); S. W. Warren, "Striking Teachers: Professionalism and Bureaucracy" (Ph.D. dissertation, Teachers College, Columbia University, 1974); and G. D. Wood, "The Bureaucratic-Professional Role Orientations of the Public School Teacher as Perceived by Teachers and Principals" (Ph.D. dissertation, North Carolina State University at Raleigh, 1971).

Bibliography

Supervision: Works Published Before 1940

Alberty, H. B., and Thayer, V. T. *Supervision in the Secondary School.* New York: D.C. Heath and Company, 1931.

Anderson, C. J.; Barr, A. S.; and Bush, M. G. *Visiting the Teacher at Work: Case Studies of Directed Teaching.* New York: D. Appleton and Company, 1925.

Ayer, F. C., and Barr, A. C. *Organization of Supervision.* New York: D. Appleton and Company, 1928.

Barr, A. S. *An Analysis of the Duties and Functions of Instructional Supervisors: A Study of the Detroit Supervisory Organization.* Bureau of Educational Research Bulletin, no. 7, Madison: University of Wisconsin, 1926.

———. *An Introduction to the Scientific Study of Classroom Supervision.* New York: D. Appleton and Company, 1931.

———. *Characteristic Differences in the Teaching Performance of Good and Poor Teachers of the Social Studies.* Bloomington, Ill.: Public School Publishing Company, 1929.

———, and Rudiseill, M. *An Annotated Bibliography on the Methodology of Scientific Research as Applied to Education.* Bureau of Educational Research Bulletin, no. 13, Madison: University of Wisconsin, 1931.

———, and Burton, W. H. *The Supervision of Instruction: A General Volume.* New York: D. Appleton-Century Company, 1926.

———; Burton, W. H.; and Brueckner, L. J. *Supervision: Democratic Leadership in the Improvement of Learning.* New York: D. Appleton-Century Company, 1938.

Bobbitt, Franklin. "Some General Principles of Management Applied to the Problems of City School Systems." *Twelfth Yearbook of the National Society for the Study of Education,* part 1, The Supervision of City Schools. Chicago: University of Chicago Press, 1913.

Boyce, Arthur C. "Methods for Measuring Teachers Efficiency." *Fourteenth Yearbook of the National Society for the Study of Education,* part 2. Chicago: University of Chicago Press, 1915.

Burton, William E. *Supervision and the Improvement of Teaching.* New York: D. Appleton and Company, 1922.

Chancellor, William E. *Our City Schools: Their Direction and Management.* Boston: D.C. Heath & Company, 1908.

———. *Our Schools: Their Administration and Supervision.* Boston: D.C. Heath and Company, 1904.

Clement, J. A., and Clement, J. H. *Co-operative Supervision in Grades Seven to Twelve.* New York: Century Company, 1930.

Collings, Ellsworth. *School Supervision: Theory and Practice*. New York: Century Company, 1927.

———. *Supervisory Guidance of Teachers in Secondary Schools*. New York: Macmillan Company, 1934.

Cubberley, Ellwood P. *Principal and His School*. Boston: Macmillan Company, 1923.

———. *Public School Administration*. Boston: Houghton Mifflin Company, 1916.

Dotterer, J. B. "An Experiment in Supervision." Master's thesis, Columbia University, 1926.

Douglass, Harl R., and Boardman, Charles W. *Supervision in Secondary Schools*. Boston: Houghton Mifflin Company, 1934.

Draper, A. S. *The Supervision of Country Schools*. New York: C. W. Bardeen, 1904.

Dyer, William Penn. *Activities of the Elementary School Principal for the Improvement of Instruction: The Kind of Supervisory Program which a City Superintendent Should Set Up for His Elementary School Principals*. New York: Bureau of Publications, Teachers College, 1927.

Elliott, Charles H. "Types of Supervision in American Cities." Master's thesis, Columbia University, 1908.

Elliott, E. C. *City School Supervision*. Yonkers-on-Hudson, New York: World Book Company, 1914.

———. *Tentative Scheme for the Measurement of Teaching Efficiency*. Madison, n.p., 1910.

Fellow, H. C. *A Study of School Supervision*. Topeka: Crane and Company, 1896.

Fitzpatrick, F. B. *Supervision of Elementary Schools*. New York: Owen Publishing Company, 1931.

Fry, M. B. "Supervision." Master's thesis, Columbia University, 1931.

Gist, A. S. *The Administration of Supervision*. Boston: Houghton Mifflin Company, 1934.

———. *Elementary School Supervision*. Boston: Houghton Mifflin Company, 1926.

Hughes, A. M., and Melby, E. O. *Supervision of Instruction in High School*. Bloomington, Ill.: Public School Publishing Company, 1930.

Johnson, Franklin W. *The Administration and Supervision of the High School*. Boston: Ginn and Company, 1925.

Joint Committee on Curriculum of the Department of Supervisors and Directors of Instruction and the Society for Curriculum Study. *The Changing Curriculum*. New York: D. Appleton-Century Company, 1937.

Judd, Charles H. *Introduction to the Scientific Study of Education*. Boston: Ginn and Company, 1918.

Kyte, George C. *How to Supervise*. Boston: Houghton Mifflin Company, 1930.

———. *Problems in School Supervision*. Boston: Houghton Mifflin Company, 1931.

Lancelot, W. H., and Barr, A. S. *The Measurement of Teaching Efficiency*. New York: Macmillan Company, 1935.

Lefkowitz, Abraham. *A Study of the Rating and Supervision of Teachers.* New York: N.Y. Council of the American Federation of Teachers, 1925.

Marble, Albert P. *The Powers and Duties of School Officers.* New York: C. W. Bardeen, 1887.

Matthews, W. L. "Supervising the Recitation By Lesson Analysis." Master's thesis, George Peabody College, 1927.

McMurray, F. M. *Elementary School Standards.* Yonkers-on-Hudson, New York: World Book Company, 1917.

Melby, Ernest O. *A Critical Study of the Existing Organization and Administration of Supervision: A Study of Current Practice.* Bloomington, Ill.: Public School Publishing Company, 1929.

Moore, B. F. "Supervision of Instruction in Cities From 15,000 to 50,000 Population." Master's thesis, Columbia University, 1913.

Mowry, William A. *Recollections of a New England Educator, 1838–1908.* New York: Silver, Burdett, 1908.

National Conference on Educational Method. "Educational Supervision." *First Yearbook.* New York: Teachers College, Columbia University, 1928.

National Conference of Supervisors and Directors of Instruction. "Current Problems of Supervisors." *Third Yearbook.* New York: Teachers College, Columbia University, 1930.

———. "Scientific Method in Supervision." *Second Yearbook.* New York: Teachers College, Columbia University, 1929.

NEA, Department of Supervisors and Directors of Instruction. "Effective Instructional Leadership." *Sixth Yearbook.* New York: Teachers College, Columbia University, 1933.

———. "The Evaluation of Supervision." *Fourth Yearbook.* New York: Teachers College, Columbia University, 1931.

———. Scientific Method in Supervisory Programs." *Seventh Yearbook.* New York: Teachers College, Columbia University, 1934.

NEA, Department of Superintendence. "The Status of the Superintendent." *First Yearbook.* Washington, D.C.: NEA, 1923.

———. "The Superintendent Surveys Supervision." *Eighth Yearbook.* Washington, D.C.: NEA, 1930.

National Society for the Study of Education. "The Relation of Principals and Superintendents to the Training and Improvement of Their Teachers." *Seventh Yearbook.* Chicago: University of Chicago Press, 1908.

Neidert, L. J. "The Administrative Aspects of Supervisory Organization in 44 American Cities." Master's thesis, University of Washington, 1926.

Nutt, H. W. *Current Problems in the Supervision of Instruction.* New York: Johnson Publishing Company, 1928.

Payne, William Harold. *Chapters on School Supervision: A Practical Treatise on Superintendency: Grading; Arranging Courses of Study; the Preparation and Use of Blanks, Records and Reports; Examination for Promotion, etc.* New York: Van Antwerp Bragg and Company, 1875.

———. *Contributions to the Science of Education.* New York: Harper, 1887.

Peeler, A. L. "The Stenographic Report of a Classroom Activity in Improving Instruction." Master's Thesis, George Peabody College, 1930.

Philbrick, John D. *City School Systems in the United States.* U.S. Bureau of Education, Circular of Information, no. 1. Washington, D.C.: U.S. Government Printing Office, 1885.

Pierce, Paul R. *The Origin and Development of the Public School Principalship.* Chicago: University of Chicago Press, 1935.

Pittman, H. *The Value of Supervision.* Baltimore, n.p. 1921.

Poret, George Cleveland. *The Contributions of William Harold Payne to Public Education.* Peabody Contributions to Education, no. 81. Nashville, n.p., 1930.

Prince, John T. *School Administration.* New York: C. W. Bardeen, 1906.

Rice, Joseph Mayer. *The Public School System of the United States.* New York: Century Company, 1893.

Risk, T. M. "Supervisory Organization and Procedure in Public Schools." Master's thesis, University of Wisconsin, 1925.

Scott, C. E. *Educational Supervision.* Milwaukee: Bruce Publishing Company, 1924.

Stone, C. R. *Supervision of Elementary School.* Boston: Houghton Mifflin Company, 1929.

Suzzalo, Henry. *Supervision of Teaching.* Boston: Houghton Mifflin Company, 1913.

Trainer, John. *How to Grade and Teach a Country School.* Burgess, Trainer, and Company, 1885.

Wagner, C. A. *Common Sense in School Supervision.* Milwaukee: Bruce Publishing Company, 1921.

Supervision: Works Published After 1940

Adams, Harold P., and Dickey, Frank G. *Basic Principles of Supervision.* New York: American Book Company, 1953.

Alfonso, Robert J.; Firth, Gerald R.; and Neville, Richard F. *Instructional Supervision.* Boston: Allyn and Bacon, 1975.

Association for Supervision and Curriculum Development. *Better than Rating: New Approaches to Appraisal of Teaching Services.* A pamphlet prepared by the Commission of Teacher Evaluation of the Association for Supervision and Curriculum Development, NEA, 1950.

———. *Personalized Supervision: Sources and Insights.* Edited by Louise M. Berman and Mary Lou Usery. Washington, D.C.: ASCD, 1966.

———. *Professional Supervision for Professional Teachers.* Edited by Thomas J. Sergiovanni. Washington, D.C.: ASCD, 1975.

———. "The Professionalization of Supervisors and Curriculum Workers." *A Policy Statement Report of the Commission on the Preparation of Instructional Leaders.* Washington, D.C.: ASCD, March 1962.

———. *Role of the Supervisor and Curriculum Director in a Climate of Change.* Edited by Robert R. Leeper. Washington, D.C.: ASCD, 1965.

———. *Supervision: Emerging Profession.* Edited by Robert R. Leeper. Washington, D.C.: ASCD, 1969.

———. *Supervision: Perspectives and Propositions.* Edited by William H. Lucio. Washington, D.C.: ASCD, 1967.

———. *The Supervisor: Agent for Change in Teaching.* Edited by James Raths and Robert R. Leeper. Washington, D.C.: ASCD, 1966.

———. *The Supervisor: New Demands, New Dimensions.* Washington, D.C.: ASCD, 1969.

———. *Toward Professional Maturity of Supervisors and Curriculum Workers.* Edited by R. P. Wahle. Washington, D.C.: ASCD, 1967.

———. "Working Paper of the ASCD Committee on the Preparation of Instructional Leaders." Washington, D.C., 1960. (Mimeographed)

Ayer, Fred C. *Fundamentals of Instructional Supervision.* New York: Harper and Brothers, 1954.

Bartky, John A. *Administration as Educational Leadership.* Stanford, Conn.: Stanford University Press, 1956.

———. *Supervision as Human Relations.* Boston: D. C. Heath and Company, 1953.

Bennie, William A. *Supervising Clinical Experience in the Classroom.* New York: Harper and Row, 1972.

Berman, Louise M. *Supervision, Staff Development, and Leadership.* Columbus, Ohio: Charles E. Merrill Publishing Company, 1971.

Blumberg, Arthur. *Supervisors and Teachers: A Private Cold War.* Berkeley, Calif.: McCuthchan Publishing Company, 1974.

Bradfield, Luther E. *Supervision for Modern Elementary Schools.* Columbus, Ohio: Charles E. Merrill Publishing Company, 1964.

Briggs, Thomas H., and Justman, Joseph. *Improving Instruction through Supervision.* New York: Macmillan Company, 1952.

Broadwell, Martin M. *Supervising Today: A Guide for Positive Leadership.* CBI Publication, 1979.

Burnham, Reba M., and King, Martha L. *Supervision in Action.* Washington, D.C.: ASCD, 1961.

Burton, William H., and Brueckner, Leo J. *Supervision: A Social Process.* New York: Appleton-Century-Crofts, 1955.

Caruso, Joseph J., and Fawcett, M. Temple. *Supervision in Early Childhood Education: A Developmental Perspective.* New York: Teachers College Press, 1986.

Cogan, Morris. *Clinical Supervision.* Boston: Houghton Mifflin Company, 1973.

Cooper, Joyce, and Miel, Alice, eds. "Personal Experiences with Supervision: Excerpts from Professional Diaries," n.p., Spring 1948. (Mimeographed)

Cramer, R. V., and Domian, O. E. *Administration and Supervision in the Elementary School.* New York: Harper and Brothers, 1960.

Crosby, Muriel. *Supervision as Co-operative Action.* New York: Appleton-Century-Crofts, 1957.

Curtin, James. *Supervision in Today's Elementary Schools.* New York: Macmillan Company, 1964.

Daresh, John C. *Supervision as a Proactive Process.* New York: Longman, 1989.

Doll, Ronald C. *Curriculum Improvement: Decision-Making and Process.* Boston: Allyn and Bacon, 1964.

Douglass, H. R.; Bent, R. K.; and Boardman, C. W. *Supervision in Secondary Schools.* Boston: Houghton Mifflin Company, 1961.

Dull, Lloyd W. *Supervision: School Leadership Handbook.* Columbus, Ohio: Charles E. Merrill Publishing Company, 1981.

Dussault, Gilles. *A Theory of Supervision in Teacher Education.* New York: Teachers College Press, 1970.

Educational Supervision: A Leadership Service, A Report of the Southern States Work Conference on Educational Problems. Tallahassee, Fla.: State Department of Education, 1955.

Elsbree, W. S., and McNally, H. J. *Elementary School Administration and Supervision.* New York: American Book Company, 1959.

Eye, Glenn, and Netzer, Lanore A. *Supervision of Instruction: A Phase of Administration.* New York: Harper and Row, 1965.

Feyereisen, Kathryn; Fiorino, A. J.; and Novak, A. T. *Supervision and Curriculum Renewal: A Systems Approach.* New York: Appleton-Century-Crofts, 1970.

Flanders, Ned. *Analyzing Teaching Behavior.* Reading, Mass.: Addison-Wesley Publishing Co., 1970.

Fleming, T. "Management by Consensus: Democratic Administration and Human Relations, 1929–1954." Ph.D. dissertation, University of Oregon, 1982.

Franseth, Jane. *Learning to Supervise Schools: An Appraisal of the Georgia Program.* Washington, D.C.: U.S. Office of Education, U.S. Government Printing Office, 1952.

———. *Supervision as Leadership.* Evanston, Ill.: Row, Peterson, 1961.

George, Claude S., Jr. *Supervision in Action: The Art of Managing Others.* Englewood Cliffs, N.J.: Prentice-Hall, 1981.

Glickman, Carl. *Supervision of Instruction: A Developmental Approach.* Boston: Allyn and Bacon, 1985.

Goldhammer, Robert. *Clinical Supervision: Special Methods* for the Supervision of Teachers. New York: Holt, Rinehart, and Winston, 1969.

Gorton, Richard A. *School Administration and Supervision: Leadership Challenges and Opportunities.* Dubuque, Iowa: William C. Rown, 1983.

Gross, Neal, and Herriott, R. E. *Staff Leadership in Public Schools: A Sociological Inquiry.* New York: John Wiley and Sons, 1965.

Gwynn, J. M. *Theory and Practice of Supervision.* New York: Dodd, Mead and Company, 1961.

Hammock, R. C., and Owings, R. S. *Supervising Instruction in Secondary Schools.* New York: McGraw-Hill Book Company, 1955.

Harman, Allan C. *Supervision in Selected Secondary Schools.* Philadelphia: University of Pennsylvania Press, 1947.

Harris, Ben M. *Supervisory Behavior in Education.* Englewood Cliffs, N.J.: Prentice-Hall, 1963.

Harrison, Raymond H. *Supervisory Leadership in Education.* New York: American Book Company, 1968.

Heald, James E.; Romano, L. C.; and Georgiady, N. P. *Selected Readings on General Supervision.* New York: Macmillan Company, 1970.

Hicks, H. J. *Educational Supervision in Principle and Practice.* New York: Ronald Press Company, 1960.

Hughes, Larry W., and Ubben, Gerald C. *The Elementary Principal's Handbook: A Guide to Effective Action*. Boston: Allyn and Bacon, 1984.

Hunter, Madeline, and Russell, Doug. *Mastering Coaching and Supervision*. California: TIP Publications, 1989.

Joyce, Bruce, and Weil, Marsha. *Models of Teaching*. Englewood Cliffs, N.J.: Prentice-Hall, 1972.

Kapp, O. W., and Dufelt, D. L. *Personalized Curriculum through Excellence in Leadership*. Denville, Ill.: Interstate Printers and Publishers, 1974.

Kyte, George C. *The Principal at Work*. New York: Ginn and Company, 1941.

Lewis, Arthur J., and Miel, Alice. *Supervision for Improved Instruction: New Challenges, New Responses*. Belmont, Calif.: Wadsworth Publishing Company, 1972.

Lipman, James M; Rankin, Robb E.; and Hoeh Jr., James A. *The Principalship: Concepts, Competencies, and Cases*. New York: Longman, 1985.

Lucio, William H., and McNeil, John D. *Supervision: A Synthesis of Thought and Action*. New York: McGraw-Hill Book Company, 1962.

Mackenzie, Gordon N. "The Professionalization of Supervisors and Curriculum Workers." *Report of the Commission on the Preparation of Instructional Leaders*. ASCD, March 1962, revised May 1963.

Mackenzie, Gordon N., and Corey, Stephen M. *Instructional Leadership*. New York: Teachers College Press, 1954.

Manis, James R. et al. *Handbook of Educational Supervision*. Boston: Allyn and Bacon, 1985.

Marks, Sir Robert James; Stoops, Emery; and Stoops-King, Joyce. *Handbook of Educational Supervision*. Third Edition. Boston: Allyn and Bacon, 1985.

Martinez, Corine, ed. *A Selected Bibliography for Professional Supervisory Competencies*. Austin: Department of Educational Administration, University of Texas, 1975.

McKean, Robert C., and Mills, H. H. *The Supervisor*. Washington, D.C.: Center for Applied Research in Education, 1964.

McNally, H. J., and Passow, A. H. *Improving the Quality of Public School Programs*. New York: Teachers College Press, 1960.

Miel, Alice. *Changing the Curriculum: A Social Process*. New York: Appleton-Century-Crofts, 1946.

Mosher, Ralph L. "The Process of Supervision in Professional Training: A Survey of Selected Professions." Special paper, Harvard Graduate School of Education, 1962.

Mosher, Ralph L., and Purpel, David E. *Supervision: The Reluctant Profession*. New York: Houghton Mifflin Company, 1972.

Neagley, Ross L., and Evans, N. Dean. *Handbook for Effective Supervision of Instruction*. Englewood Cliffs, N.J.: Prentice-Hall, 1964.

Neville, Richard F. "The Supervisory Function of the Elementary School Principal as Perceived by Teachers." Ph.D. dissertation, University of Connecticut, 1963.

Oliva, Peter F. *Supervision for Today's Schools*. New York: Longman, 1989.

Plunkett, W. Richards. *Supervision: The Direction of People at Work*. Dubuque, Ind.: William C. Brown Company, 1981.

Reeder, E. H. *Supervision in the Elementary School.* Boston: Houghton Mifflin Company, 1953.

Rorer, John Alexander. *Principles of Democratic Supervision.* Contributions to Education, no. 858. New York: Teachers College, Columbia University, 1942.

Sarason, Seymour B. *The Culture of the School and the Problem of Change.* Boston: Allyn and Bacon, 1971.

Sergiovanni, Thomas J., and Starrett, Robert J. *Emerging Patterns of Supervision: Human Perspectives.* New York: McGraw-Hill Book Company, 1971.

Spaulding, Frank E. *School Superintendent in Action in Five Cities.* Ringe, N.H.; Richard R. Smith Publisher, 1955.

Spears, Harold. *Improving the Supervision of Instruction.* Englewood Cliffs, N.J.: Prentice-Hall, 1953.

———. *Secondary Education in American Life.* New York: American Book Company, 1941.

Stoler, Nathan. *Supervision and the Improvement of Instruction.* Englewood Cliffs, N.J.: Educational Technology Publications, 1978.

Stoops, E. *Elementary School Supervision.* Boston: Allyn and Bacon, 1965.

Swearingen, Mildred E. *Supervision of Instruction: Foundations and Dimensions.* Boston: Allyn and Bacon, 1962.

Taba, Hilda. *Curriculum Development: Theory and Practice.* New York: Harcourt, Brace, and World, 1962.

Tanner, Daniel, and Tanner, Laurel N. *Curriculum Development: Theory into Practice.* New York: Macmillan Company, 1975.

———. *Supervision in Education: Problems and Practices.* New York: Macmillan Company, 1987.

Tuttle, F. B. "The Theory of Supervision of Instruction." Ph.D. dissertation, Yale University, 1942.

Unruh, Adolph, and Turner, Harold E. *Supervision for Change and Innovation.* New York: Houghton Mifflin Company, 1970.

Vigilante, N. J. "A Role Perception Study of Elementary Principals and Elementary Supervisors in the State of Ohio." Ph.D. dissertation, Ohio State University, 1964.

Wiles, Jon, and Joseph Bondi. *Supervision: A Guide to Practice.* Columbus, Ohio: Charles E. Merrill Publishing Company, 1986.

Wiles, Kimball. *Supervision for Better Schools.* Englewood Cliffs, N.J.: Prentice-Hall, 1967.

———. *Supervision in Physical Education: A Guide to Principles and Practices.* Englewood Cliffs, N.J.: Prentice-Hall, 1956.

Wilhelms, Fred T. *Supervision in a New Key.* Washington, D.C.: ASCD, 1973.

Williamson, Margaret. *Supervision: New Patterns and Processes.* New York: Associated Press, 1961.

———. *Supervision: Principles and Methods.* New York: Woman's Press, 1960.

Wilson, L. Craig; Byar, T. Madison; Shapiro, Arthur S.; and Schell, Shirley H. *Sociology of Supervision: An Approach to Comprehensive Planning in Education.* Boston: Allyn and Bacon, 1969.

Index

Abbott, Andrew, 25
Abbott, Max G., 155
Administration, 88, 108, 110, 114, 118–20, 127; autocracy in, 104
Administrative supervision, 118, 119
Alfonso, Robert J., 158
Allen, Richard D., 112
American Federation of Teachers (AFT), 101, 102
American School Board Journal, 41
American Teacher, 101, 102
Anderson, William H., 72
Arnold, Sarah L., 71
Assistant principal, 23, 88
Assistant superintendent, 20, 87, 88, 111, 151
Association for Supervision and Curriculum Development (ASCD), 16, 143–44, 150, 151, 152, 153, 154, 160
Atlantic Monthly, 41–42
Ayer, F. C., 128

Bagley, William C., 103
Balliet, T. M., 49
Bamberger, Florence E., 112, 117
Bardeen, Charles W., 72
Barnard, Henry, 82
Barr, Alvin S., 93, 114, 115, 116, 127, 128, 152
Bennis, Warren G., 155
Bent, Robert K., 152
Block, Louis J., 68
Blumberg, Arthur, 157
Boardman, Charles W., 152
Bobbitt, Franklin, 69, 88, 89–95, 134
Bowles, Samuel, 17
Boyce, Arthur C., 96–97
Bradford, Mary D., 122
Brim, Orville G., 104, 114
Brooklyn Teachers Association, 102
Bruce, William G., 41

Brueckner, L. J., 98, 114, 117
Bryan, William Jennings, 80
Buber, Martin, 157
Burke, John, 52
Burton, William H., 93, 114, 117, 123–24, 126, 138
Butler, Nicholas M., 14, 82, 134
Button, Henry Warren, 74

Calkins, Norman A., 59
Carlson, Evelyn F., 19
Carnegie, Andrew, 38
Carter, James, 82
Caswell, Hollis L., 139, 142
Cates, E., 49
Centralization, 14, 37, 44, 47, 56, 66, 71, 72, 74–75
Chalmers, W. W., 51–52
Chancellor, William, 53, 62, 65–66, 85, 88
Charters, W. W., 134
Chicago Teachers Federation, 70
Chubb, John E., 155–56
Coburn, W. G., 111
Cocking, Walter D., 105, 134, 140, 141
Committee of Fifteen, 46
Corson, Oscar T., 71
Corwin, Ronald, 28–31
Costa, Arthur, 108
Counts, George, 16, 134–35
Courtis, Stuart A., 90–91, 126, 136, 141
Crabtree, J. W., 99
Cremin, Lawrence A., 81
Cubberley, Ellwood, 21, 88
Cunningham, Ruth, 150
Curriculum, 16, 89, 133–44, 149, 151, 152–53
Curriculum Journal, 141, 144, 150
Cushman, C. L., 142

Dale, Edgar, 134, 141

209

Dalthorp, Charles J., 95
Davidson, William M., 95
Department of Supervision and Curriculum Development, 144, 150
Department of Supervisors and Directors of Instruction, 16, 114, 125, 138, 141, 142, 143, 149
Dewey, John, 16, 76, 81, 112, 122, 130–31, 147
Douglass, H. R., 152
Draper, Andrew S., 14, 45, 46, 48, 57, 75
Dunn, Fannie W., 112
Dutton, Larkin, 56
Dutton, Samuel T., 76

Eaton, John, 44
Edson, A. W., 48
Education, 46
Educational Leadership, 150, 153, 156, 158
Educational Method, 150
Elliott, Edward C., 96
Elsbree, Williard S., 19, 24, 98
Evans, N. Dean, 108

Faulkner, William, 149
Firth, Gerald R., 158
Foote, John M., 119
Forum, 40
Freidson, Eliot, 27–28

George, Henry, 81
Gintis, Herbert, 17
Gove, Aaron E., 45, 51, 54, 57, 70
Green, Clyde C., 95
Greenwood, James, 48, 50, 51, 52, 56
Guditus, Charles, 108
Gwynn, J. M., 111

Haley, Margaret A., 70
Hanna, Paul, 141
Harap, Henry, 134, 138, 140, 141, 142, 143
Harden, Francis E., 69–70
Harris, William Torrey, 16, 49, 53, 54, 57, 62, 64, 68, 75, 82, 88, 133, 134, 147
Hart, Albert B., 67–68
Heffernan, Helen, 138, 143
Henderson, Ruth H., 150

Herbartian philosophy, 133
Hervey, Henry D., 96
Heubauer, Dorothy, 139
Hill, Sallie, 69, 102–3
Hinsdale, Burke A., 69
Horall, A. H., 137
Hosic, James F., 76, 93, 110, 112, 122–23
Hughes, J. L., 54

Illich, Ivan, 17

Johnson, Earl S., 157
Johnson, Franklin, 98
Jones, Lewis H., 41
Journal of Education, 46
Journal of Educational Method, 110, 111, 118, 119, 120, 137
Journal of Speculative Philosophy, 62
Judd, Charles H., 116

Katz, Michael B., 74, 155
Kaufman, Bel, 25
Keller, Frank J., 102
Kerr, Stephen T., 149
Keyes, R. K., 120
Kilpatrick, William H., 134
King, Leroy A., 98
Klohr, Paul R., 157
Krajewski, Robert J., 153
Kyte, George C., 111–12

Lancaster, Joseph, 55
Lancasterian Monitoral System, 55
League of Teachers Association, 69
Lefkowitz, Abraham, 102
Leonard, J. Paul, 143
Lewis, Arthur J., 153, 156
Lewis, E. E., 116
Lindquist, Rudolph, 134, 142
Lloyd, Henry D., 81
London, Jack, 81

McAndrew, William, 93
Macdonald, James B., 155
McGuffey, William, 82
Mackenzie, Gordon N., 138, 151
McKinley, William, 80
McMurray, Charles A., 134
MacRae, David, 55
Madden, Margaret, 119

INDEX

Mann, Horace, 16, 39, 82
Marble, Albert, 59, 73
Markowitz, Shirley, 158
Maxwell, William, 46, 57, 67, 75, 82, 147
Melby, E. O., 120
Melchior, William T., 120
Merriam, Charles E., 81
Merton, Robert K., 26
Michigan Teacher, 57
Miel, Alice, 143, 147, 155, 156
Mowry, William A., 39, 41

National Association of Secondary School Principals, 116
National Conference on Educational Method, 110, 111, 114
National Conference of Supervisors and Directors of Instruction, 114, 129
National Education Association (NEA), 45, 46, 53, 59, 68, 69, 70, 150
National Herbart Society, 54
National Society for the Study of Education, 69, 90, 134
National Society of Curriculum Workers, 140
National Teacher, 69
Neagley, Ross L., 108
Neville, Richard F., 158
Newlon, Jesse H., 71, 100–101, 125, 136
News Bulletin, 140, 141
New York Times, 155
Norris, Frank, 81

Oberholtzer, E. E., 115

Parker, Francis W., 39, 82, 133
Parrott, Ava L., 99–100
Patri, Angelo, 101
Payne, William H., 19, 21, 53, 57–59, 60, 62, 64, 65, 66, 67, 75, 82, 87, 134, 147
Peres, Israel H., 45
Philbrick, John D., 44
Pickard, Josiah L., 19, 59, 64, 68
Playground and Recreation, 109
Poret, G. C., 57
Prince, John T., 48, 118
Principal, 15, 20, 21–23, 51, 65, 85, 86, 87, 88, 91, 99, 101, 102, 111, 126, 127, 128, 148, 150, 158
Professions, 27; power model of, 28–29, 107; trait model of, 28–29
Progressivism, 80–81, 83

Rankin, Paul, 142
Rating, 15, 62, 79, 92, 94–103, 104, 106, 109–10, 116, 117, 127, 131–32, 152
Reutter, E. Edmund, 22
Rice, Joseph Mayer, 40–41, 74
Riis, Jacob, 81
Roosevelt, Theodore, 80
Rossman, John D., 105
Rugg, Harold O., 97, 134–35

Sabin, Henry, 71, 72
Salisbury, Ethel I., 112
Saylor, Galen, 141, 150, 153
School and Society, 76, 112, 122
School Review, 67
Schools: as bureaucracies, 66, 107, 126, 154; corruption of, 48; critique of, 40–43; function of, 82; as hierarchies, 59, 65, 126, 159; importance of, 82; inspection of, 48; size of, 21–22
Seeley, David S., 75–76, 154
Seeley, Homer, 56
Sex (gender), 21, 49–50, 65–66, 85, 86–87, 144
Shaheen, Thomas A., 155
Shepard, Herbert A., 158
Shores, J. Harlan, 151, 153
Sinclair, Upton, 81
Sloyer, M. W., 120
Smith, William A., 124–25
Snedden, David, 124
Society for Curriculum Study, 16, 140, 141, 142, 149
Society for Curriculum Workers, 127
Soldan, F. Louis, 39, 48, 57
Spaulding, Frank E., 85, 88
Steffens, Lincoln, 81
Stenographic reports, 104–6
Stevens, Romiett, 104–6
Stevens, Thaddeus, 82
Stone, C. W., 115
Stone, T. W., 90–91
Storm, H. C., 100, 101

Stover, Franklin G., 150
Stowe, Calvin, 82
Stratemeyer, Florence B., 105
Strayer, George, 88, 134
Strober, Myra, 87
Superintendent: and curriculum, 133; as expert, 64; function of, 15, 52, 60, 87; as inspector, 48, 60; as manager, 58; methods of, 50–53, 62, 64–65, 91; as supervisor, 15, 44–53, 80, 83; as teacher of teachers, 47–48, 58
Supervision: autocratic, 49, 69, 71, 73, 99, 101, 103, 104, 108, 114, 148; bureaucracy and, 73–76, 107, 108, 154; clinical, 106; cooperative, 102, 106, 112, 114, 122, 125, 137, 147; criticism of, 69, 70, 71, 99–103, 128; democratic, 65, 69, 76, 106, 109, 112, 114, 118, 120–26, 138, 151, 152; as distinct from administration, 118–20, 127; as a form of control, 53, 56, 65, 66, 74, 106; as a function, 18–19, 20, 47; as inspection, 48, 49–50, 51, 60, 96, 117, 120, 152; methods of, 49, 52, 64–65, 91–99, 104–6, 110–11, 151; as an occupation, 110; practice of, 56, 88; as a profession, 111, 114; scientific, 42, 90–94, 97, 115–18, 127, 129–32; sexual bias in, 49–50; status of, 88, 95, 126–28, 144, 154; by superintendent, 15, 52, 83–84
Supervisors: authority of, 85, 87, 88, 128; criticism of, 99–103, 132; as curriculum specialists, 128; and curriculum workers, 133–44, 149–54; general and special, 15, 20, 21–23, 85, 86, 87, 88, 91, 111, 144, 150–60; numbers of, 83–84, 86; professional status of, 106, 107, 108, 126–28, 129, 144; qualifications of, 111; training of, 112
Swearingen, Mildred E., 151

Tanner, Daniel and Laurel, 18–19
Tarbell, Ida, 81
Taylor, Frederick Winslow (also Taylorism, scientific management), 89, 90, 94, 95
Taylor, Joseph S., 95
Teachers: critique of rating, 97–98, 99–100; critique of supervision, 15, 29, 95, 99–103, 157; efficiency of, 60, 95–106; incompetence of, 47, 48–49, 58, 62, 92, 94; inspection of, 50; numbers of, 21–22, 83–84, 86; rating of, 92; status of, 30–31, 92
Terman, L., 134
Thorndike, E. L., 134
Threlkeld, A. L., 136
Trainer, John, 54–55
Tyack, David, 14–15, 20, 87

Unruh, Glenys G., 152
Urban education: growth of, 38–39, 73; problems of, 15, 20, 27, 38–40, 49, 147; reforming, 37, 42–43, 45, 66, 72–73, 82–83, 133; superintendent, 15, 47

Van Til, William, 154

Wagner, Charles A., 119
Walker, Decker, 148–49
Ward boards, 14, 20, 37, 40, 41–42, 66
Warriner, E. C., 67
Weber, Max, 26–27, 75
White, Emerson E., 45, 68–69
Whyte, William H., 156
Wickershan, J. P., 46
Wiley, W. E., 115
Wilhelms, Fred T., 158
Wilson, Woodrow, 122
Winship, A. E., 46